Baseball Fathers
Baseball Sons

From Orator Jim to Cal, Barry, and Ken... every one a player.

by
LARRY EKIN

BETTERWAY PUBLICATIONS, INC.
WHITE HALL, VIRGINIA

Published by Betterway Publications, Inc.
P.O. Box 219
Crozet, VA 22932
(804) 823-5661

Cover design by Rick Britton
Topps and Bowman cards reprinted by permission,
© The Topps Company, Inc.
Typography by Park Lane Associates

Library of Congress Cataloging-in-Publication Data
Ekin, Larry
    Baseball fathers, baseball sons : from Orator Jim to Cal, Barry, and Ken
--every one a player / Larry Ekin.
        p. cm.
    Includes index.
    Summary: Discusses the statistics and accomplishments of fathers and
sons who have played professional baseball.
    ISBN 1-55870-226-1 : $13.95
    1. Baseball players--United States--Biography--Juvenile
literature. 2. Fathers and sons--United States--Biography--Juvenile
literature. [1. Baseball players. 2. Fathers and sons.]
I. Title.
GV865.A1E37 1992
796.357′092′2--dc20
[B]   91-43113
                                                            CIP
                                                            AC

Printed in the United States of America
0 9 8 7 6 5 4 3 2 1

This one is for Dave — as fine a companion as a boy could hope for
and as fine a man as a brother can claim . . .
AND
Adam and Nathan, whose wide-eyed exuberance
reminds us all why we love this game.

Two baseball card dealers deserve special mention for their contributions to this project. Steve Rogers and Orv Johannson know baseball history and convey a love for the game. In addition, they both possess an encyclopedic knowledge of baseball cards and collectibles. Both encouraged this project from the very beginning and willingly lent it their expertise.

I conducted much of the research for this book at the University of Florida Library and the Library of Congress. In both places, the staff provided valuable assistance, Dave Kelley of the Library of Congress in particular.

Contents

Introduction

A four-year-old boy steps blinking into the bright sunlight of a late spring afternoon. He hitches up his shorts and hefts a baseball bat half his own size. A few yards away, his father arcs an underhanded, looping toss towards the boy's bat. The boy traces the ball's arc with his eyes and jerks the bat forward. The bat makes contact with the ball, and the ball rockets past his father. Father and son share a moment of delighted surprise. Then, with an exuberance bordering on instinct, the boy flings the bat to the ground and begins to run. He runs in random patterns, directionless, and with herky-jerky abandon, not because he has been told to do so, but because, somehow, it simply seems the thing to do. A lifelong love affair is being born; a love affair of sunlight and sinew.

If that boy is lucky, someone (his father, a brother or sister, an older kid on the block, or the neighborhood "tomboy") will take that boy under his or her wing. Together, they will refine his skills and develop his understanding of the game. That boy will soon be running with the same exuberance, but in the sequence ordained by his elders and followed by generations.

Within a few short years, he will have developed an enthusiasm for a particular team and, most probably, for a particular player or players on that team. One day, while on summer vacation, his father packs him and Grandpa into the family station wagon. "Where are we going?" he inquires. The two adults, silent conspirators, exchange furtive glances but remain evasive. Traffic thickens. Soon, their destination becomes apparent as the sight of a big-league ballpark overwhelms the horizon. They park their vehicle and merge with a crowd exuding excitement. The lucky boy is already drinking in the atmosphere, satiating his young senses with the sights, sounds, and smells that will leave an unerasable imprint, which, in America, seems to bond one generation to another.

He will consume peanuts and a hot dog. As we are discussing a *lucky* boy, he will witness his hero perform some magical deed, bringing the crowd to its feet. Thereafter, with all the undiminished imagination youth can bring to bear, when he knocks a ball around his backyard or playground, he will be that player, or at least a teammate, and the roar of the crowd he hears in his mind will be as real as Santa Claus on Christmas morning.

If that boy proves skillful as well as lucky, he will be given the opportunity to play the game in front of real crowds; perhaps not as large and as vocal as the phantom crowds of his childhood's mind, but real people will be applauding his skills. He will continue to hone his skills and learn new dimensions of this game. Perhaps he will get the chance to play on a championship team. Every boy should have this chance at least once in his life, because, as they say in the cliché business, it's something that can never be taken away from you. He will still have his heroes, and, in a sense, they will still be his companions. Only now, instead of existing solely in his head, they will take on the ephemeral reality of the smell of bubblegum and the transient reality of pasteboard images. What's more, when the extended family gathers for a holiday picnic and it comes time to choose up sides for softball, he'll now be expected to carry his own weight at bat and in the field.

In time, one of three absolutely predictable things will transpire. The boy's interest may dwindle, replaced by other passions. In time, he may return as a casual fan. Or his interest and his baseball ambitions may rage unchecked, but he will slowly, reluctantly accept the limitation of his own skills. He will probably continue to play and follow the game. At odd moments in his life, he will recall a perfectly executed double play, a well-placed hit, an unexpected snare of a line drive... Sometimes, if he cocks his head and listens carefully, he just might once again hear the imaginary roar of his childhood. You can be certain that one of the first presents he will buy for his offspring will be a baseball mitt, probably several years before it can be properly worn on the infant's hand. In this day and age, of course, it might be his son or his daughter who, in his or her turn, will stand blinking in the sunlight of a late spring afternoon. And in that sunlight and warmth, a blinking father will remember, a blinking child will dream, and an American cycle will renew itself.

Finally, a tiny handful of young men who are both extraordinarily talented and extraordinarily lucky will earn the opportunity to keep testing their skills (and their luck), perhaps one day stepping out in a major league uniform. If their extraordinary luck and their talent hold up, they might even get to put in a full season, or two, or even a real career. Perhaps they will bring their own boy out to the ballpark and that boy will realize, "Hey, my dad's a big leaguer."

Let us briefly recollect the 1903 season. The first moving picture portraying baseball players at work was made this year and featured Nap Lajoie and Harry Bay. The established National League and upstart American League settled into an uneasy truce and stopped raiding one another for talent. Honus Wagner won his second batting crown with a .355 mark, as Pittsburgh cruised to its third straight National League championship. Over in the American League, the legendary Cy Young, 36 years old, led a Boston pitching staff of six pitchers, one of whom appeared in only one game. Young compiled a record of 28-9, leading Boston to its first pennant. Ed Delahanty's mysterious death on July 4 marred the mid-season mark. Boston defeated Pittsburgh five games to three in the first modern World Series.

Overlooked by most baseball historians, another singular event took place this season, though the Society of American Baseball Researchers has yet to determine the precise day. But sometime during that long-ago season, a six-foot, one-inch 22-year-old left-hander hitched up his Chicago Cubs' flannels, blinked in the sunlight, and hiked out to the mound for his first major league start. He pitched 3 innings, walked 2, struck out 5, gave up 6 hits, took a loss, and was saddled with a 12.00 ERA. Never mind. Jack Doscher had just completed the American cycle. Jack Doscher, of Troy, New York, became the first son of a major league ballplayer to become a major league ballplayer himself.

Jack's father, John Henry (Herm), was born in December of 1852 and appeared in his first big-league game in the National Association during the 1872 season. That made him a 19-year-old rookie—a heady feat, even in those days.

In the final analysis, Herm's career spanned 10 years; a decade spent toiling for a succession of really bad major league teams. And in a major league career that spanned a decade, Herm appeared in only 80 games, compiled only 325 at-bats, recorded no home runs, and logged a career batting average of .225. Even back then a .225 average wasn't going to take you far. One interesting footnote to Herm's career stands out. Whether he voluntarily took the time off, or whether he was involuntarily demoted remains unclear. But the fact of the matter is that Herm disappeared from the major leagues during the first year of Jack's life. Perhaps he was trying to instill in his son the desire to throw rather than hit. Whatever the reason, Herm reappeared in 1881, and 1882 proved to be his last season on a major league roster.

Young Jack undoubtedly benefited from his father's tutelage. Unfortunately, his career as a major league pitcher seems to have mirrored his father's hitting career. Shortly after Jack's debut, the Cubs sold him to the Brooklyn Superbas, the team that became the Dodgers in 1913. In Brooklyn, young Jack appeared in three games but managed to reduce his ERA to 7.71. He pitched in only two games the next season and suffered through a 1-5 campaign for the 1905 Brooklyn team, a team that finished last, 56½ games out of first. Jack jumped the team in 1906; we don't know why. He resurfaced with Cincinnati in 1908, but, following a broken leg, was out of organized major league baseball forever. He left with a respectable 2.86 ERA.

The problem was, he couldn't seem to win. He posted a 2-11 career record with 13 starts, 10 complete games, and 145 innings over 27 games.

What matters is that young Jack was the first, but far from the last, baseball son to appear in a major league uniform. Does that mean that Herm Doscher was the first major league father? Well, if you mean, was he the first to have his son play in the majors, then, obviously, the answer is yes. But if by "first father" you mean the major leaguer who played earliest and later had a son appear in a major league uniform, then baseball's first father was Orator Jim O'Rourke.

O'Rourke's major league career began for Boston in the National Association in 1872, the same year as Doscher's. However, Doscher didn't appear in the majors until September 5th, whereas O'Rourke's debut came on April 26th. When the National League was organized, Boston joined as a charter member, and O'Rourke recorded the first hit in National League history, a single with two out in the top of the first.

Orator Jim's nickname stemmed from his tendency to make speeches and use flowery language—apt attributes for a graduate of Yale Law School. His proficiency on the playing field carried him into the Hall of Fame. In addition to playing the game, O'Rourke spent time as a player/manager, an umpire, a minor league owner, and president of the Connecticut League. At the age of 52, O'Rourke caught all nine innings in the pennant-clinching game for the 1904 Giants.

Since Orator Jim logged modern major league baseball's first hit, either 120 or 121 major league fathers sired major league sons. This discrepancy in numbering stems from how you choose to regard the Ripkens. You see, while Cal Ripken, Sr. managed at the major league level, he never played, or even appeared in a major league uniform as a player.

The cumulative experience of baseball's fathers and sons presents an astonishing microcosm of major league history, illustrating virtually every facet of the game. Recorded playing time, for example, ranges from one game (Jack Aragon, Joe Berry, Sr., John Corriden, and others) to *25 years* (Eddie Collins).

The careers of baseball's fathers and sons offer studies in major league frustration and futility as well as breathtaking accomplishments. On-field exploits include triple plays, no-hitters, batting crowns, stolen base championships, MVP awards, and a host of individual game, season, and career records. When their playing days were over, baseball fathers and sons who stayed in the game became scouts, coaches, managers, umpires, executives, and even owners. Sometimes the father's career overshadowed the son's; sometimes vice versa. Occasionally, their careers seem mirror images of one another.

Consider Willie and Art Mills. Wee Willie appeared for New York (NL) in 1901. He started two games and is credited with two complete games. He also lost them both. Son Art, a pitcher like his father, was called up by Boston (NL) in 1927. He managed to get in playing time the following season as well, and eventually appeared in nineteen games. In 46 innings, he gave up 58 hits, walked 26, struck out 7, and finished his career with a record of 0-1.

Or how about Ralph and Don Savidge, another pair of pitchers. Ralph, known as The Human Whipcord, came up for Cincinnati as a 29 year old in 1908 and also appeared in 1909. After five major league games, he left baseball with an 0-1 record. Twenty years later, son Don got the

call from the Washington Senators. His career covered 3 games, 6 innings, 12 hits, 2 walks, and 2 strikeouts and ended 0-0.

Baseball son Guy Morton, Jr. must claim some sort of record for major league futility. Boston (AL) brought Moose up for the tail end of the 1954 campaign. September 17th, Moose stepped to the plate and struck out. It proved to be the sum total of Moose's major league career: one game, one at-bat, and one strikeout. Nevertheless, there are undoubtedly a lot of us who would trade considerable segments of our lives for just that one moment of futility.

However, if our careers were to be limited to one game, our fantasies would likely run more along the lines of John Corriden's career. Corriden, son of Red Corriden, appeared in one game for the 1946 Brooklyn Dodgers. He had no at-bats, but he is credited with scoring a run. That proved to be both the beginning and the end of young Corriden's career. One game, with no at-bats, but he *scored a run*! Chuck Lindstrom, son of Hall of Famer Fred Lindstrom, also had a one-game career and also scored a run. However, showing real style, Chuck smashed a triple and picked up an RBI as well, to start and end his major league career with a perfect 1.000 batting average and an astonishing 3.000 slugging percentage.

At the opposite end of the major league longevity spectrum, you find baseball father (and legend) Connie Mack, The Tall Tactician. When Mack's playing days ended, he stayed in the game as manager and, eventually, owner/manager of the Philadelphia Athletics. Mack ended up managing for 50 years. Mack's son Earle was brought up to the parent club during three different seasons. His debut was October 5, 1910, and his father must have been proud as the 20 year old went two for four with a triple. Unfortunately, it was the apex of Earle's playing career. In 1911 he went zero for four and in 1912 he went zero for eight. Never mind, though. In 1924, he joined the Athletics as a coach and spent the next 26 years working with the senior Mack.

The other anchor in the baseball father-son longevity chain is Eddie Collins. Appropriately, Collins was a Connie Mack protégé. A graduate of Columbia University, Eddie's playing career stretched from 1906 to 1930. The early part of Collins' playing career was spent in Philadelphia as part of Mack's "$100,000 infield." A pittance, of course, in this day and age, but at the time it was a mind-boggling sum to pay grown men to play a children's game. When financial considerations caused Mack to break up his infield, Collins went to the White Sox. A few seasons later, the infamous

"Black Sox" scandal rocked organized baseball, but Collins emerged with his reputation intact. Collins' son, Eddie, Jr., played the outfield, but had his career interrupted by World War II and never reappeared in a major league uniform.

In between the one-gamers and the astonishing records of Mack and Collins lie the career records of baseball's fathers and sons, running the gamut of experience between those parameters. Eight baseball fathers played or managed their way into the Hall of Fame. To date, no baseball sons occupy space in Cooperstown, but at the rate some of today's sons are playing, a baseball son is likely to be elected sometime early next century. Our baseball fathers and sons also include other stars, some players who recorded one or two seasons of glory, and a considerable number of respectable journeymen. There are players who proved to be disappointments, early retirements due to injuries, and a few genuinely inspiring baseball stories, like that of Smokey Joe Wood.

Wood was a pitcher, and a good one at that. He pitched a no-hitter in 1911, logged 16 consecutive victories in 1912, and went on to win three World Series games that season. An injury resulting in chronic thumb pain forced Wood to abandon pitching a few seasons later. For most people, it would have meant the end of a baseball career, but not Wood. He went back to work, retrained himself as an outfielder, and fought his way back to the major leagues to record 695 games in the outfield with a career batting average of .283.

Reviewing the records of baseball fathers and sons provides plenty of fodder for baseball trivia buffs as well. Here are a few examples. When Big Ed Walsh helped pitch the 1906 "Hitless Wonder" White Sox to the world championship, his battery-mate was Billy Sullivan. Just over twenty years later, Ed Walsh (the son) pitched for the White Sox to catcher Billy Sullivan, Jr. Marty and Matt Keogh constitute the only American father-son combination to have played in Japan. Jim Bagby, Jr. was the pitcher who ended Joe DiMaggio's hitting streak. Ted Williams hit home runs off of *both* father Thornton Lee *and* son Donald.

We could and will go on, but first, let's take a look at the all-time list of major league baseball fathers and baseball sons on the next page.

FATHER-SON BASEBALL QUIZ

Now that you've had a chance to scan the list, let's test your knowledge of baseball history a bit.

1. This baseball father was known as "Slats Mc-Gillicuddy" in his playing days. (1 point.)

2. This baseball father is the only player in major league history to have lost a no-hitter in his first and only major league pitching appearance. (1 point.)

3. This father-son combination was the first to play professionally on the same team at the same time. (1 point.)

4. When Billy and Cal Ripken, Jr. played for Cal, Sr., they were not the first sons to play under their father as manager. Who was the first major leaguer to play for his father as manager? Hint: The father is a Hall of Famer. (1 point.)

5. Name another son who played for his father in the major leagues. (1 point.)

6. They were the first father-son combination to each record seasons with at least 30 home runs and 30 stolen bases. (1 point.)

7. Two major league fathers hit home runs in the 1954 All-Star Game. Hint: Both produced All-Star sons. Bonus: Another father appeared in this game; name him. (2 points; 1 Bonus point.)

8. Name the father credited with a win in an All-Star Game. (1 point.)

9. Name the father credited with a loss in an All-Star Game. (1 point.)

10. This Hall of Fame father's career is often overshadowed by the line drive he hit off the toe of Dizzy Dean in the 1937 All-Star Game, effectively ending Dean's career. Who was he? (1 point.)

11. The 1951 Cleveland Indians featured these three fathers in their regular starting lineup. (1 point for each you can name.)

12. The 1989 Kansas City Royals featured three baseball sons in their regular lineup. (1 point for each you can name.)

13. They are the only American father-son com-

MAJOR LEAGUE FATHER-SON ROSTER

Father	Son(s)	Father	Son(s)
Bobby Adams	Mike	Harl Maggert	Harl
Sandy Alomar	Roberto & Sandy, Jr.	Charlie Malay	Joe
Felipe Alou	Moises	Barney Martin	Jerry
Ruben Amaro	Ruben, Jr.	Wally Mattick	Bobby
Angel Aragon	Jack	Dave May	Derrick
Earl Averill	Earl	Pinky May	Milt
Jim Bagby, Sr.	Jim, Jr.	Hal McRae	Hal
Clyde Barnhart	Vic	Frank Meinke	Bob
Charlie Beamon	Charlie	Willie Mills	Art
Gus Bell	Buddy	Rene Monteagudo	Aurelio
Yogi Berra	Dale	Eugene Moore, Sr.	Eugene, Jr.
Charlie Berry	Charlie	Guy Morton, Sr.	Guy, Jr.
Joe Berry, Sr.	Joe, Jr.	Manny Mota	Andy & Jose
Bobby Bonds	Barry	Walter Mueller	Don
Ray Boone	Bob	Bill Narleski	Ray
Fred Brickell	Fritz	Julio Navarro	Jaime
Earle Brucker, Sr.	Earle, Jr.	Chet Nichols, Sr.	Chet, Jr.
Mike Brumley	Mike	Ron Northey	Scott
Dolph Camilli	Doug	Frank Okrie	Len
Al Campanis	Jim	Orator Jim O'Rourke	Queenie
Cam Carreon	Mark	Patsy O'Rourke	Joe
Joe Coleman	Joe	Tiny Osborne	Bobo
Eddie Collins, Sr.	Eddie, Jr.	Steve Partenheimer	Dan
Ed Connolly, Sr.	Ed, Jr.	Herman Pillette	Duane
Jimmy Cooney	Jimmy & Johnny	Mel Queen	Mel
Red Corriden	John	Cal Ripken, Sr.	Cal, Jr. & Billy
Bill Crouch	Bill	Walt Ripley	Allen
Herm Doscher	Jack	Ralph Savidge	Don
Dick Ellsworth	Steve	Ducky Schofield	Dick
Jim Eschen	Larry	Joe Schultz, Sr.	Joe, Jr.
Tito Francona	Terry	Diego Segui	David
Len Gabrielson	Len	Earl Sheely	Bub
John Ganzel	Babe	Dick Siebert	Paul
Larry Gilbert	Charlie & Tookie	George Sisler	Dick & Dave
Peaches Graham	Jack	Bob Skinner	Joel
Fred Green	Gary	Roy Smalley, Jr.	Roy, III
Ken Griffey, Sr.	Ken, Jr.	Ed Sprague	Ed
Ray Grimes	Oscar	Ebba St. Claire	Randy
Ross Grimsley	Ross	Dave Stenhouse	Mike
Sam Hairston	Jerry & Johnny	Joe Stephenson	Jerry
Larry Haney	Chris	Ron Stillwell	Kurt
Jim Hegan	Mike	Mel Stottlemyre	Todd
Ken Heintzelman	Tom	Billy Sullivan, Sr.	Billy, Jr.
Wally Hood, Sr.	Wally, Jr.	Haywood Sullivan	Marc
Randy Hundley	Todd	George Susce	George
Julian Javier	Stan	Chuck Tanner	Bruce
Adam Johnson	Adam	Jose Tartabull	Danny
Ernie Johnson	Don	Ricardo Torres	Gil
Bob Kennedy	Terry	Mike Tresh	Tom
Marty Keogh	Matt	Hal Trosky, Sr.	Hal, Jr.
Lew Krausse, Sr.	Lew, Jr.	Paul (Dizzy) Trout	Steve (Rainbow)
Bill Kunkel	Jeff	Al Unser	Del
Joe Landrum	Bill	Ozzie Virgil, Sr.	Ozzie, Jr.
Max Lanier	Hal	Howard Wakefield	Dick
Vern Law	Vance	Dixie Walker	Dixie & Harry
Thornton Lee	Don	Ed Walsh	Ed
Dutch Lerchen	George	JoJo White	Mike
Glenn Liebhardt	Glenn	Maury Wills	Bump
Fred Lindstrom	Chuck	Bobby Wine	Robbie
Jack Lively	Bud	Smokey Joe Wood	Joe
Connie Mack	Earle	Del Young	Del

bination who both played professionally in Japan. (1 point.)

14. Name the eight fathers who occupy positions in the Hall of Fame. (1 point for each you can name.)

15. Name the eight major-league fathers who sired more than one son to play in the big leagues. (1 point for each you can name.)

16. Three major-league sons have been named Rookie of the Year. Who were they? (1 point for each.)

17. Few major leaguers can claim a career spanning fourteen years. Age slows down even those who last this long, and they lose a step on the base paths and their swing slows down. However, this baseball father (whose career lasted even longer) won a league base-stealing title *fourteen years after* his first stolen base crown. (1 point.)

18. These two sons of a big league pitcher are the only brothers to have both won batting titles. What's the family? (1 point.)

19. Following a short and lackluster career as a pitcher, this major league father went on to have a distinguished career as a major league umpire and was still active when his son first appeared in the major leagues. (1 point.)

20. These two baseball fathers went from the dugout to the penthouse. Following their playing days, they became major league owners. (1 point.)

21. He is the only father—or son—to receive a Cy Young Award. (1 point.)

22. Baseball son Jim Bagby retired Joe DiMaggio to end the Yankee Clipper's 56-game hitting streak. However, that was not DiMaggio's longest hitting streak. In the Pacific Coast League, he once turned in a 61-game streak for the San Francisco Seals. What baseball son held him hitless to end that streak? (1 point.)

23. Name the first baseball father and son to have both played in a World Series. (1 point.)

24. Name the first African-American father-son combination. (1 point.)

25. In 1990, Barry Bonds became the second baseball son to win the MVP award (Cal Ripken, Jr. won in 1983). Name the five baseball fathers who have won MVP honors. (1 point for each you can name.)

Bonus. Name a father and son who have both managed in the major leagues. (1 point for each pair you name.)

Answers

1. Connie Mack.

2. Peaches Graham.

3. Okay, it's a trick question. The Griffeys were the first to play together *in the major leagues* when they became teammates in Seattle in 1990. But the first father and son to play together *professionally* were the O'Rourkes. In 1903, Orator Jim, player-owner of the Bridgeport team in the Connecticut League, lured his son Jim away from the Yale baseball team.

4. Earle Mack played for his father, Connie.

5. Dale played for Yogi Berra in New York.

6. Bobby Bonds was a five-time 30/30 player; Barry accomplished the feat for the first time in the 1990 season.

7. Ray Boone's solo home run in the third inning made the score 4-0. In the eighth, Gus Bell's two RBI pinch-hit shot gave the NL a 9-7 lead. The AL won the game in the ninth when Yogi Berra and Mickey Mantle scored on Nellie Fox's single.

8. On July 13, 1960, Vern Law started and won that season's second All-Star game.

9. Mel Stottlemyre lost the 1969 All-Star game.

10. Earl Averill hit Dizzy Dean with a line drive that broke Dean's toe in the 1937 All-Star contest. Dean tried to come back too soon, and his career ended shortly thereafter.

11. Jim Hegan caught, Ray Boone played short, and Bob Kennedy was in the outfield.

12. Bob Boone caught, Kurt Stillwell played short, and Danny Tartabull played in the outfield.

13. Marty and Matt Keogh.

14. The players, in order of their years of election are: Connie Mack (1937), George Sisler (1938), Eddie Collins (1938), Orator Jim O'Rourke (1945), Ed Walsh (1946), Yogi Berra (1972), Earl Averill (1975), and Fred Lindstrom (1976).

15. Sandy Alomar—Roberto and Sandy; Jimmy Cooney—Jimmy and John; Larry Gilbert—Charlie and Tookie; Sam Hairston — Jerry and John; Cal Ripken—Billy and Cal; George Sisler — Dick and Dave; Mel Stottlemyre — Todd and Mel; Dixie Walker — Dixie and Harry.

16. Tom Tresh was AL Rookie of the Year in 1962, Cal Ripken in 1982, and Sandy Alomar in 1990.

17. Eddie Collins stole 81 bases in 1910 and 42 in 1924; he also led the league in 1919 and 1923.

18. Dixie and Harry Walker.

19. Bill Kunkel gave up a mediocre pitching career for an outstanding career as an umpire.

20. Connie Mack and Haywood Sullivan. Both had sons who played for their franchises.

21. Vern Law.

22. Ed Walsh, Jr., pitching for Oakland, retired DiMaggio five times on July 25, 1933.

23. Billy Sullivan caught for the "Hitless Wonder" White Sox in 1906; Billy, Jr. caught for the Tigers in the 1940 World Series.

24. The Hairstons.

25. Eddie Collins won the Chalmers Award in 1914. George Sisler won the 1922 AL MVP; Dolph Camilli the 1941 NL award. Yogi Berra was named AL MVP in 1951, 1954, and 1955, and Maury Wills was named the NL MVP in 1962.

Bonus. George and Dick Sisler. Connie and Earle Mack. While Earle never had a managerial contract, he did manage a few games.

Scoring. There are 50 possible points and three possible bonus points. If you scored 45 or more, you probably should have written this book. Anything else, you grade yourself.

ALL-TIME FATHER-SON TEAMS

Before there was fantasy baseball, before there was computer baseball, and before baseball cards were available all year long, baseball fans employed an imaginative array of ways to while away the off-season. They relived the season, studied stats, became imaginary general managers as they argued trades. And they constructed fantasy teams. These might be all-time all-stars, or the greatest array of players ever fielded by a particular team. In fact, baseball fans seem to have conjured up just about every conceivable type of fantasy team — all rookie, all switch-hitter, all born outside the continental U.S., etc. There's even a book devoted solely to listing various combinations of all-time teams.

So, scan the register of baseball fathers and sons. Peek ahead to the records section. Think it over for a minute. At least four types of fantasy father-son teams present themselves; you may think of others. You can select an all-father team and an all-son team. You can select an all-time team from all the fathers and sons. The fourth possibility may be the most challenging. Compile a roster in which you have to use both the father and the son. In the case of multiple sons, we'll say you can designate one or both sons.

Okay, before we take a look at this writer's choice for the all-time father-son baseball team, let's set a few ground rules. For our all-time fantasy team, let's say we can select any player whose father—or son—was active at the major league level. This way we can include the Ripkens. Of course, if you want to be a purist, you can simply decide that you want to select your own all-time team on the basis that they had to have played at the major league level. If so, I would suggest you simply substitute Maury Wills for Cal Ripken at shortstop. I'm not including a DH, but there are plenty of candidates to choose from if you want one on your team. Now, without further ado, here is one man's selection for the all-time, father-son team.

	ALL-TIME FATHER-SON TEAM												

Pos.	G	AB	R	H	2B	3B	HR	RBI	BB	SO	SB	BA	SA
Yogi Berra													
C	2,120	7,555	1,175	2,150	321	49	358	1,430	704	414	30	.285	.482
George Sisler													
1B	2,055	8,267	1,284	2,812	425	164	102	1,175	472	327	375	.340	.468
Eddie Collins													
2B	2,826	9,949	1,818	3,311	437	186	42	1,299	1,503	286	743	.333	.428
Buddy Bell													
3B	2,405	8,995	1,120	2,514	425	56	201	1,106	836	776	55	.279	.406
Cal Ripken													
SS	1,476	5,655	871	1,552	294	28	225	828	635	701	33	.274	.456
Earl Averill													
OF	1,669	6,358	1,224	2,020	401	128	238	1,165	775	518	69	.318	.533
Bobby Bonds													
OF	1,849	7,043	1,258	1,886	302	66	332	1,024	914	1,757	461	.268	.471
Dixie Walker													
OF	1,905	6,740	1,037	2,064	376	96	105	1,023	817	325	59	.306	.437
Totals:													
	16,305	60,562	9,787	18,309	2,981	773	1,603	9,050	6,656	5,104	1,825	.302	.460

Reserves:
Bob Boone: C; Dolph Camilli: 1B; Roberto Alomar: 2B; Fred Lindstrom: 3B; Maury Wills: SS; Ken Griffey, Jr.: OF; Jim O'Rourke: C, INF-OF

Pitchers:

W	L	Pct	Sv	G	GS	CG	IP	H	BB	SO	ShO	ERA
Starter: Ed Walsh (RHP)												
194	128	.602	40	430	315	250	2,965	2,346	617	1,736	58	1.82

Other Pitchers:
Jim Bagby, Sr. (RHP), Hal Lanier (LHP), Vern Law (RHP), Thornton Lee (LHP), Ray Narleski (RHP), Mel Stottlemyre (RHP), Dizzy Trout (RHP), Joe Wood (RHP/Outfielder)

Discussion

This team would win a lot of games. Five Hall of Famers provide the backbone, and you've got two Hall of Famers on the bench! They won't hit as many home runs as some fantasy teams, but you're going to get production up and down the lineup. Let's take this a step further. How does this look for a batting order? Bobby Bonds leads off, who was perhaps the most disruptive lead-off hitter in baseball history until Ricky Henderson came along. Eddie Collins bats second, one of baseball's premier contact hitters. Let's put George Sisler in the third slot. How about Berra batting cleanup and Cal Ripken in the fifth slot? Berra ranks 37th on the all-time home run list, and Ripken is the first shortstop in history to homer 20 or more times in nine consecutive seasons. Frankly, the rest of the order doesn't matter all that much since you've got two left-handed hitters with career averages over .300 and a right-handed hitting third baseman with over 1,100 career RBIs.

Big Ed Walsh anchors the pitching staff. If this team has a weakness, it's here. Thornton Lee and Hal Lanier are the only lefties, although Ross Grimsley or Dick Ellsworth must be given some consideration. At least one of them would probably be included if you were building a 25-man roster. Others might be inclined to include Joe Coleman. We're a little short on relief specialists, with Ray Narleski being the only one who made a career of relief pitching. On the other hand, a lot of these guys pitched at a time when a good pitcher was expected to start and also come into crucial games at key moments in a relief role. Relief pitchers just weren't used as they are today. This is also a fantasy staff used to winning, as their cumulative record attests.

As far as the reserves go, Bob Boone provides a reliable backup; if Sandy Alomar keeps playing like he did in 1990, he may turn out to be a serious contender for this position on our hypothetical roster. Dolph Camilli was a tough choice over Hal Trosky at first. Both were great sluggers and impressive RBI men, but Camilli's RBI totals are just too impressive. Roberto Alomar and Maury Wills provide speed. Lindstrom is a Hall of Fame third baseman. Orator Jim O'Rourke is a bit of a sentimental choice over someone like Don Mueller, but he's also another Hall of Famer and, in a pinch, he can play anywhere. Assuming Ken Griffey, Jr. remains healthy, he may turn out to be another one who will make the first team in the future. Bobby Bonds, of course, could also emerge as a choice.

Okay, let's take a look at some other variations. What do you think of these choices for the All-Father and All-Son teams?

All-Father Team

- C: Yogi Berra
- 1B: George Sisler
- 2B: Eddie Collins
- 3B: Fred Lindstrom
- SS: Maury Wills
- OF: Earl Averill
- OF: Bobby Bonds
- OF: Jim O'Rourke
- P: Big Ed Walsh

All-Son Team

- C: Bob Boone or Sandy Alomar, Jr.
- 1B: Mike Hegan
- 2B: Roberto Alomar
- 3B: Buddy Bell
- SS: Cal Ripken, Jr.
- OF: Dixie Walker
- OF: Barry Bonds
- OF: Ken Griffey, Jr.
- P: Ross Grimsley

Just putting these teams together provides lots of fun, and you may have already developed a few arguments with these selections. However, now that you're warmed up, we've saved the most challenging for last. Try assembling a complete roster—either 24 or 25 players—with the stipulation that the roster must include both the fathers and their sons.

MY MOM PLAYED THIS GAME

The Montreal Expos signed Casey Candaele as an undrafted free agent out of the University of Arizona in 1982. The switch-hitting utility infielder made his major league debut for the Expos on June 5, 1986 and became the first major league baseball player to have a mother who also played professional baseball. Casey's mother, Helen Callaghan Candaele, played in the All-American Girls Professional Baseball League.

The AAGPBL was the brainchild of chewing gum magnate (and Cubs owner) P.K. Wrigley. The league opened play in 1943 with the Rockford Peaches, South Bend Blue Sox, Racine Belles, and Kenosha Comets playing a 108-game schedule. The league proved popular; it expanded to 10 teams and in 1948 it drew a million fans. The league folded in 1954. For more information on the AAGPBL, see "Women and the Game" in John Bowman and Joel Zoss' *Diamonds In The Rough*, Debra Shattuck's "Women in Baseball" in *Total Baseball*, or the television documentary, "A League of Their Own," produced by Kelly Candaele. The Hall of Fame opened a special exhibit on women in baseball in 1988.

While the AAGPBL proved the most durable, it was far from the first effort to organize a women's baseball league. The first known "professional" women's game took place in Springfield, Illinois on September 11, 1875. Three men organized and promoted a game between the "Blondes" and the "Brunettes." The idea was copied or adapted by promoters and entrepreneurs, and around the turn of the century "Bloomer Girl" teams toured out of Kansas City, New York, Texas, and Boston. These were barnstorming teams of both men and women who played exhibitions against local teams. Baseball father Smokey Joe Wood got his start in organized baseball playing for the Kansas City Bloomer Girls. This makes him the first major league father to play professionally for a "girls'" team!

In this day and age, it seems only a matter of time before some talented female ballplayer breaks baseball's sex line. No doubt it will seem sensational at the time, but within a few years everyone will probably wonder what all the fuss was about.

GRANDPAS AND LITTL'UNS

Baseball genes have skipped a generation five times. George Brinton McClellan Rooks went into the Boston Beaneaters' outfield for the first time on May 5, 1891. Boston won the National League that season, but it's doubtful that Rooks was there to celebrate since his total major league career lasted a mere five games. He batted two for sixteen, walked four times, struck out once, and scored a run.

Almost halfway through the next century, George's grandson strode onto a major league diamond for the first time. Lou Possehl made his pitching debut for the Phillies on August 25, 1946. Lou spent portions of five seasons with the Phillies—extremely small portions. He appeared in 1946-48, missed the next two years including the Whiz Kids pennant of 1950, then reappeared in 1951-52. All in all, Lou appeared in 15 games, started 8 of them, won 2, lost 5, and left baseball with a 5.19 ERA.

Shano Collins played first and the outfield for the White and Red Sox teams between 1910 and 1925. Since he spent the 1919 season with the White Sox, you could say that he was probably the only player in major league history to have played with the White, Red, and Black Sox. Shano was part of the clean Sox faction and so was able to stay in baseball. He managed Boston during the 1931 and part of the 1932 seasons. Perhaps Shano taught his grandson his positions—Bob Gallagher played first and the outfield for the Red Sox, Astros, and Mets.

Bill Brubaker first came up for the Pirates in 1932. He won the regular third base job in 1936 and led the major leagues that season with 96 strikeouts. He offset this with 102 RBIs and hit .289. This proved to be Bill's career year, and things slid downhill from then until he left baseball in 1943. Fifty-one years and eight days later, grandson Dennis Rasmussen pitched for the San Diego Padres.

Sometime during a game on July 10, 1918, Martin John Herrmann took the mound for the NL's Brooklyn Robins. Marty pitched an inning without giving up a hit or a walk and, somewhat mysteriously, never appeared in the major leagues again. The White Sox brought grandson Ed up for a cup of coffee in 1967 before making him their regular catcher in 1969. A pretty good defensive catcher, he spent the next few seasons behind the plate, swatting down Wilbur Wood's knuckleball. After brief stops with the Yankees and Angels, he landed with Houston in time to spend time snatching J.R. Richards' fast ball out of thin air.

Lloyd Spencer, an outfielder, played just eight games for the 1913 Washington Senators. Grandson Jim exceeded grandpa's career his first season (1968) and went on to spend 15 years in the American League with California, Texas, Chicago, New York, and Oakland.

It seems highly probable that the second grandfather-grandson pitcher-catcher combination will develop in the next few years. Bill Salkeld started plying his trade as a professional ballplayer in 1934 and gave it up after 1936. He came out of retirement to sign on as a playing manager for Tucson in the Arizona-Texas League. He batted his way back into the Pacific Coast League and was finally called up by the Pirates in 1945; he proceeded to hit .311 in 95 games. Bill appeared in 356 games for the Pirates, Red Sox, and White Sox. His grandson Roger was the Seattle Mariners' first round draft pick in 1990, and the third player taken in the draft. In $314^2/_3$ innings of high school ball, Roger posted a 38-9 won-lost record, struck out 456 while walking just 194 batters, and threw 7 one-hitters and a no-hitter.

PART I

Fathers and Sons in the Majors

THE EARLY YEARS (1870s-1900)

Prior to the creation of the National League (1876), Orator Jim O'Rourke was already an established professional base ball (they used two words in those days) player. O'Rourke played for the Middletown, Connecticut Mansfields in 1872. When they disbanded, he signed on with the Boston Red Stockings and helped them win National Association Championships in 1873, '74, and '75.

The Boston Red Stockings joined the National League as a charter member, and on April 24, 1876, O'Rourke recorded the first hit in league history. The Orator displayed a keen batting eye, hitting .327 that season and registering 15 walks, second in the league.

The Red Stockings won the 1877 championship (42-18), and Orator Jim led the NL in runs (68), on-base percentage (.407), and walks (20). This latter achievement seems modest at first glance. But, remember that it took nine balls to walk a batter in those days PLUS the batter instructed the pitcher as to where he wanted the ball pitched. What's more, pitchers were restricted to a stiff-arm delivery. Seen in this light, O'Rourke's base-on-balls total reveals an extraordinary patience at the plate that must have exasperated opposing teams. The Red Stockings, incidentally, eventually metamorphosed into the Atlanta Braves.

But if O'Rourke exasperated his opponents, the penny-pinching ways of the Boston ownership exasperated O'Rourke. When they tried to collect a $20 uniform fee from their players, it proved the last straw for O'Rourke and shortstop Harry Wright. They took their talents to Providence for the 1879 season. Orator Jim apparently stopped waiting on walks and started slamming the ball that season, as he powered the Grays to a league championship. He smashed 11 triples (fourth in the league) and six home runs (second in the league), led the league in on-base percentage (.371), and tied Charley Jones of Boston for the league lead in RBIs with 62. This RBI total stands as the most produced in a single season during the 1870s.

O'Rourke's offensive production tapered off slightly during the ensuing decade, as he spent seasons with the Red Stockings (1880), the Buffalo Bisons (Player-Manager, 1881-1884), and the New York Gothams. Still, he batted .300 or above during six seasons and led the league in hits in 1884 (162) and triples in 1885 (16). By the end of his active major league career, Orator Jim had recorded games at every position and could boast of a .312 career batting average in 1,761 games. James Henry O'Rourke also spent time as an umpire, a minor league founder, a minor league playing owner, and a minor league president. He added another major league game to his career totals in 1904 when he caught a complete game for the Giants; he was then 52.

The notion of postseason play began to take hold during the 1880s, originally in the form of city or regional championships staged after the regular season. In 1884, the winner of the National League took on the winner of the American Association, and what we now know as the World Series was born. These championships varied from six to 15 games.

Baseball's longest World Series pitted the NL's Detroit Wolverines (79-45) against the American Association's St. Louis Browns (95-40) and was staged in 10 different cities between October 10 and 26, 1887. The Wolverines chewed up the Browns, 10 games to five. Baseball father Charlie Ganzel divided his time between first base (10 games) and catching (seven games) for the Wolverines; a couple times even playing both positions in one game. In 58 at-bats, he had 13 hits (.224), scored 5 runs, drove in 2 runs, and stole 3 bases.

Ganzel played his first major league ball with the St. Paul White Caps of the Union Association before joining the Phillies in 1885; he came to Detroit in 1886. During the regular season, the Wolverines used him mainly as a catcher, although they also employed him at first, third, and the outfield. He hit .260 in 57 games. When the Wolverines disbanded after the 1888 season, Ganzel caught on with the Red Stockings and played the remainder of his 14-year major league career in proximity to his Quincy, Massachusetts boyhood home.

The 1888 championship was pared back to a best of 10 format with games in New York, Brooklyn, Philadelphia, and St. Louis. Orator Jim O'Rourke played for his third different championship team as the Giants prevailed six games to four over the Browns.

In 1889, the number of balls required for a walk was established at the now accepted number of four. O'Rourke and the Giants returned to the Series. They stood up and proved they were better men than the Brooklyn Bridegrooms, six games to three.

Prior to the start of the 1890 season, The Orator lent his rhetorical skills to the creation of the Players Association. He was one of dozens of established stars who jumped to the new league. He registered his highest batting average that season. Although it enjoyed widespread fan support, financial difficulties forced the Players Association to fold after just one season and O'Rourke rejoined the Giants.

After the American Association folded, the National League experimented with a split-season format in 1892. The resulting postseason match-up featured the Boston club against Cleveland, a club that had been absorbed from the now defunct AA. Boston (are you ready for this?) was now known as the Beaneaters; Beaneater Charlie Ganzel caught two games and went four of eight at the plate in the series. The first game against the Spiders was an 11-inning scoreless tie called due to darkness. The Beaneaters won the next five games. Just what do you suppose their team symbol looked like?

Okay, the Beaneaters may have had one of the most hysterical team names in baseball history (the Bridegrooms are right up there too), but they were credited with generally playing smart, heads-up, and clean baseball. And in an era when there was only one umpire on the field, and players tripped, spiked, held, punched, and spat, the fact that the gentlemanly Beaneaters won five pennants during this rowdy decade must surely count for something.

1901-1919

The creation of the American League, its success, and Commissioner Ban Johnson's determination to clean up the game eventually prompted the National League to follow suit. As part of this process, the American League introduced the two-umpire system in 1906; by 1912 it became standard in both leagues. Other rule changes continued to encourage the evolution of the game towards its modern form.

The game remained a thump and run endeavor with hitters brandishing heavy bats in choked-up hands. Not only were the balls dead, but they were used and used and used during the course of a game. As if that weren't enough, players and pitchers took plenty of inventive liberties in scratching and scuffing the ball as well as exercising considerable creativity in discoloring and dousing the ball with all manner of imaginative substances. Things began to change with the introduction of the cork center ball in 1911, but it would be several more years before ballplayers and managers fully realized the difference.

The century's opening decades also provided the stuff for fashioning plenty of baseball legends. Exciting names carried out deeds on (and sometimes off) the playing field that continue to elicit awe from the devotees of today. One has only to recite the names Ty Cobb, Honus Wagner, Nap Lajoie, Cy Young, Walter Johnson, Christy Mathewson ... to conjure up thrilling images of those days. Several baseball fathers loom among these early giants and it is to them that we now pay our respects.

Cornelius McGillicuddy, known to baseball history as Connie Mack, took the helm of the Philadelphia Athletics during their first year in existence and didn't relinquish it until half a century later. During the interim he assembled and disassembled one of baseball's greatest teams, endured years of baseball drought, and assembled a second dynasty. Throughout it all he presided over the dugout with such dignity and decorum that he was invariably referred to as Mister Mack. This was a man who seldom missed church, even after the general acceptance of Sunday baseball.

As a player, Mack became one of the first catchers to adopt the practice of playing directly behind the hitter rather than 10 to 20 feet away as was then customary. He quickly developed a reputation for his ability to distract hitters with his conversation, asking just the right question or making just the right remark to distract their concentration. He also learned how to use his glove to make the sound of a foul tip and created quite a few "caught" foul tip third strike strike-outs.

When he moved into the dugout, Mister Mack never adopted the custom of donning a uniform, preferring instead somber business suits, starched collars, and a straw skimmer. Of course, because he wasn't wearing a uniform, he couldn't come onto the field. Some historians wonder whether this might help explain why he was thrown out of so few games.

Early baseball writers dubbed Mack "The Tall Tactician," but he might just as well have been "The Taciturn Tactician." Like any legend, stories about Mack abound, and this one may or may not stand up to scrutiny. A volatile ballplayer was once enraged when Mack chastised him for an errant throw. "What did you want me to do," he thundered, "stick it up my ass?" "Well," replied Mack, who virtually never used any sort of strong language himself, "you have to admit it would have been safer there."

When Connie's son Earle made the A's, they became the first father-son manager-player combination. Earle didn't carve out much of a playing career, but he did end up coaching with the A's for 26 years.

One of the keys to Connie Mack's early success with the A's was keystone sacker Eddie Collins. Mack signed Collins while he was still a student at Columbia University. Eddie's athletic career there began in the fall of 1903 when the 16-year-old, 140-pound freshman won the varsity quarterback position. He came to Mack's attention while playing semipro baseball to earn money for his tuition. The Sad Sack second baseman with the Jumbo ears played six games for the A's in the 1906 season under the name of Sullivan. He lost his collegiate eligibility—not for this, but because he had played semipro ball under his own name. Nevertheless, Columbia University hired the popular Collins to coach their 1907 team.

"Cocky" played his first full season in the majors in 1908 and quickly displayed one of those behavior quirks that become a batting trademark. Just before he came to the plate, he would park his gum under the bill of his hat. But if he got two strikes, he would reach up, put the gum back in his mouth, and begin chewing furiously.

In 1909, his name appeared among the offensive (and defensive) league leaders for the first time when he finished second to Ty Cobb in hits, batting average, and on-base percentage. Collins and Mr. Mack's A's proceeded to play championship baseball in 1910, 1911, and 1913. They won the AL in 1914 but lost to Boston in the World Series. When financial constraints forced Mack to break up his "$100,000 infield," Collins went out west to Chicago, where he helped the White Sox win a championship in 1917.

In 1919, Collins captained the White Sox team that became embroiled in baseball's greatest scandal. Collins emerged unscathed but for the rest of his life spoke contemptuously and unsympathetically of his crooked and/or stupid teammates. Eddie returned to Philadelphia in the twilight of his career and completed his 25-year playing career back with Mack as a playing coach. Mack considered Collins "the greatest second baseman that ever lived." Even today, he remains one of the two or three best the game has ever seen.

When Eddie stepped up to the plate for the first time in the majors (September 17, 1906), it was in Chicago against another Ed. He singled in his first at-bat, but Big Ed Walsh and the White Sox went on to win the game 5-4 in 11 innings. The "Hitless Wonders" also proceeded to win the AL pennant and the World Series despite the fact that both their team batting average (.230) and total hits (1,132) registered dead last in the league. Over the next few years Walsh would hurl his way into the Hall of Fame. His lifetime 1.82 ERA and opponents' on-base percentage of .270 remain all-time major league records.

Question. What pitcher led the major leagues in winning percentage during the 1911-1920 decade? The great Walter "Big Train" Johnson? The incomparable Christy "Big Six" Mathewson? The unpredictable Grover Cleveland Alexander? All wrong. It was baseball father Smokey Joe Wood. In 1912 Wood's 34-5 record established an .872 winning percentage, the best single season mark in the first two decades of the 20th century. His 104-49 cumulative provided a .680 percentage, best in the decade. If that weren't enough, baseball analyst Bill James, in his *Historical Baseball Abstract*, named Smokey Joe the "Best-Looking Player" of the decade.

Now let's begin taking a season-by-season look at our national pastime, highlighting the roles played by baseball's fathers and sons.

A Season-by-Season Look

1901

April 24—Billy Sullivan is the Chicago catcher in the first game ever played in the American League; the White Stockings beat the Cleveland Bronchos 8-2, and Sullivan goes two for four and scores a run.

With a slogan of "clean baseball, beer, and plenty of twenty-five cent seats," the American League opens play with clubs in eight cities. Catchers are required to stay behind the batters within 10 feet of home plate, and the National League adopts the foul strike rule. A Spalding bat sells for $1.00; their best ball (warrantied to last a full game) retails for $1.25. Their top-of-the-line catcher's mitt costs $6.00, and an all-leather, boy's infielder glove can be purchased for 25 cents.

With Sullivan as their regular catcher, the Chicago White Stockings proceed to capture the first American League championship with a record of 83 wins and 53 losses. No postseason play-off ensues as the National League remains disdainful of its new competitor. Still, the White Stockings outdraw their established crosstown rivals.

Active Fathers/Sons: Billy Sullivan and Willie Mills.

1902

The National League requires batsmen to attempt to get out of the way of a pitched ball and disallows a free base when hit by a slowly pitched ball. Connie Mack's Athletics win their first pennant with a record of 83-53.

Active Fathers/Sons: Joe Berry, Sr., Peaches Graham, and Billy Sullivan.

1903

September 18—In his only major league pitching appearance, baseball father Peaches Graham has a no-hitter thrown against him.

The American League adopts the foul strike rule. Jack Doscher becomes the first son of a major leaguer to play in the big leagues; he goes 0-1 pitching for Chicago (NL) and 0-0 in three games for Brooklyn. The AL champion Boston Pilgrims defeat the NL's Pittsburgh Pirates five games to three in the first World Series.

Active Fathers/Sons: Jack Doscher, Peaches Graham, and Billy Sullivan.

1904

May 5 — Cy Young hurls the American League's first perfect game against Connie Mack's Philadelphia Athletics.

September 22—The New York Giants clinch their first pennant since 1888 as Orator Jim O'Rourke catches a complete game at the age of 52 years, 29 days. He gets a hit and scores a run for good measure. The Giants refuse to meet the AL champs and so no Series is played.

The AL adopts the 154-game schedule and requires clubs to use home and road uniforms. The American Sabbath Union opposes Sunday baseball. Several rule changes take effect, including: "The baserunner is out if one or more members of the team at bat stand or collect at or around a base for which a baserunner is trying, thereby confusing the fielding side and adding to the difficulty of making such a play."

During the winter meetings of the Connecticut League, Orator Jim O'Rourke protested against the participation in four games of a New Haven player named Tuckey. The Orator said that Tuckey had been "farmed out"; that is, a major league club actually owned his playing contract.

It had been an exceedingly tight three-way race between New Haven, Springfield, and O'Rourke's Bridgeport team. New Haven won the pennant on the final day of the season. Springfield edged into second place past Bridgeport by defeating league doormats Meriden in a *quadruple-header*, while Bridgeport managed only a split in a doubleheader against Holyoke.

Now, with the league upholding O'Rourke's protest and throwing out the games Tuckey played for New Haven, O'Rourke's club was entitled to the championship. However, O'Rourke demurred, insisting that his protest had been made on principle rather than as a ploy to win the pennant. Complying with Orator Jim's desires, the Connecticut League owners awarded New Haven the pennant.

Active Fathers/Sons: Jack Doscher, Jim O'Rourke, Billy Sullivan, and Ed Walsh.

1905

Connie Mack's Philadelphia Athletics win the AL for the second time in four years. World Series play resumes and the A's lose to Christy Mathewson and the New York Giants, four games to one.

Active Fathers/Sons: Jack Doscher, Charlie Malay, Billy Sullivan, Howard Wakefield, and Ed Walsh.

1906

Rule changes this season include one stating: "Foul lines are to be clearly visible from any part of the diamond, and no wood or other hard substances shall be used in construction of such lines." The White Sox start August in fourth place, with the Athletics in first. But the Pale Hose win 19 consecutive games and go on to clinch the AL pennant by three games. The "Hitless Wonders" record a team batting average of .228 and hit only three home runs all season—one by pitcher Ed Walsh. In the World Series, behind the pitching of Big Ed Walsh, the Hitless Wonders outplay the mighty Cubs in the first crosstown World Series. One of Walsh's two victories is a shutout; he hurled 10 shutouts during the regular season to lead the majors. He also tied for the league lead in saves with three.

Active Fathers/Sons: Eddie Collins, Jack Doscher, Glenn Liebhardt, Billy Sullivan, Howard

Wakefield, and Ed Walsh.

1907

A fine of $5 is imposed on any player, other than the pitcher, who intentionally discolors or damages the ball. Batters are out if they step from one batter's box to the other after the pitcher takes his position. Ed Walsh posts a 24-18 record. He leads the major leagues in innings pitched (422), games (56), and complete games (37), and leads the AL in ERA (1.60).

Active Fathers/Sons: Eddie Collins, Glenn Liebhardt, Harl Maggert, Billy Sullivan, Howard Wakefield, and Ed Walsh.

1908

June 13—Ed Walsh steals home in the seventh inning of a game against New York.

September 29—Ed Walsh pitches both games of a doubleheader, winning both. In 18 innings of work, he gives up one run, seven hits, and walks one.

October 2—Ed Walsh strikes out 15 in eight innings, but ends up on the losing end of a 1-0 score as Cleveland's Addie Joss throws a perfect game.

Pitchers are prohibited from scuffing or discoloring new balls. Roger Bresnehan uses shin guards.

Big Ed Walsh pitches 464 innings, wins 40 games, and records 42 complete games and 11 shutouts. His mark includes nine wins against both the Yankees and the Red Sox.

Active Fathers/Sons: Eddie Collins, Jack Doscher, Peaches Graham, Glenn Liebhardt, Queenie O'Rourke, Ralph Savidge, Billy Sullivan, Ed Walsh, and Smokey Joe Wood.

1909

June 2—Ed Walsh steals home against the St. Louis Browns.

Players or managers ejected from games are required to go directly to the clubhouse or leave the grounds. Umpires are given the authority to accept or reject special ground rules.

Ed Walsh leads the AL with eight shutouts and is second in ERA with 1.41. Opponents can muster only a .203 batting average against him, and an on-base percentage of only .253. Eddie Collins finishes second in the AL in hits (198), walks (62), average (.346), and on-base percentage (.416). Collins' season marks also include 104 runs (third in the AL), 30 doubles (third in the AL), and 257 total bases (third in the AL).

Active Fathers/Sons: Eddie Collins, Peaches Graham, Glenn Liebhardt, Gene Moore, Sr., Ralph Savidge, Billy Sullivan, Dixie Walker, Sr., Ed Walsh, Smokey Joe Wood, and Del Young.

1910

August 24—Billy Sullivan catches three of 39 baseballs dropped from the top of the Washington Monument.

Teams are required to deliver their batting order prior to the start of the game. Also, "In case of spectators overflowing on the playing field, the home captain shall make special ground rules to cover balls batted or thrown into the crowd."

Connie Mack's "$100,000 infield," featuring Eddie Collins, wins the AL and World Series against the Cubs, 4-1; Collins hit .429 and swiped four bases. The season provided Collins with his first base-stealing crown, with 81 thefts. "Cocky" finished fourth in the AL in average (.322) and on-base percentage (.381). Earle Mack becomes the first major leaguer to be managed by his father. Big Ed Walsh leads the league with 45 games and five saves, and leads baseball with an ERA of 1.26 and the fewest walks per game (1.48). He is among the league leaders in innings pitched (370), shutouts (7), and strikeouts (258).

Active Fathers/Sons: Eddie Collins, Red Corriden, Bill Crouch, Peaches Graham, Dutch Lerchen, Earle Mack, Bob Meinke, Eugene Moore, Billy Sullivan, Dixie Walker, Ed Walsh, and Smokey Joe Wood.

1911

The Spalding Company introduces the cork center ball to the general market. "Base ball today is no hapazzard [sic] amusement, it is a scientific pastime, a sport of almost geometric exactitude," reads their advertisement for the product. It continues, "It commands the best that is in men of national prominence, and gives in return the plaudits of millions. . ." The ball retailed for $1.25. Spalding retailed its top-of-the-line catcher's mitt for $8.00; its first baseman's mitt for $4.00, the same price as its top fielder's mitt. A youth's "professional style leather glove" sold for 50 cents; a youth economy model could be had for 25 cents. The company offered uniforms from $4.00 to $15.00 with a discount for supplying a whole team. To improve their batting, a movable batting cage was available at a cost of $50.00; "tarred nets with this backstop instead of plain nets" cost an extra $3.00.

Smokey Joe Wood and Big Ed Walsh both threw no-hitters during the season. On July 29th, Wood no-hits the St. Louis Browns, allowing only two walks and a hit batsman to win 5-0. On August 27th, Walsh hurls his only career no-hitter. Pitching at Comiskey Park against the Red Sox, only one man reached first (a walk) as he also wins 5-0.

Walsh's season record is 27-18, while Wood's

is 23-17. Walsh leads the league in games (56), innings (369), saves (4), and strikeouts (255). Wood placed second in strikeouts (231) and saves (3). Both men threw five shutouts.

Connie Mack's Athletics win the World Series in six games. Mack employs only three pitchers against John McGraw's New York Giants, and Frank Baker homers in the second and third games to become "Home Run Baker."

Active Fathers/Sons: Eddie Collins, Peaches Graham, Jack Lively, Billy Sullivan, Dixie Walker, Ed Walsh, and Smokey Joe Wood.

1912

May 18—Eddie Collins collects five hits and steals four bases as the Athletics trounce a standby team assembled by Detroit manager Hughie Jennings when his regulars stage a strike over Ty Cobb's suspension for fighting with a fan. The Athletics win 24-2.

September 11—Eddie Collins steals six bases in a game; he repeats the feat on September 22nd.

Joe Wood leads Boston to the AL title with a 34-5 record, including 16 consecutive wins. He leads the majors in wins, winning percentage (.872), complete games (35), and shutouts (10). In the World Series, he wins three and loses one as Boston overcomes the New York Giants. Ed Walsh pitches in 62 games, registering 32 complete games, 6 shutouts, and 10 saves—the most in the majors that season. Wood and Walsh finish second and third behind Walter Johnson in numerous pitching categories, including fewest hits per game, strikeouts, ERA, and opponents' batting average and on-base percentage.

Active Fathers/Sons: Jim Bagby, Sr., Eddie Collins, Red Corriden, Peaches Graham, Ernie Johnson, Harl Maggert, Chick Mattick, Guy Morton, Sr., Eugene Moore, Sr., Joe Schultz, Sr., Billy Sullivan, Dixie Walker, Ed Walsh, and Smokey Joe Wood.

1913

July 4—Smokey Joe Wood ties a major league record for hitting by a pitcher by smacking two doubles in the fourth inning.

Early in the season, Smokey Joe Wood slips on wet grass while fielding a bunt. He breaks the thumb on his pitching hand. After this, Wood never completely recovers his fast ball and pitches in constant pain. For the season, Eddie Collins leads the majors with 125 runs, and compiles 184 hits, 242 total bases, 85 walks, a .345 average, a .411 on-base percentage, and 54 stolen bases.

Connie Mack's Athletics defeat the New York Giants in the World Series, 4-1. Eddie Collins stars in Game Three with three hits (including a triple) and three RBIs.

Active Fathers/Sons: Eddie Collins, Red Corriden, Wally Mattick, Guy Morton, Steve Partenheimer, Joe Schultz, Ed Walsh, and Smokey Joe Wood.

1914

Rule changes continue as a batter hitting a home run or ground rule double is required to touch the bases in regular order. Now, don't you just have to stop and wonder for a moment what prompted this change? Were there perhaps a few screwball players who ran the bases in random order after a home run? Third base coaches are prohibited from running in the direction of home plate for the purpose of decoying the defense, and they cannot hold runners, although they are permitted "to address words of assistance and direction" to base runners.

The Federal League opens with franchises in eight cities. The league lures a number of stars from established NL and AL teams and creates opportunities for lesser players to compete at the major league level.

Philadelphia wins the AL by eight and a half games, but falters in the Series to be swept by the Boston Braves. The Braves, languishing in last place well into July, suddenly start winning and keep winning until they are World Champs. Baseball father Larry Gilbert contributes by playing sixty games in the outfield and hitting .268 with 25 RBIs. Gilbert goes zero for one as a pinch hitter in the Series. Eddie Collins leads the majors in runs with 122, and has a .344 batting average and a .452 on-base percentage. Despite a sub-par Series (3/14), Collins is named winner of the Chalmers Award (the Most Valuable Player award at the time).

Active Fathers/Sons: Angel Aragon, Eddie Collins, Red Corriden, Larry Gilbert, Earle Mack, Guy Morton, Billy Sullivan, Ed Walsh, Smokey Joe Wood, and Del Young.

1915

Prior to the start of the season, financial pressure forces Connie Mack to disband his "$100,000 infield." Eddie Collins is sold to the White Sox for $50,000, a remarkable sum at the time. Mack's once-proud A's tumble into the cellar, finishing the season with a 43-109 record, 58½ games out of first. George Sisler makes his debut as a pitcher/first baseman. Joe Wood leads the AL with a 1.49 ERA and a .750 winning percentage, but doesn't pitch in that year's Series. The Red Sox have five pitchers who won 14 or more games, including a young Babe Ruth (18-6). In the Series, the Red Sox utilize only three pitchers to dispatch the Phillies, four games to one.

Active Fathers/Sons: Eddie Collins, Red Corriden, Jim Eschen, Larry Gilbert, Ernie Johnson, Joe Schultz, George Sisler, Ed Walsh, Smokey Joe Wood, and Del Young.

1916

Smokey Joe Wood sits out the entire season. Some sources indicate that the reason was he now suffered pain so severe, he could not raise his right arm. Other sources report that he chose to hold out after Boston management sold his friend and roommate Tris Speaker to Cleveland. The truth may well be a combination of these two factors. What remains certain is that at the age of 26, Smokey Joe Wood's career as a pitcher is virtually over. Despite the departure of Speaker and the absence of Wood, Boston, behind the pitching of a young Babe Ruth, claims the AL pennant and the World Series. Connie Mack's Athletics end the season with a 36-117 record, including a span of 20 consecutive losses from July 21st to August 8th. Eddie Collins, now with Chicago, logs another fine season among the American League leaders with 17 triples, 86 walks, a .405 on-base percentage, and 40 stolen bases.

Active Fathers/Sons: Angel Aragon, Jim Bagby, Sr., Eddie Collins, Ernie Johnson, Joe Schultz, George Sisler, Billy Sullivan, and Ed Walsh.

1917

Smokey Joe Wood is dealt to Cleveland. He appears in only one game. George Sisler makes his mark on the AL with 190 hits (second behind Cobb's 225), 30 doubles (fourth), 244 total bases (fourth), a .353 average (second to Cobb's .383), and a .453 slugging average (fourth). Sisler's .390 on-base percentage lodges him fourth in the AL, one point ahead of Eddie Collins. Also in the AL, Jim Bagby asserts himself with 23 wins and 8 shutouts in 49 games and 321 innings of work. He registers seven saves for good measure.

In the sixth (and final) game of the World Series, Eddie Collins races home from third ahead of Giant third baseman Heinie Zimmerman. Collins was on third with Joe Jackson on first. When teammate Hap Felsch hit one back to the box, Collins faked a dash for the plate to draw a throw and prevent the double play. Collins let himself get caught in a rundown while Jackson ran from first to third and Felsch headed for second. Then, when Giants' catcher Bill Rariden flicked the ball to Zimmerman, Collins noticed that no one was backing up Rariden. When he noticed home wasn't covered, he streaked past Rariden toward the plate and forced Zimmerman into pursuit from his post at third. Collins' heads-up play

proved to be the winning run of the Series.

Active Fathers/Sons: Angel Aragon, Jim Bagby, Eddie Collins, Jimmy Cooney, Ernie Johnson, George Sisler, Ed Walsh, and Smokey Joe Wood.

1918

George Sisler leads the AL in stolen bases with 45. He is third in hits (154), fifth in total bases (199), third in average (.341), and fourth in on-base percentage (.400).

In one of baseball's most remarkable comeback stories, Smokey Joe Wood completes the transformation from pitcher to outfielder. He joins his friend Tris Speaker in the Cleveland outfield and records another 19 games at second as the Indians fight their way into second place, only two and a half games behind Boston. Smokey Joe finishes the season with 66 RBIs, tied with Babe Ruth for third in the AL.

Wood and Ruth become the fifth and sixth players in baseball history to hit more home runs than the rest of their teammates combined; Wood slams five of Cleveland's nine, while Ruth rockets eleven of Boston's fifteen.

Eddie Collins' 73 walks place him fourth in that category, and his .407 on-base puts him second to Cobb. Jim Bagby's 45 games tie him for the major league lead, and his six saves rank second in the AL; his 17 wins rank him fifth in the AL.

Active Fathers/Sons: Jim Bagby, Eddie Collins, Ernie Johnson, George Sisler, and Smokey Joe Wood.

1919

Sunday baseball is permitted in New York state.

Eddie Collins leads the AL with thirty-three stolen bases. Collins will be one of the few White Sox untainted by the "Black Sox" scandal. George Sisler enjoys another fine season with a .352 average (third in the AL), and he is also among the top five in the league in hits (180), triples (15), home runs (10), total bases (271), and slugging (.530). Jim Bagby allows a mere 1.64 walks per game.

Active Fathers/Sons: Jim Bagby, Eddie Collins, Jimmy Cooney, Joe Schultz, George Sisler, and Smokey Joe Wood.

1920-1940

Most of the time, history is a rather messy business. Like a rather poorly constructed run-on sentence, it lacks appropriate punctuation. One searches for the central meaning, looking for the best place to put a period or perhaps enclose a lingering afterthought in parentheses. Occasionally, though, history provides neat little punctuation marks through an event or series of events that enable historians to discern a definite transition from one period to another.

You are probably asking what all this has to do with baseball. Quite simply, this. Following the introduction of the "live" cork center ball, baseball slowly began waking up to new offensive possibilities. Symbolically, this transformation can be illustrated by examining the careers of two players named George.

Both Georges came into the American League at a time when pitchers generally had the upper hand; offense was generated one base at a time. However, astute managers realized that our Georges, both promising pitchers, had such skills with the stick that their potential value to the team was much greater with them in there swinging every day than it was with them throwing every fourth or fifth day.

And so, our two Georges became everyday players, and their subsequent career accomplishments provided ample proof that a new baseball era had begun. Conveniently for historians, during the 1920 season both performed deeds that provide a dramatic, forceful example of the new type of play ushered in by the live ball, as well as provide a convincing close to the old era.

In 1920, George Herman Ruth astounded the baseball world by smashing 54 home runs—an unheard of figure and 25 home runs more than Ruth's previous record of 29. His slugging average was an incredible .847, a mark that stands to this day. Baseball father George Harold Sisler is the other George, and he safely put the sphere into play for 257 hits, another record that stands to this day. In addition, he finished the season second to Ruth in slugging (.632), runs (137—tied with Tris Speaker), and home runs (Sisler's 19 pale in comparison with the Bambino's feat).

To put their slugging marks in some sort of perspective, keep in mind the fact that, aside from Babe Ruth's .657 mark the previous season (Sisler also finished second that year), Sisler's slugging average was the highest in either league since Nap Lajoie slugged .643 in 1901. However, the man they came to call Gorgeous George finished ahead of Ruth in total bases (399 to 388), and he won the batting crown with a .407 mark.

Consider the following. In 1915, the year Sisler first appeared in the American League, batters reached pitchers for 160 home runs. Over in the senior circuit, they displayed slightly more power, knocking 225 round-trippers. For the five-year period 1915-19, American Leaguers recorded 777 home runs; their National League counterparts hit 1,010, for a combined total 1,787. In 1920,

though, American Leaguers launched 370 home run balls to 261 in the NL. If we look at the 1920-24 seasons we see a dramatic increase to 2,287 American League and 2,207 National League home run clouts. The number of teams in the leagues and the length of the schedules remained the same for both periods, but the home run totals for either league in the latter period were greater than the combined totals from the earlier period. Other measures of the new trend in baseball could be explored, with similar results.

Today, even casual fans know of George Herman Ruth. However, even though he remains one of the game's greatest first basemen, and his single season hit record still stands, comparatively few fans remember Sisler. Perhaps that's to be expected. George Harold Sisler was as modest off the field as George Herman Ruth was flamboyant. The adjectives one bumps into most while reading about "The Sizzler" include retiring, unassuming, and sober; sober being used in this case in both meanings of the word. W.C. Fields, impressed by Sisler's ball playing, once invited George to join him in a bit of "snake-bite cure." Sisler politely refused, and a look of disappointment crossed Fields' face. "Oh well," he remarked, "not even the perfect ballplayer can have everything."

Sisler came into the big leagues from the University of Michigan campus at a time when it was still rare enough for a college man to play baseball that this was frequently mentioned. He signed with the St. Louis Browns and played for his old college coach, Branch Rickey. He was 4-4 with a 2.83 ERA as a rookie pitcher in 1915, but put in enough games at first and the outfield to record a .285 average in 274 at-bats. He swung a 42-ounce bat, and, as his records show, he swung it with authority.

After his conversion to first base, he displayed remarkable quickness and agility in the field. He once turned a suicide squeeze into a double play. Racing in from first, in one continuous motion he scooped up the ball, tagged out the runner about 15 feet from the plate, and flipped the ball to the catcher in time for him to tag out the runner streaking home from third. Branch Rickey told a story about George fielding a ground ball and tossing it softly toward first. When he discovered the pitcher wasn't covering the bag, he leaped forward to catch his own throw and baseball's only 3-3 putout. The story may or may not be true, but the combination of baseball skills that Sisler brought to the diamond made him the best first baseman in baseball prior to Lou Gehrig, and one of the finest ever.

George produced three sons who played

professionally, two of them in the major leagues. George, Jr. played a year in the Browns' organization; eventually he became president of the International League. Dick played for the Cardinals and Phillies, and Dave pitched for Boston, Detroit, Washington, and Cincinnati.

A careful examination of Sisler's playing record reveals another parallel to the changes in baseball strategy. As the uppercut aimed at the seats steadily replaced the chop placed between fielders or the bunt dragged down the line, stolen bases also steadily declined. Sisler led the league in stolen bases four times. In 1918, the first time he won the base-stealing title, Sisler stole 45 of the 960 bases stolen in the American League.

In 1927, his last year to win the title, he led the league with the modest total of 27. This marked the lowest stolen base total for a league leader since the American League was founded. At the same time, the league total was down to 788.

Again, to show that these facts represent trends rather than aberrations, let's compare a few five-season totals. Between 1915 and 1919, runners stole a combined total of 11,869 bases in the American and National leagues. (We are not including the 1915 Federal League totals here.) The total decreased to 7,712 between 1920 and 1924. By the 1935-39 period, home runs *outnumbered* stolen bases. The table below shows this information.

Period	AL HRs	NL HRs	Total	AL SBs	NL SBs	Total
1915-19	777	1,010	1,787	6,008	5,861	11,869
1920-24	2,207	2,287	4,494	3,607	4,105	7,712
1935-39	3,887	3,163	7,050	2,726	1,985	4,711

Okay, enough history. Let's resume our season-by-season review of baseball history and baseball fathers' and sons' roles.

A Season-by-Season Look

1920

Baseball gets tough with pitchers. A host of new rules prohibit pitchers from applying: "rosin, paraffin, licorice, or any other foreign substance . . ." Licorice? Other rules outlaw the spitball, the "emery ball," etc., but established spitball pitchers are "grandfathered" into the game. Other rule changes include the infield fly rule, refined balk rules, and a prohibition against runners running the bases backwards or "making a travesty of the game."

An official Spalding ball now costs $2.50 per ball, a whopping sum when one stops to consider that a bat costs $2.00 and a boy's fielder's glove can be purchased for $1.00. Spalding offers catcher's mitts ranging from the "Boys' Amateur" at $1.50 to the "Honor" at $22.00; their "Stick on the Hand" first baseman's glove retails for $13.50.

Baseball father Jim Bagby leads the majors with a 31-12 record, a .721 winning percentage, and 48 games. He leads the AL with 30 complete games and 340 innings pitched. His efforts help Cleveland clinch the AL. In the subsequent World Series, Bagby slammed the first World Series home run by a pitcher, but his feat is overshadowed by Bill Wambsganss' unassisted triple play. Cleveland goes on to win the Series against the Brooklyn Robins 5-2, with Bagby winning the

second and historic fifth games. George Sisler leads the majors with .407 average and 257 hits, a still-standing major league record for hits in a season. He reaches first safely 305 times.

Active Fathers/Sons: Jim Bagby, Clyde Barnhart, Eddie Collins, Ray Grimes, Wally Hood, Sr., Frank Okrie, Joe Schultz, George Sisler, Ricardo Torres, and Smokey Joe Wood.

1921

August 9—In a nineteen-inning game, George Sisler goes six for nine, making him one of the few ballplayers ever to record six hits in a single game. He finishes the season with an AL-leading 35 stolen bases, and once again places in the top five in runs (125, fourth), hits (216, third), triples (18, second), and average (.371, fourth).

Active Fathers/Sons: Jim Bagby, Clyde Barnhart, Joe Berry, Jr., Eddie Collins, Johnny Cooney, Ray Grimes, Wally Hood, Ernie Johnson, Joe Schultz, Earl Sheely, George Sisler, Ricardo Torres, and Smokey Joe Wood.

1922

George Sisler leads the majors with a .420 average, and leads the AL with 134 runs, 246 hits, 18 triples, and 51 stolen bases. Baseball father Ray Grimes records seventeen consecutive RBI games. Baseball father Herman "Old Folks" Pillette's 2.85 ERA is good enough for second in the AL, and his opponents' batting average is only .258—fifth lowest in the league.

Before Bo Jackson, there was . . . Nig? The New York Giants utilize 27-year-old baseball son

Howard (Nig) Berry as a pinch runner in six games; Berry also plays halfback for the NFL's Rochester Jeffersons.

Active Fathers/Sons: Jim Bagby, Clyde Barnhart, Joe Berry, Eddie Collins, Jimmy Cooney, Ray Grimes, Wally Hood, Ernie Johnson, Walt Mueller, Tiny Osborne, Herman Pillette, Joe Schultz, Earl Sheely, George Sisler, Ricardo Torres, and Smokey Joe Wood.

1923

George Sisler is sidelined the entire season while recuperating from an eye operation. Eddie Collins reappears among the league leaders with 84 walks, a .360 average, and a .455 on-base mark; he leads the AL with 49 stolen bases.

Active Fathers/Sons: Jim Bagby, Clyde Barnhart, Eddie Collins, Jimmy Cooney, Ray Grimes, Ernie Johnson, Walter Mueller, Tiny Osborne, Herman Pillette, Joe Schultz, and Earl Sheely.

1924

George Sisler comes back as a player-manager and hits .305. Eddie Collins leads the AL with 42 stolen bases and is fourth in walks (89) and batting average (.349). Baseball father Whitey Sheely's .426 on-base percentage ranks fifth in the junior circuit. In early October, a headline proclaims, "Mack's Patience Netting Rewards," while the sub-headline reads, "Putrid Outfit of Early Months Finishes Fifth in Race." And you thought today's headline writers were cruel.

In one of the most exciting World Series ever played, a bad hop on a ball hit to Fred Lindstrom made Walter Johnson a winner in the seventh game. Eighteen-year-old Lindstrom found himself inserted into the Giants' lineup after an injury to regular third baseman Heinie Groh. *The Sporting News* (October 23, 1924) reported: "When Heinie Groh's trick leg went back on him before the World Series, supporters of the Giants groaned and wondered what McGraw would do. Could the youthful Freddy Lindstrom take care of the difficult three-quarter station in the World Series? Would he mess up things in general for the National League champions? These were some of the questions the fans asked themselves."

During the regular season, the young Lindstrom played a mere 11 games at third and hit a meager .253 in 79 at-bats. He responded to his opportunity in the Series by going 10 for 30 at the plate and cleanly handling all 25 chances. However, bad hops twice victimized him in the Seventh Game, accounting for the Senators' tying and winning runs.

Nevertheless, young Lindy caught the fancy of America's sporting public and was featured in an October 30, 1924 profile in *The Sporting News.*

"Fred Lindstrom An Ideal Boy Who Sends His Earnings Home" reads the headline, while below we are informed, "Young Giant Star Comes from Humble Family of Swedish-Irish Mixture; Mother Was Disappointed When He Failed to Become Lawyer."

Active Fathers/Sons: Clyde Barnhart, Eddie Collins, Jimmy Cooney, Johnny Cooney, Ray Grimes, Ernie Johnson, Fred Lindstrom, Walter Mueller, Tiny Osborne, Joe Schultz, Earl Sheely, and George Sisler.

1925

April 14-May 19—George Sisler starts the season by batting safely in 34 consecutive games, an AL record.

July 11—Sisler establishes an AL single game record by smashing a home run and a triple, both with the bases loaded.

Connie Mack's rebuilt Athletics battle the Senators for the AL championship, but falter in August, finishing the season in second place with an 88-64 record, 8½ games off the pace. Whitey Sheely observes a career year with a .315 average, 43 doubles (second in AL), and 111 RBIs (fifth in the AL). Gorgeous George Sisler's name reappears among the AL leaders in hits (fourth, with 224), triples (third, with 15), and total bases (fifth, with 311). Baseball father Clyde (Pooch) Barnhart helps the Pirates win their first NL championship since 1909 by playing 138 games in the outfield and hitting .325 with 114 RBIs during the regular season. He plays all seven Series games for the victorious Bucs, going seven for 28.

Active Fathers/Sons: Clyde Barnhart, Charlie Berry, Eddie Collins, Jimmy Cooney, Johnny Cooney, Ernie Johnson, Fred Lindstrom, Tiny Osborne, Joe Schultz, Earl Sheely, and George Sisler.

1926

May 20th, 21st, and 22nd—Earl Sheely ties a National League record, slashing seven doubles during three consecutive games. He adds a home run for good measure.

On Opening Day, Connie Mack's Athletics battle the Senators for 15 innings, the longest Opening Day duel on record; the Mackmen succumb 1-0.

The National League introduces the rosin bag.

Active Fathers/Sons: Clyde Barnhart, Fred Brickell, Eddie Collins, Jimmy Cooney, Johnny Cooney, Ray Grimes, Fred Lindstrom, Walter Mueller, Chet Nichols, and Earl Sheely.

1927

May 30—Baseball son Jimmy Cooney completes an unassisted triple play for the Cubs, catching Paul Waner's line drive, stepping on second to double Lloyd Waner, and tagging baseball father Clyde Barnhart.

George Sisler leads the AL with 27 stolen bases. Freddie Lindstrom's 36 doubles place him third in the NL. Pooch Barnhart registers another fine season for the NL champion Pirates, by hitting .319 in 108 games.

In the World Series, the hapless Pirates must go against the team many consider the greatest in baseball history—the famed Yankees won 110, lost 44, and finished 19 games above their nearest competition. The Bronx Bombers sweep the Bucs, but Barnhart plays well, going five for 16 (.313) and producing four of the Pirates' 10 RBIs.

Active Fathers/Sons: Clyde Barnhart, Fred Brickell, Eddie Collins, Jimmy Cooney, Johnny Cooney, Babe Ganzel, Fred Lindstrom, Art Mills, Chet Nichols, Earl Sheely, and George Sisler.

1928

June 25—Fred Lindstrom ties a major league record by rapping out nine hits during a doubleheader.

Over the course of the season, Lindstrom leads the NL in hits with 231; he's second in total bases with 330, third in batting average with a .358, fourth in doubles with 39, and fifth in RBIs with 107. Connie Mack's Athletics find themselves in a dogfight with the Yankees for the pennant, pulling even on September 7th and overtaking the Bronx Bombers on the next day. On September 9th, 85,264 people—the largest crowd in baseball history—pack Yankee Stadium. The Yankees sweep a doubleheader to reclaim first and never relinquish it, clinching on September 28th. The A's finish 2½ games out with a 98-55 record. Forty-one-year-old Eddie Collins, back with the White Elephants, appears in 36 games, mostly as a pinch hitter or runner.

Active Fathers/Sons: Clyde Barnhart, Charlie Berry, Fred Brickell, Eddie Collins, Jimmy Cooney, Johnny Cooney, John Ganzel, Fred Lindstrom, Art Mills, Chet Nichols, George Sisler, and Ed Walsh, Jr.

1929

April 16—In his first major league at-bat, Earl Averill launches a career that will lead to the Hall of Fame by hitting a home run.

Let's take another look at some equipment. The Spalding Company offers a selection of seven catchers' mitts, priced from $1.00 for the "Boy's Amateur" to $16.00 for the "Spalding Honor." First basemen can equip themselves for between $1.00 and $11.00. Somewhat incongruously, the company offers a "Babe Ruth Home Run Special" fielder's glove for $6.00. Aren't gloves supposed to prevent home runs? A boy's leather (sheepskin) glove still runs less than a dollar—75 cents.

Their best bat costs $2.50. "Double oil tempered in boiling oil, hard filled, thoroughly seasoned, hand polished, new satin finish, smooth as silk velvet. Best second growth specially selected northern white ash of the finest quality obtainable without reference to cost," reads their ad. Still, they apparently felt constrained to add the disclaimer, "We do not guarantee bats against breaking." Oh, yes, their best ball costs $2.00.

Connie Mack's revamped Athletics dethrone the mighty Yankees and go on to win the World Series four games to one against the Cubs. In Game One, Mack startles everyone when he announces 35-year-old Howard Ehmke as his starting pitcher. This produces one of the most famous Mack stories. Ehmke reportedly approached Mack with the declaration that "This old arm has one great game left." Mack assigned him to scout the Cubs during the waning days of the season. Then, he came out and pitched the A's to a 3-1 victory in the Series opener. During Game Four, at Philadelphia, the Mackmen overcame an 8-0 deficit with an astonishing 10-run rally in the bottom of the seventh inning.

Active Fathers/Sons: Earl Averill, Charlie Berry, Fred Brickell, Eddie Collins, Ed Connolly, Jimmy Cooney, Fred Lindstrom, Chet Nichols, Joe O'Rourke, Don Savidge, Earl Sheely, George Sisler, George Susce, and Ed Walsh, Jr.

1930

September 17—Earl Averill wallops three consecutive home runs and establishes the AL record for RBIs in a doubleheader with eleven.

The Reach Company, Spalding's major competition, offers an Eddie Collins model fielder's glove. The "finest and most serviceable glove made" retails for $8.50.

Connie Mack's Athletics win their second consecutive pennant and World Series. During baseball's hittingest season, the A's finish with a team average of .294, eight points above the League average, but nine points below the incredible .303 National League average. The White Elephants defeat St. Louis four games to two. Fred Lindstrom is fourth in the NL in hits with 231 and fifth in batting average with .379, a mark that establishes a NL record for the highest batting average for a third baseman (in more than 100 games).

Active Fathers/Sons: Earl Averill, Charlie Berry, Fred Brickell, Eddie Collins, Jimmy Cooney, Johnny Cooney, Glenn Liebhardt, Jr., Fred Lindstrom, Chet Nichols, George Sisler, and Ed Walsh, Jr.

1931

Baseball's rule makers instruct umpires to call "No game" if a game is called before five innings, or "legally drawn" if called after five innings with a tie. They prohibit glass buttons and polished metal on uniforms.

Connie Mack's Athletics win their third consecutive AL title, but succumb to the Cardinals four games to three in the Series rematch. Mack's team finished 13½ games ahead of the second-place Yankees, and this marks their third consecutive season of 100+ wins. It also marked the last time that The Tall Tactician would witness the World Series from the dugout.

During the season, 19-year-old rookie Lew Krausse pitched a 1-0 season for the A's, but did not appear in postseason play. Earl Averill established himself amongst other heavy-hitting Hall of Famers; he finished behind Gehrig and Ruth in runs with 140, second to Gehrig in hits with 209, and third behind the Yankee sluggers in homers with 32, total bases with 361, and RBIs with 143.

Active Fathers/Sons: Earl Averill, Charlie Berry, Fred Brickell, Lew Krausse, Sr., Fred Lindstrom, Gene Moore, Jr., Chet Nichols, Earl Sheely, Billy Sullivan, Jr., and Dixie Walker.

1932

Bill Terry succeeds John "The Little Napoleon" McGraw as manager of the New York Giants, much to the distress of Fred Lindstrom who had expected the position. Earl Averill collects 198 hits, 32 home runs, 359 total bases, 124 RBIs, and a .569 slugging percentage, again lodging himself firmly among the league leaders.

Active Fathers/Sons: Earl Averill, Charlie Berry, Fred Brickell, Lew Krausse, Sr., Fred Lindstrom, Chet Nichols, Dick Siebert, Billy Sullivan, Jr., George Susce, JoJo White, and Ed Walsh, Jr.

1933

May 7—Earl Averill ties a major league record by hitting eight singles in a doubleheader.

July 6—Connie Mack manages the AL to a 4-2 victory in the first All-Star Game. Eddie Collins coaches third for Mack. Managing against John McGraw, Mack regards the game seriously and uses his bench sparingly. Earl Averill successfully pinch-hits for pitcher General Crowder in the sixth, driving in a run. Aside from the pitching changes, Averill is the only sub used by Mack.

During the regular campaign, Fred Lindstrom slugs 39 doubles, third in the NL.

Active Fathers/Sons: Earl Averill, Charlie Berry, Fred Brickell, Dolph Camilli, Thornton Lee, Fred Lindstrom, Joe Malay, Gene Moore, Jr., Billy Sullivan, Jr., Hal Trosky, Dixie Walker, and JoJo White.

1934

May 30—Hal Trosky smashes three consecutive home runs.

July 10—Earl Averill goes two for four with a run and three RBIs in the All-Star Game.

Earl Averill teams up with Hal Trosky to make one of the league's most formidable duos. Averill finishes with 128 runs, 48 doubles, 31 homers, 340 total bases, and a .569 slugging mark; Trosky logs 206 hits, 45 doubles, 35 round-trippers, 374 total bases, 142 RBIs, and a .598 slugging percentage. Trosky becomes the third batter in AL history to record more than 200 hits, establishes AL records for most total bases in a rookie season and most long hits in a rookie season, and ties the AL record (during a 154-game season) for doubles by a rookie. JoJo White patrols the outfield in 100 games for Detroit, as the Tigers claw their way to their first pennant since the glory days of 1907-09. White hits .313 in 384 at-bats, and his 28 stolen bases lodge him second in the league.

In the fall classic, the Dean brothers, Dizzy and Daffy (really Jerome and Paul), and the Cardinals tame the Tigers four games to three. Dizzy wins two and loses one, while brother Paul wins two. This series may provide baseball fans with one of the greatest assemblies of names and nicknames in baseball history. The Cardinals boast *Ripper* Collins (first base), *Spud* Davis (pinch hitter), Leo *The Lip* Durocher, Frankie *The Fordham Flash* Frisch, *Pepper* Martin, and *Ducky* Medwick to go along with the Dean boys. Detroit, not to be outdone, counter with hurlers *General* Crowder, *Chief* Hogsett, *Firpo* Marberry, and *Schoolboy* Rowe, as well as *Goose* Goslin, *Gee* Walker, and JoJo White. White, incidentally, plays all seven games of the Series, but can only scratch out three hits in 23 at-bats. He does walk eight times and score six of Detroit's 23 runs.

Active Fathers/Sons: Earl Averill, Charlie Berry, Dolph Camilli, Thornton Lee, Fred Lindstrom, Gene Moore, Jr., Hal Trosky, Dixie Walker, and JoJo White.

1935

May 24—Dolph Camilli and Billy Sullivan, Jr. both play in the first night game in the major leagues, in Cincinnati.

Camilli's 25 home runs place him third in the NL. Hal Trosky hits 26, good enough for fifth in the AL; his 113 RBIs prove good enough for fourth place in the league. Despite the presence of three .300+ hitters, a .299 hitter, and a .296 hitter in their starting lineup, the Athletics plunge to the bottom of the American League standings. Detroit repeats as AL champs, again with JoJo White in their regular lineup. His hitting is off, but his 19 stolen bases suffice to place him fourth in the AL. In the NL, the Cubs, bolstered by the off-season addition of Freddie Lindstrom, win 21 straight in September, including three straight over the second-place Cardinals the last week of the month, to clinch the title.

During the World Series, White plays five of the six games in the Detroit victory, getting five hits in 19 at-bats and scoring three runs. Lindstrom plays in four games, hitting a poor three for 15 and neither scoring nor driving in a run.

Active Fathers/Sons: Earl Averill, Charlie Berry, Dolph Camilli, Johnny Cooney, Thornton Lee, Fred Lindstrom, Joe Malay, Gene Moore, Jr., Walt Ripley, Billy Sullivan, Jr., Hal Trosky, Dixie Walker, and JoJo White.

1936

Earl Averill leads the majors in hits with 232 and triples with 15; Hal Trosky leads the majors with 162 RBIs and *405* total bases. Averill is also among league leaders in runs (136), triples (15), home runs (28), total bases (385), batting average (.378), on-base percentage (.438), and slugging percentage (.627). Trosky's marks rank him among the leaders in hits (216), home runs (42), and slugging (.644). Despite the Herculean efforts of this dynamic Cleveland duo, the Indians only muster an 80-74 record to finish in fifth place, 22½ games behind the Yankees.

Over in the NL, Dolph Camilli puts up some impressive numbers for the last-place Phillies. Dolph slugs 13 triples and 28 round-trippers, both figures second on the circuit, and he complements these efforts with 116 walks, also a league second. Camilli's 306 total bases and .441 on-base percentage place him fourth in those categories.

Active Fathers/Sons: Earl Averill, Charlie Berry, Dolph Camilli, Johnny Cooney, Max Lanier, Thornton Lee, Glenn Liebhardt, Fred Lindstrom, Gene Moore, Jr., Dick Siebert, Billy Sullivan, Jr., Hal Trosky, Dixie Walker, and JoJo White.

1937

July 5—For the second time in his career, Hal Trosky smashes three home runs in a game.

July 7—Earl Averill smashes a line drive off the toe of Dizzy Dean in the All-Star Game; the injury effectively ends Dean's career.

Dixie Walker ties Mike Kreevich for the AL

crown in triples. Connie Mack is elected to the Hall of Fame. Dolph Camilli again emerges as one of the most productive NL hitters, leading the league in on-base percentage (.446) and standing among the leaders with 27 home runs (third place), 279 total bases (fifth place), 90 walks (second place), a .339 average, and a .587 slugging average.

Active Fathers/Sons: Earl Averill, Earle Brucker, Dolph Camilli, Johnny Cooney, Ken Heintzelman, Max Lanier, Thornton Lee, Gene Moore, Jr., Dick Siebert, Billy Sullivan, Jr., Hal Trosky, JoJo White, and Del Young.

1938

Camilli ends the season third in the NL in runs with 106 and fourth in home runs with 24. In the AL, Trosky's 40 doubles tie him for third, while Averill's 15 triples are second. Averill also records the junior circuit's fourth-best on-base percentage (.429). Something of a workhorse like his father, Jim Bagby pitches in 43 games for the Red Sox, tying him for third in the league. Bagby begins the season by pitching Opening Day, a rare honor for a rookie. Baseball father Thornton Lee's name appears among the league-leaders for the first time; his 245 innings and 3.49 ERA for the White Sox rank fifth for the season. Baseball father Bobby Mattick plays a minor role in the Cubs' title, going one for one and playing one game at shortstop. He does not appear in the Series, which the Yankees sweep.

Active Fathers/Sons: Earl Averill, Jim Bagby, Jr., Charlie Berry, Earle Brucker, Dolph Camilli, Eddie Collins, Jr., Johnny Cooney, Oscar Grimes, Ken Heintzelman, Max Lanier, Thornton Lee, Glenn Liebhardt, Harl Maggert, Bobby Mattick, Gene Moore, Jr., Dick Siebert, Billy Sullivan, Jr., Mike Tresh, Hal Trosky, Dixie Walker, JoJo White, and Del Young.

1939

Eddie Collins is chosen to manage the AL All-Star team; they lose 4-2 to a NL team managed by Honus Wagner. The teams are known as the "Collinses" and the "Wagners." George Sisler and Eddie Collins are elected to the Hall of Fame. The Spalding Company retails its top-of-the-line "Marvel" fielder's glove for $10.35. "This ready-broke, ready-to-play mitt is all that its name implies," boasts their advertising copy, "It conforms to the hand right from the start and satisfies the whims, wishes and requirements of the player whom it serves."

Dolph Camilli remains one of the batting leaders in the NL, leading the league in walks (110), and ranking in the top five in runs (105), triples (12), homers (26), total bases (296), RBIs

(104), on-base percentage (.409), and slugging percentage (.524). Hal Trosky hits .335 and slugs .589, fourth and fifth best in the AL. Thornton Lee hurls 235 innings, fourth in the AL.

Active Fathers/Sons: Earl Averill, Jim Bagby, Jr., Earle Brucker, Dolph Camilli, Bill Crouch, Len Gabrielson, Oscar Grimes, Ken Heintzelman, Bob Kennedy, Max Lanier, Thornton Lee, Bobby Mattick, Pinky May, Gene Moore, Jr., Joe Schultz, Jr., Dick Siebert, Billy Sullivan, Jr., George Susce, Mike Tresh, Hal Trosky, Dizzy Trout, Dixie Walker, and Del Young.

1940

April 16 — Bob Kennedy, playing for the White Sox, goes zero for four against Bob Feller during Feller's Opening Day no-hitter; Hal Trosky plays first and bats cleanup for the victorious Cleveland nine.

Thornton Lee throws 24 complete games, second to Feller's 31 in the American League. In an extremely tight race, Detroit (90-64) edges out Cleveland by one game and the Yankees by two games to break a Yankee chain of four years. Billy Sullivan, the Tigers' backup catcher, contributes by hitting .309 and driving in 41 runs. Thirty-eight-year-old Earl Averill chips in with a .280 batting mark and 20 RBIs, while Dizzy Trout wins three but loses seven. Camilli once again has a productive season for the senior circuit's Brooklyn Dodgers, ending the year tied for third in triples with 13. He finishes fourth in home runs (23), total bases (271), and on-base percentage (.397), while his walks (89) and slugging average (.529) prove good enough for third.

The Tigers succumb to the Reds in the Series, three games to four. Sullivan appears in five games and scores three runs, but bats a dismal .077 (one for 13). Averill proves unsuccessful in three pinch-hit attempts. Trout starts and loses Game Four.

Active Fathers/Sons: Earl Averill, Jim Bagby, Jr., Earle Brucker, Dolph Camilli, Johnny Cooney, Charlie Gilbert, Oscar Grimes, Jim Hegan, Ken Heintzelman, Bob Kennedy, Max Lanier, Thornton Lee, Bobby Mattick, Pinky May, Gene Moore, Jr., Joe Schultz, Jr., Dick Siebert, Billy Sullivan, Jr., George Susce, Gil Torres, Mike Tresh, Hal Trosky, Dizzy Trout, Dixie Walker, Harry Walker, and Del Young.

1941-1945

By 1942, 71 major leaguers and hundreds of ballplayers from the minor leagues traded one kind of uniform for another. Like the general population, some volunteered and some were drafted. And while it's true that some of them spent their time in the service playing ball, a lot of them witnessed some pretty tough action as well. By 1945, 384 major leaguers wore Uncle Sam's uniforms. Rationing and the lack of quality material deadened the baseball itself. Major league rosters filled with physical rejects, and older players didn't do much to enhance the quality of play either. One result was that stolen bases increased and home runs decreased again. There were still some pretty good ballplayers left though, and just because a player might have had his best years during the war is no reason to dismiss him as a lesser star.

Sixteen baseball fathers and sons left major league rosters and served in the wartime military. They were: Jack Aragon, Dolph Camilli, Al Campanis, Eddie Collins, Jr., Joe Coleman, Sr., Jim Hegan, Ken Heintzelman, Bob Kennedy, Pinky May, Ron Northey, Mel Queen, Joe Stephenson, Billy Sullivan, Jr., Dick Wakefield, Harry Walker, and Joe Wood, Jr. Others served, but became major leaguers later.

A Season-by-Season Look

1941

For the season, baseball father Thornton Lee leads the AL in ERA (2.37) and compiles a 22-11 record for a White Sox club that goes 77-77 and finishes in third place. Lee also pitches 30 complete games, most in the majors. Baseball father Dolph Camilli receives NL MVP honors as he leads the league in homers with 34 and RBIs with 120. He anchors an energized Brooklyn nine who brought joy to that borough with their first pennant since 1920. Baseball son Dixie Walker patrols their outfield for 146 games. "The People's Cherce" batted .311 in 531 at-bats and knocked in 71 runs.

During the World Series, the Dodgers lose handily to their crosstown rivals, managing to win only Game Two against the hated Yankees. Pinstripe pitching limits Brooklyn to a collective 29 for 159 (.182). Neither Camilli nor Walker prove able to do much to dispel Dodger heartbreak. Both play all five games and both end the Series with 18 at-bats. Dolph manages three hits, Dixie four. Walker scores three of Brooklyn's 11 total runs.

Active Fathers/Sons: Jack Aragon, Earl Averill, Jim Bagby, Jr., Dolph Camilli, Eddie Collins, Jr., Bill Crouch, Charlie Gilbert, Oscar Grimes, Jim Hegan, Ken Heintzelman, Bob Kennedy, Max Lanier, Thornton Lee, Bobby Mattick, Pinky May, Gene Moore, Joe Schultz, Jr., Dick Siebert, Billy Sullivan, Jr., George Susce, Mike Tresh, Hal Trosky, Dizzy Trout, Dick Wakefield, and Harry Walker.

1942

The war effort begins to claim more and more ballplayers. A young Cardinal squad wins 43 of its last 51 games to fly past the Dodgers. Harry (The Hat) Walker, Dixie's brother, aids the Redbirds off the bench and hits .314, while appearing in 56 games in the outfield and two at second base. Baseball father Max Lanier wings his way to 13 victories, losing eight. For second-place Brooklyn, Camilli smashes 26 home runs (he ties Mize for second in the NL) and finishes second to Mize for the RBI lead (110 to 109). He also records 247 total bases (fifth) and 97 walks (third).

St. Louis wins the Series four games to one against the Yankees, with Max Lanier getting credit for the win in Game Four. The New Yorkers tied that game with a five-run rally in the bottom of the sixth. St. Louis battled back with two runs in their half of the seventh. Lanier entered the game in the bottom of the seventh and silenced the booming Yankee bats, shutting them out for the final three innings of play. At the plate, Lanier was one for one with a run batted in.

Active Fathers/Sons: Jim Bagby, Jr., Dolph Camilli, Joe Coleman, Eddie Collins, Jr., Larry Eschen, Charlie Gilbert, Oscar Grimes, Jim Hegan, Ken Heintzelman, Bob Kennedy, Max Lanier, Thornton Lee, Bobby Mattick, Pinky May, Gene Moore, Jr., Ron Northey, Mel Queen, Dick Siebert, Billy Sullivan, Jr., George Susce, Mike Tresh, Dizzy Trout, Al Unser, and Harry Walker.

1943

Opening Day—In Cleveland, Jim Bagby drives in the only run with a sacrifice fly to win a 1-0 decision against Detroit.

August 24—Connie Mack's Athletics lose 6-5 to the White Sox, establishing a mark of 20 consecutive losses.

Baseball son Dick Wakefield leads the AL in hits with 200 and doubles with 38. Father Dizzy Trout posts a 20-12 record, including a league-leading five shutouts in 247 innings (fifth in the AL) over 44 games (second in the league). Max Lanier's 1.90 ERA leads the NL; he's fourth in strikeouts with 123, and his 15-7 record helps St. Louis cruise to a pennant. The Cardinals finish the season 105-49, 18 games beyond the reach of the second-place Reds. Harry Walker, now established as a regular Cardinal flychaser, hits .295 with 53 RBIs and 76 runs.

Max Lanier loses the opening game of the World Series to Spud Chandler of the Yankees, 4-2. In a reversal of the previous year, the Yankees whip the Cardinals four games to one. Lanier pitches in three games, starting two. In 15.1 innings, he strikes out 13, the highest strikeout total

in the series. He finishes with a highly respectable 1.76 ERA. Harry the Hat Walker plays all five games but hits miserably, a meager three for 18 (.167), with no runs and no RBIs.

Active Fathers/Sons: Jim Bagby, Jr., Earle Brucker, Sr., Dolph Camilli, Al Campanis, Johnny Cooney, Charlie Gilbert, Oscar Grimes, Don Johnson, Max Lanier, Thornton Lee, Pinky May, Bobby Moore, Ron Northey, Joe Schultz, Jr., Dick Siebert, Joe Stephenson, George Susce, Mike Tresh, Dizzy Trout, Al Unser, Dick Wakefield, Harry Walker, and JoJo White.

1944

Dizzy Trout wins 27 games, but teammate Hal Newhouser wins 28; it is the first time since 1920 (when Stan Coveliski and baseball father Jim Bagby accomplished the feat) that two pitchers rack up 55 wins for a club in one season. Trout's final attempt at his 28th win comes on October 1st—the closing day of the season—with Detroit and St. Louis tied in the standings at 88-65. Trout and the Tigers lose 4-1 to Washington, while the Browns defeat Yankee rookie (and baseball father) Mel Queen, giving the Brownies their first championship in 44 years in the American League. Trout leads the majors with a 2.12 ERA and seven shutouts. Dixie Walker wins the NL batting crown, leading the majors with a .357 average. Dixie's brother Harry is now in military service, but the Redbirds still rule the National League roost. A top-notch pitching staff includes Max Lanier (17-12) as the Cardinals finish 105-49 to set up an all-St. Louis World Series.

No doubt you've heard of a "subway Series," and you've heard of the "I-75 Series," but what do you suppose today's sportswriters would have made of this one? Not only is this the only all-St. Louis World Series, but it is a one-park series. The Browns own Sportsmen's Park, but the Cardinals also play their home games there that season. A Dugout Series? The Cardinals beat the Browns in six and Max Lanier turns in another good postseason performance. Lanier starts Game Two. He is relieved in the eighth with a 2-2 ballgame that the Cardinals win in the 11th inning. He starts and wins the climactic sixth game for a Cardinal championship. Lanier again helps himself with the bat, going two for four and driving in one of the Cardinals' sixteen runs in the Series. For the Browns, baseball son Gene (Rowdy) Moore, in the next-to-last year of a 14-year journeyman career, scores four of the Browns' 12 Series runs despite hitting only .182.

Active Fathers/Sons: Jim Bagby, Jr., Vic Barnhart, Johnny Cooney, Oscar Grimes, Don Johnson, Max Lanier, Thornton Lee, Gene Moore, Jr.,

Ron Northey, Stan Partenheimer, Mel Queen, Joe Schultz, Jr., Dick Siebert, Joe Stephenson, George Susce, Gil Torres, Mike Tresh, Hal Trosky, Dizzy Trout, Al Unser, Dick Wakefield, Dixie Walker, JoJo White, and Joe Wood.

1945

"Orator Jim" O'Rourke is elected to the Hall of Fame. Baseball son Oscar Grimes' 97 walks (third in the AL) help him reach a .395 on-base mark (fourth in the AL). Father Mike Tresh achieves a dubious distinction when he establishes an AL record for the fewest long hits in a season by a player in 150 or more games. Tresh has 12 doubles. Dizzy Trout helps pitch the Tigers back to the top with an 18-15 record.

In the World Series, Dizzy spins a complete game win in Game Four and loses Game Six in relief. The Tigers mangle the Cubs in Game Seven.

Active Fathers/Sons: Jim Bagby, Jr., Vic Barnhart, Dolph Camilli, Bill Crouch, Oscar Grimes, Don Johnson, Max Lanier, Thornton Lee, Gene Moore, Jr., Stan Partenheimer, Joe Schultz, Jr., Gil Torres, Mike Tresh, Dizzy Trout, Al Unser, and Dixie Walker.

1946-1972

Stodgy. That's the word that keeps coming to mind when trying to analyze and describe the baseball strategy of the post-war era. Basically, guys got on base and then just kind of roosted there, waiting for someone to swat one into the seats. During the war years, major leaguers parked 5,348 balls in the stands and committed 4,744 base path thefts. This established a ratio of 1.1 home runs to steals. After the war, the boys reverted back to the type of baseball that had been gaining acceptance since 1920. For the 1946-50 period, there were 8,113 home runs and 3,836 stolen bases, for a ratio of 2.1 home runs for every stolen base in the major leagues.

This trend continued, reaching a peak in the half decade between 1955-59 when the 11,210 home runs established a 2.97 ratio compared to the 3,774 stolen bases during that same time. If you still need convincing that major leaguers just weren't running like they used to, consider these additional tidbits. In 1950, Dom DiMaggio, a great ballplayer by anyone's standards, won the AL base stealing title with *15* stolen bases! We're talking about a league-leading season total here, folks. That same year in the AL, Washington and Philadelphia tied for the team stolen base lead with 42 steals. In 1955, the leaders in both leagues ranged between 11 and 25. Only three teams recorded 100 or more steals for a season during the entire *decade*, and that was the Chicago White Sox of 1957-59.

Predictable. That's another word that comes to mind. In the 23 seasons played after the war and prior to the introduction of divisional play in 1969, the New York Yankees won 15 American League championships. Now, of course, this was a great thing if you were a Yankee fan and, with the generosity of hindsight, most of us can admit there were some very fine Yankee teams during their dynastic rule. But if you weren't a Yankee fan . . . well, if you followed baseball during the time, then you remember that the world was divided into Yankee fans and Yankee haters. You were either one or the other; no middle ground existed and passions ran deep whichever side you came down on.

In the world of pre-parity baseball, things weren't a whole lot different over in the National League, although success was distributed a bit more evenly. The Dodgers took six pennants while they were in Brooklyn and another four after making the move to L.A. The Cardinals won four league championships, the Braves won three (one in Boston, two in Milwaukee), and the Giants won the three pennants (two in New York, one in San Francisco). Philadelphia, Pittsburgh, and Cincinnati claimed one flag each; only the lowly Cubs failed to win at least once during these years.

Off the field, though, enormous changes proved to be the rule rather than the exception. In 1947, Branch Rickey brought Jackie Robinson to the Dodgers. If the 1919 World Series was baseball's greatest scandal, its greatest shame was in its abiding inability or unwillingness to integrate its ranks. Franchise shifts occupy another important portion of the history of the era. Boston moved to Milwaukee (1953); the St. Louis Browns became the Baltimore Orioles (1954); the Athletics fled Philadelphia for Kansas City (1955); and, of course, major league baseball migrated to the West Coast when the Dodgers and Giants relocated themselves in Los Angeles and San Francisco (1958). The American League embraced expansion in 1961 (Los Angeles Angels and Minnesota Twins), and the National League followed suit in 1962 (Houston and New York). Both leagues adopted divisional play in 1969.

But if the strategy was stodgy and the seasons generally predictable, don't think for a minute that there wasn't a wealth of talent on the field. It's been said that every generation of fans develops an undying attachment for the stars of its own era. That's probably true, and the generations that grew up with the likes of Joe Dimaggio, Ted Williams, Mickey Mantle, Willie Mays, Duke Snider, Jackie Robinson, Warren Spahn, Whitey

Ford, Bob Feller, Stan Musial, Pee Wee Reese, and a host of other baseball idols certainly claim plenty of icons in baseball's pantheon. There were an awful lot of good baseball players around.

The Career of Yogi Berra

Lawrence Peter Berra was one of them. Now, what comes immediately to mind for most people is a squatty guy with a goofy grin known for his malapropisms. And while it may be true that he inspired the "Yogi Bear" cartoon character, Yogi the ballplayer was no joke.

To begin with, Berra was surprisingly nimble and quick for a catcher, particularly when he was younger. And while he didn't jump over any candlesticks, he did pounce on quite a few bunts. In 1947, for example, he turned an attempted suicide squeeze into an unassisted double play.

A St. Louis Browns' hitter laid a bunt down the first-base line with the runner from third headed for the plate. Berra leaped from behind the plate, fielded the ball, tagged the batter headed for first, and dove back to the plate in time to tag the runner. "I just tagged everything in sight, including the umpire," Yogi explained. Berra was a good handler of pitchers and exhibited an uncanny knack for outguessing hitters. What's more, Berra possessed a long, detailed, and accurate memory, which he employed against American League hitters for 18 seasons.

Yogi established major league records for most consecutive chances handled by a catcher without an error (950) and consecutive games by a catcher without an error (148). In fact, Berra's only liability behind the plate seemed to be his short, stubby fingers—pitchers complained that they had trouble picking up his signals. Berra attempted to compensate by tinting his fingers with iodine but gave up that practice after Yankee relief pitcher Joe Page told him that just made it look like his wrists were bleeding.

However, it is Yogi's hitting that most people remember. Despite being one of the most notorious bad-ball hitters in baseball history, Berra seldom struck out. In fact, he lists 7,555 career at-bats and only 414 strikeouts. The most he ever fanned in one season came in 1959 when he struck out 38 times. In 1950, Berra's career year in terms of average, he whiffed a mere 12 times in 597 at-bats! He also displayed impressive power, as evidenced by his 358 career home runs; 313 of those came as a catcher, a number that stood as a major league record until it was broken by Johnny Bench.

Yankee greats Joe Dimaggio and Mickey Mantle attracted greater glory, but no player's career paralleled the great Yankee teams of that era like Berra. He played on 14 of their 15 pennant winners during this period and *managed* the team during that other pennant-winning season. Yet it's easy to imagine that things might have turned out differently.

Berra was born and raised on Elizabeth Street in St. Louis in a neighborhood people called "Dago Hill" in those days. He loved playing baseball and grew up rooting for the Cardinals. According to some sources, his bad-ball hitting was inspired by his idol Ducky Medwick. Throughout his youth, he teamed up with neighborhood pal Joe Garagiola, and the boys played some impressive baseball for the Stag Athletic Club. Garagiola caught then, and Yogi usually played third or the outfield.

Anyway, both boys attracted the attention of the hometown Cardinals and were given a workout. But the Cardinals liked Garagiola better. They offered him $500 to sign, but Branch Rickey was only willing to offer Berra $250. Yogi's pride stung, he refused the Cardinals' offer, and played for a Junior American Legion team called the Stockhams; they moved him behind the plate. He was quick and daring enough that he stole home in a 1942 American Legion tournament game. Yogi pulled this feat off against a catcher named Gene Mauch who later made his mark in the major leagues as a manager.

Shortly thereafter, the Yankees did offer Yogi a $500 signing bonus. He accepted and agreed to a $90 a month contract to play at Norfolk in the Piedmont League. He discovered that he didn't get the bonus money unless he completed the season. He also found out that his salary wasn't enough to live on. People talk about "hungry" ballplayers, but they don't mean it literally. For Yogi, though, it was sometimes a reality. He confided this in letters to his mother, and Mom secretly sent him a few extra dollars. They kept this from Yogi's father, Pietro, because they knew he would order young "Lawdie" (as his mother called him) to give up baseball and come home. Berra enlisted in the Navy and served aboard a rocket launcher that capsized off Omaha Beach during the Normandy invasion.

Berra returned to baseball in 1946 and hit .314 in 77 games for Newark. The Yankees called him up for seven games that season, and in 1947 he went back up to stay. In 83 games he hit .280 with 11 home runs and 54 RBIs—pretty good marks for a rookie. At the time, only one Rookie of the Year award was given, and that year the baseball writers gave it to Jackie Robinson. Berra didn't even place among the top five in the balloting. Still, the Yankees won the pennant and Berra began compiling his postseason records when he hit the first pinch-hit home run in World Series history in Game Three.

"If you can't imitate him," Yogi once said, "don't copy him." In the case of Lawrence Peter Berra, few would even dare to try. He was a one and only, and he was also one of the greatest catchers ever to play the game.

Yogi's son Dale made it to the major leagues when the Pirates called him up in 1977. Dale was only 20 years old at the time; consequently he can boast of making it to the major leagues at an earlier age than his father. But, while he was good enough to stick around for 11 major league seasons, he never achieved the notoriety of his father. The two teamed up in 1985 when Dale played shortstop and Yogi managed the Yankees.

Other Fathers and Sons

Forty-seven other baseball fathers and 55 baseball sons played major league ball at some point between 1946 and 1973. And, while none of them have records that can match Yogi Berra, each of them made his own contribution. None of them enjoyed playing careers as long as Yogi but, on the other hand, few of them retired after such a short career as John Corriden either.

On April 20, 1946, the Brooklyn Dodgers used Corriden as a pinch runner. He scored, but he never appeared in another major league game. John's run came 36 years, 5 months, and 12 days after his father, Red, made his major league debut for the St. Louis Browns. That may seem like quite a while, but it's not the longest period of time between Dad's and Junior's debuts. Just four days earlier, those same Dodgers played 29-year-old Jack Graham at first base. This was 43 years, 6 months, and 27 days after his dad, Peaches, played second for the first time for the Cleveland Bronchos, forerunners of the Indians.

Unfortunately, Peaches had already died at the time so he never witnessed his boy's accomplishment. Sadly, this same fate befell six other baseball fathers—Cam Carreon, Ed Connolly, Sr., Guy Morton, Sr., Ebba St. Claire, Dizzy Trout, and Howard Wakefield. Cam Carreon's death seems the most tragic in this regard. He died in Tucson on September 2, 1987. Son Mark made his debut for the Mets just six days later.

On the average, about 27 years and five months expire between the major league debuts of fathers and the debuts of their sons, with an average of about 19½ years passing between the last season a father was active in the major leagues and his son's debut. The Bruckers claim credit for the shortest period elapsed between debuts. Earle, Sr. caught his first game for Connie Mack's Athletics on April 19, 1937. Mack liked the 36-year-old rookie well enough that he kept him around for another 706 games in four more seasons. Earle, Jr. made his debut on October 2, 1948, just 11 years, 5 months, and 13 days after his dad. Junior was a catcher, too, and he also appeared for the A's. This makes them one of only three father-son combinations to have played for the same manager — Eddie Collins' son also played for Mr. Mack and the Griffeys, of course, both played for Seattle's Jim Leyland.

The promotion of Earle Brucker, Jr. to the big time might have been a bit of a sentimental gesture by Connie Mack. The Athletics were well out of the race and Earle, Sr. was coaching for the A's that season. Further evidence of this can be seen in the fact that Junior's career lasted a total of two games. Then again, perhaps Mack just liked having around guys named "Earle" who spelled their name the same way his son's name was spelled. Since Mack's son was also an A's coach that season, Mr. Mack must have devised some sort of system to differentiate among his Earles, but I haven't yet discovered what it was. The chart below shows the length of time between debuts and length of time between dad's last active and junior's first season.

Time between Dad's & Junior's Debuts					
Seasons 0-9	10-19	20-29	30-39	40+	Average
Father/Son Pairs 0	5	71	29	7	27.4

Time Between Dad's Last Active Season and Junior's First					
7	46	40	17	2	19.65

Stolen Bases Increase Again

Toward the latter part of the 1946-1972 period, another shift in baseball strategy began to occur. To put it simply, baseball began to rediscover the stolen base. The ratio of home runs to stolen bases began moving back toward some sort of equilibrium. Two baseball fathers possessed the proper combination of skills to have a profound impact on the way the game was played and to influence these strategic trends. And, again, taking a brief look at their careers proves instructive in understanding these developments. Take a quick look at the chart below.

YEARS	AL HRs	NL HRs	Total	AL SBs	NL SBs	Total	Ratio
1941-45	2,629	2,719	5,348	2,627	2,117	4,744	1.1/1
1946-50	3,784	4,329	8,113	1,812	2,024	3,836	2.1/1
1955-59	5,208	6,002	11,210	1,800	1,974	3,774	2.97/1
1961-65	7,212	6,389	13,885	2,934	3,321	6,255	2.2/1
1968-72	7,158	6,782	13,940	4,425	4,420	8,845	1.57/1
1983-87	10,985	7,477	18,432	7,507	8,843	16,350	1.1/1

Why did we look at these particular five-year blocks? To begin, 1941-45 are the war years; 1946-50 represent the return to pre-war baseball. The last years of the fifties represent the era with the fewest stolen bases. The years 1961-65 are the first five years of expansion baseball, and for this reason the idea of a ratio becomes more useful than comparing the actual numbers. The 1968-72 period was selected because it represents the final years before the introduction of the designated hitter rule. Finally, the 1983-87 period simply presents some stats for comparison from a more recent, possibly more familiar, period.

Now, can you guess which two baseball fathers' careers symbolize the changes outlined above? They are Maury Wills and Bobby Bonds.

After eight seasons in the minors, Maury Wills played his first full season in the majors for the 1960 Dodgers. He played 145 games at shortstop, hit .295, and led the league with 50 steals, but was overlooked by the sportswriters voting for Rookie of the Year. They selected Wills' teammate Frank Howard, and a second Dodger teammate, Tommy Davis, placed fifth in the voting; Wills was not even among the top five. He led the league in stolen bases again in 1961 and won his first Gold Glove that year.

In 1962, he electrified the baseball world when he erased Ty Cobb's single season stolen base record (96) and set a new standard with 104. The Dodgers lacked power that year—their home run total registered among the league's lowest—but they utilized a balanced attack to lead the league most of the season. This included 198 team stolen bases, the highest team total in either league since 1918 when Brooklyn stole 200 collective bases. The Dodgers were the only team with at least 100 steals that season and for two seasons more, but the idea was catching on that this was something that might make your offense more potent.

Los Angeles won the NL pennant in 1965 and recorded 172 team thefts, but four other teams registered at least 100 steals that season. Wills played his last season in 1972. Six major league teams stole at least 100 bases that year, and the Dodgers weren't even one of them. Evidence, if not proof, that baseball had rediscovered the stolen base.

Bobby Lee Bonds came out of Riverside, California and into the National League after minor league stops at Lexington, Fresno, Waterbury, and Phoenix. Athleticism ran in the Bonds family. He had a sister (Rosie) who was a member of the 1964 U.S. Olympic team and a brother (Robert) who played for the Kansas City Chiefs. Bobby reached the Giants in 1968 and patrolled Candlestick Park's right field for the next six seasons before becoming a baseball Bedouin, playing with seven teams in the final seven years of his career. He struck out a lot, never won the MVP award, and played for only one division winner in a 14-year career. What Bobby Bonds did best was combine speed and power in a way that no ballplayer before him ever did.

In 1969, his first full season in the majors, Bobby hit 32 home runs and stole 45 bases to become only the fourth man in baseball history to hit 30 homers and steal 30 bases. It was a feat he repeated four more times, something no other baseball player has ever accomplished. He did it twice in the NL and three times in the AL, making him the first to accomplish 30/30 in both leagues. And, if you look at his season records, you'll see he came pretty close several other times.

In 1973, he barely missed reaching a loftier baseball milestone when he stole 43 bases and hit 39 home runs. Now, *that* was a career year. He led the league in runs and total bases and was fifth in home runs and fourth in stolen bases. In fact, his figures were remarkably similar to those that garnered Jose Canseco his 1988 MVP. But he didn't play for a pennant winner, and, so it seems, voters simply didn't give his accomplishments as much attention as Canseco later received. He finished a distant third behind Pete Rose and Willie Stargell in that year's MVP vote.

One other fact should be considered regarding Bobby's career. He slugged 35 of those home runs as a lead-off hitter. Basically, Bobby was the prototype for the disruptive type of lead-off hitter who could beat you on the base paths or park your mistake in the seats.

Now, once again, let's take a look at some of the season-by-season accomplishments of baseball's fathers and sons.

A Season-by-Season Look

1946

July 9—Baseball son Dixie Walker strikes out in a pinch-hitting appearance during the All-Star Game.

Big Ed Walsh is elected to the Hall of Fame. The boys are home from the war, but all is not happy in baseball land. Philadelphia outfielder Rene Monteagudo and Cardinal pitcher Max Lanier are among 17 National Leaguers and six American Leaguers who "jump" to the Mexican League. Lanier was disgruntled because after winning 17 regular season games and the sixth game of the World Series, he was offered only a $500 raise.

Dizzy Trout pitches 23 complete games for Detroit, fourth-best in the AL; his 151 k's rank fifth. Dixie Walker's 184 hits rank second in the National League, his 258 total bases fourth, and his 116 RBIs second. His 14 stolen bases rank fifth, just behind baseball father Bobby Adams.

On a base hit by baseball son Harry Walker, Enos Slaughter races home from first with what proves to be the winning run of the Series in one of the most thrilling climaxes ever witnessed to a World Series contest. Walker's six Series RBIs lead all contestants, and his .412 average paces the Cardinals as they triumph over the Red Sox.

Active Fathers/Sons: Bobby Adams, Jim Bagby, Jr., Vic Barnhart, Yogi Berra, Joe Coleman, John Corriden, Charlie Gilbert, Jack Graham, Oscar Grimes, Jim Hegan, Ken Heintzelman, Don Johnson, Bob Kennedy, Max Lanier, Thornton Lee, Ron Northey, Mel Queen, Joe Schultz, Jr., Dick Sisler, Gil Torres, Mike Tresh, Hal Trosky, Dizzy Trout, Dick Wakefield, Dixie Walker, and Harry Walker.

1947

Harry the Hat Walker captures the NL batting title, the only player to win a batting championship while playing for two teams in the same season (St. Louis and Philadelphia). He hit .363 (20 points above Ted Williams in the AL) and led the majors in triples with 16. Harry's brother Dixie hits .306 for Brooklyn as the Dodgers win the NL with a 94-60 record.

Yogi Berra hits the first pinch-hit home run in World Series history in Game Three. Dixie Walker and the Dodgers go down to defeat at the hands of the Yankees, four games to three.

Dixie Walker opposes Jackie Robinson's entry into major league baseball and the Dodgers'

lineup. In a letter to Brooklyn General Manager Branch Rickey, the popular Walker requests a trade. Rickey obliges and dispatches Walker to Pittsburgh. Years later, when asked about the matter, Walker said, "I've said all I'm going to say on that subject." Walker paused, then continued, "There is one more thing I'll add. Jackie Robinson was a great ballplayer."

Active Fathers/Sons: Bobby Adams, Jim Bagby, Jr., Yogi Berra, Joe Coleman, Charlie Gilbert, Jim Hegan, Ken Heintzelman, Don Johnson, Bob Kennedy, Thornton Lee, Bud Lively, Ron Northey, Mel Queen, Joe Schultz, Jr., Dick Sisler, Joe Stephenson, Billy Sullivan, Jr., Mike Tresh, Dizzy Trout, Dick Wakefield, Dixie Walker, and Harry Walker.

1948

Mike Tresh registers his first home run in 787 games; he had only one previous round tripper in ten years in the majors. Baseball father Jim Hegan performs backstop duties in 142 games for the Cleveland Indians, a team that also includes father Bob Kennedy, who came over in a trade with the White Sox, and father Ray Boone, just coming into the league. The Indians end the season tied with Boston, overcoming the Red Sox in a special one-game play-off.

The Indians face the other Boston team in an Indians versus Braves World Series, one that must have kept sportswriters and headline writers up at night inventing clichés. In Game Five, Boston backup catcher Bill Salkeld, grandfather of 1990 pitching prospect and No. 1 draft pick Roger Salkeld, homers in the sixth inning to tie a game that the Braves went on to win with a six-run seventh inning. Finally, though, the Tribe prevailed against the Braves to bring Cleveland its first world championship since 1920. Jim Hegan caught all six games and drove in five of the Tribe's 16 Series runs.

Active Fathers/Sons: Bobby Adams, Yogi Berra, Ray Boone, Earle Brucker, Jr., Joe Coleman, Jim Hegan, Ken Heintzelman, Don Johnson, Bob Kennedy, Thornton Lee, Bud Lively, Don Mueller, Ron Northey, Len Okrie, Mel Queen, Joe Schultz, Jr., Dick Sisler, Roy Smalley, Mike Tresh, Dizzy Trout, Dick Wakefield, Dixie Walker, and Harry Walker.

1949

Eighteen of the 26 players who "jumped" to the Mexican League, including Max Lanier, are reinstated. Baseball son Ray Narleski sets a major league record, giving up four grand slams in a season. Baseball father Ken Heintzelman turns in a sparkling season. He ties three others for the NL shutout title with five; he also throws 250 innings (fourth in the NL) with a 3.02 ERA (fifth in the NL). Yogi Berra cracks the Yankees' starting lineup for the first time. Despite missing a month with a broken finger, Berra drives in 91 runs as Casey Stengel's Yankees hold off a late Boston charge.

The Bronx Bombers meet the Bums from Flatbush in a rematch of the 1947 Series, with the uptowners besting the Dodgers four games to one. Berra catches four games, but has a miserable Series at the plate, going one for 16 (.063).

Active Fathers/Sons: Bobby Adams, Yogi Berra, Ray Boone, Joe Coleman, Jack Graham, Jim Hegan, Ken Heintzelman, Wally Hood, Jr., Bob Kennedy, Max Lanier, Bud Lively, Don Mueller, Ron Northey, Mel Queen, Dick Sisler, Roy Smalley, Mike Tresh, Dizzy Trout, Dick Wakefield, Dixie Walker, and Harry Walker.

1950

Yogi Berra's name appears among the top AL hitters for the first time, with 116 runs (fourth place), 192 hits (third place), 318 total bases (third place), and 124 RBIs (third place). He finishes third in the MVP voting. Baseball bid adieu to one of its living legends. After fifty years as manager of the A's, and a baseball career that began in 1887, Cornelius McGillicuddy, known to the world as Connie Mack, retires. Mr. Mack left baseball with 3,776 wins and 4,025 losses and a legacy that can never be matched.

A nail-biting NL pennant race comes to a dramatic conclusion when baseball son Dick Sisler clouts a tenth-inning, three-run homer that beats Brooklyn and clinches the pennant for the Philadelphia "Whiz Kid" Phillies, their first since 1915.

The Whiz Kids can't keep it up though; the swaggering Yankees swept the Series. Yogi Berra clouts one of the two home runs in the Series.

Active Fathers/Sons: Bobby Adams, Gus Bell, Yogi Berra, Ray Boone, Joe Coleman, Tookie Gilbert, Jim Hegan, Ken Heintzelman, Bob Kennedy, Max Lanier, Vern Law, Don Mueller, Ron Northey, Len Okrie, Mel Queen, Dick Sisler, Roy Smalley, Dizzy Trout, Dick Wakefield, and Harry Walker.

1951

While the New York Yankees continue beating up the American League, baseball fans are treated to yet another NL thriller. It's almost as if the NL is intent on making up for the AL's predictability. At any rate, on October 3, the Giants' Bobby Thomson launches his famous home run. The story has been told in virtually every baseball book since and has been featured in so many television highlight films that virtually any base-

ball fan can recall the black-and-white image of Thomson rounding third. Consequently, we have no need to retell the tale. Instead, we merely note that without baseball son Don (Mandrake the Magician) Mueller singling and then sliding into third on Whitey Lockman's double, Bobby's "shot" might not have taken place at all. When Mueller is injured in his slide and the Giants are forced to replace him, Dodger manager Charley Dressen takes advantage of the delay to bring in Ralph Branca to face Thompson.

Yogi Berra wins his first MVP award this year. What's even more interesting, Berra wins without appearing among the leaders in any offensive category except total bases (269, fourth place). However, when you stop to consider that Berra had 161 hits in 547 at-bats (.294), including 27 homers, drove in 88 runs, scored 92 runs, AND caught 141 games, THEN you realize what kind of season Lawrence Peter had this year.

Other notes of interest from 1951: In his rookie season, baseball son Chet Nichols leads the NL with a 2.88 ERA. Father Gus Bell ties Stan Musial for the NL lead with 12 triples. And, in the interest of completing the category of obscure ballplayers producing notable results (there's probably a record everywhere if you just search long enough), we note that Mel Queen recorded the NL's highest ratio of strikeouts per game that season with 6.59.

Mueller is unable to play in the Series and the Yankees (yawn) win another, four games to two.

Active Fathers/Sons: Bobby Adams, Gus Bell, Yogi Berra, Ray Boone, Joe Coleman, Ross Grimsley, Sr., Sam Hairston, Jim Hegan, Ken Heintzelman, Bob Kennedy, Max Lanier, Vern Law, Don Mueller, Chet Nichols, Jr., Len Okrie, Mel Queen, Bud Sheely, Dick Sisler, Roy Smalley, Ebba St. Claire, Dizzy Trout, and Harry Walker.

1952

April 23 — Don Mueller contributes a home run to Hall of Famer Hoyt Wilhelm's first major league victory; Wilhelm himself hits his first and only major league home run in his first at-bat.

Major league baseball adopts the four man umpire crew.

Bobby Adams' 180 hits place him third in the NL. Berra's season totals place him fourth in the AL in runs (97), third in home runs (30), and fifth in RBIs (98) as (ho-hum) the Yankees win another AL race. The Indians are this year's Designated Chasers, and with Jim Hegan behind the plate and Ray Boone at shortstop, they finish a respectable two games behind the Yankee behemoth.

Active Fathers/Sons: Bobby Adams, Gus Bell,

Yogi Berra, Ray Boone, Jim Hegan, Ken Heintzelman, Bob Kennedy, Max Lanier, George Lerchen, Don Mueller, Ron Northey, Len Okrie, Mel Queen, Bud Sheely, Dick Sisler, Roy Smalley, Ebba St. Claire, and Dick Wakefield.

1953

Shibe Park in Philadelphia is renamed Connie Mack Stadium. With Ebba St. Claire as their third-string catcher, the Braves move from Boston to Milwaukee. In the NL, Gus Bell pounds out 37 doubles and safely touches 320 bases; both figures are sufficient for fifth place in the league. Yogi Berra and Ray Boone place fourth and fifth in the AL home run race with 27 and 26 respectively; their .523 and .519 slugging marks give them third and fourth place. Boone records more RBIs, 114 (third in the AL) to Berra's 108 (fourth). Berra's season contributes to the Yankees' fifth straight pennant.

In the World Series, Berra catches all six games as the pinstripes cruise to a four games to two championship over Brooklyn. Berra bats .429 (nine for 21) with a homer and four RBIs.

Active Fathers/Sons: Bobby Adams, Gus Bell, Yogi Berra, Ray Boone, Joe Coleman, Tookie Gilbert, Jim Hegan, Bob Kennedy, Max Lanier, George Lerchen, Barney Martin, Don Mueller, Dick Schofield, Bud Sheely, Dick Sisler, Roy Smalley, and Ebba St. Claire.

1954

July 13—Ray Boone and Gus Bell both smack home runs in the 21st All-Star Game.

Prior to the start of the season, Connie Mack and his family sell their interest in the A's; the franchise shifts to Kansas City.

Don Mueller leads the majors in hits with 212 and has the second-best average in the NL (.342). Yogi Berra wins his second AL MVP award and drives in 125 runs. Also in the AL, Joe Coleman's 7.49 hits per game are the fourth best, while Ray Narleski's thirteen saves are the third best. Coleman's efforts come for the new Baltimore franchise, shifted from St. Louis after Bill Veeck sold out. Narleski's rookie contributions, served up to veteran Jim Hegan, help the surprising Cleveland Indians wrest the AL title away from the New York Yankees. However, the world championship stayed in the Big Apple as the Giants sweep the Indians. Don Mueller proves his mettle in postseason play by hitting .389 and scoring four runs.

Active Fathers/Sons: Bobby Adams, Gus Bell, Yogi Berra, Ray Boone, Joe Coleman, Jim Hegan, Bob Kennedy, Vern Law, Guy Morton, Jr., Don Mueller, Ray Narleski, Chet Nichols, Dick Schofield, Bob Skinner, Roy Smalley, and Ebba St.

Claire.

1955

Ray Boone ties with Jackie Jensen for the AL RBI title with 116; Yogi Berra racks up 108 for second place. This was the only offensive category that includes Berra among the leaders. Despite this and a modest .279 batting average, Berra's overall contributions and esteem are such that he is voted his third MVP award. Ray Narleski leads the major leagues with 19 saves and ties Brooklyn's Clem Labine for the major league pitching appearance mark with 60. In the NL, Gus Bell's 188 hits are third in the senior circuit.

Active Fathers/Sons: Bobby Adams, Gus Bell, Yogi Berra, Roy Boone, Joe Coleman, Jim Hegan, Bob Kennedy, Vern Law, Don Mueller, Ray Narleski, Chet Nichols, Ron Northey, Dick Schofield, Roy Smalley, Haywood Sullivan, and George Susce.

1956

In a year when most of the NL's offensive categories are dominated by the likes of Hank Aaron, Roberto Clemente, Eddie Matthews, Stan Musial, and Duke Snider, Gus Bell's 31 doubles rate third in the league. Bell plays 149 games in the outfield and hits .292 with 29 homers and 84 RBIs for the third-place Reds, who finish a mere two games out of first. Berra produces another remarkable year for the Bronx Bombers, who once again reign in the AL. Berra knocks in 105 runs and crashes 30 homers and 29 doubles while hitting a respectable .298.

Yogi Berra rampages through the World Series. In Game Two (October 5th) he crashes a grand slam off Cy Young winner Don Newcombe. In Game Five (October 8th), he calls the pitches for Don Larsen's perfect game. The Series with Brooklyn goes a full seven games, and in the finale on October 10th, Berra smashes another two homers off Newcombe and calls a shutout. For the Series, Berra records 3 home runs, drives in 10 runs, scores 5 runs, and hits a hefty .360 (nine for 25).

Active Fathers/Sons: Bobby Adams, Earl Averill, Charlie Beamon, Gus Bell, Yogi Berra, Ray Boone, Tito Francona, Jim Hegan, Bob Kennedy, Marty Keogh, Vern Law, Don Mueller, Ray Narleski, Chet Nichols, Ron Northey, Dick Schofield, Dave Sisler, Bob Skinner, Roy Smalley, George Susce, and Ozzie Virgil, Sr.

1957

July 1—Gus Bell is cut down by Minnie Minoso while trying to reach third on Ernie Banks' hit during the ninth inning of the 24th All-Star Game.

The season ends with the Braves astride the NL standings. They go on to best the Yankees four games to three. After a mediocre regular season, Yogi Berra turns in another impressive post-season display, hitting .320 in the fall classic.

Active Fathers/Sons: Bobby Adams, Charlie Beamon, Gus Bell, Yogi Berra, Ray Boone, Tito Francona, Jim Hegan, Bob Kennedy, Marty Keogh, Vern Law, Donald Lee, Don Mueller, Ray Narleski, Ron Northey, Bobo Osborne, Dick Schofield, Dave Sisler, Bob Skinner, Roy Smalley, Haywood Sullivan, George Susce, Dizzy Trout, and Ozzie Virgil, Sr.

1958

The Dodgers and the Giants move west. Baseball father Felipe Alou cracks the Giants' starting lineup and father Bob Skinner registers one of his best years for the second-place Pirates. Skinner joins the league leaders in average (.321) and on-base percentage (.390), both marks good enough for fifth place. Also with the Pirates, Vern Law's control results in his walking only 1.74 batters per game, third best in the league that season. In the AL, Yogi Berra has begun to platoon behind the plate.

The World Series reprises the previous year as far as contenders, but the Yankees reverses the outcome, defeating the Braves 4-3. Berra catches all seven games, but hits only .222.

Active Fathers/Sons: Bobby Adams, Felipe Alou, Ruben Amaro, Earl Averill, Charlie Beamon, Gus Bell, Yogi Berra, Ray Boone, Fritz Brickell, Dick Ellsworth, Tito Francona, Jim Hegan, Marty Keogh, Vern Law, Donald Lee, Chuck Lindstrom, Don Mueller, Ray Narleski, Bobo Osborne, Dick Schofield, Dave Sisler, Bob Skinner, Roy Smalley, George Susce, Hal Trosky, Jr., and Ozzie Virgil, Sr.

1959

April 22—Ray Boone starts the ball rolling for the Go-Go Sox, spiritual heirs to the Hitless Wonders of 1906. In the seventh inning of a game against Kansas City, Boone reaches first on an error. Nearly an hour later, following some of the most bizarre baseball ever witnessed at the major league level, Boone has scored twice and the White Sox have recorded 11 runs IN ONE INNING ON ONE HIT. Shortly thereafter, the aging Boone is traded to Kansas City. The Sox Go-Go on to win the AL, a comfortable five games ahead of second-place Cleveland.

May 26—Dick Schofield plays shortstop and leads off, and Bob Skinner plays left and bats fifth for the Pirates as Harvey Haddix pitches 12 perfect innings—and loses.

August 3—Yogi Berra homers for the AL in the year's second All-Star game. (From 1959 through 1962, baseball conducts two All-Star games each season.)

Vern Law's 20 complete games are second-best in the majors, and his 18-9 record produces a .667 winning percentage, second to teammate El-roy Face. Face turns in one of the most remarkable pitching performances of recent history, going 18-1. Law again demonstrates his control as he allows only 1.79 walks per game and registers a 2.98 ERA. The Dodgers bring the first pennant to the West Coast and begin making playing time for a young shortstop named Maury Wills. The Dodgers squelch the Sox in six games during the Series.

Active Fathers/Sons: Bobby Adams, Felipe Alou, Earl Averill, Gus Bell, Yogi Berra, Roy Boone, Fritz Brickell, Camilo Carreon, Tito Francona, Freddie Green, Jim Hegan, Marty Keogh, Vern Law, Don Mueller, Ray Narleski, Bobo Osborne, Dick Schofield, Dave Sisler, Bob Skinner, Haywood Sullivan, George Susce, and Maury Wills.

1960

July 11—In Municipal Stadium, Kansas City, Vern Law enters the game in the ninth and retires Brooks Robinson and Harvey Kuenn to preserve a victory for the NL in the 28th All-Star Game.

July 13—In Yankee Stadium, New York, Vern Law starts and wins the 29th All-Star Game for the NL.

Tito Francona, playing for the Cleveland Indians, slams 36 doubles to lead the AL. In the NL, Ruben Amaro claims the starting shortstop job for the last-place Phillies. For years, stolen base totals had been declining, with as few as 16 stolen bases qualifying for the NL title (Stan Hack in 1938). Maury Wills serves notice that things are about to change as he leads the NL with 50 stolen bases, the most since 1922. Wills is caught stealing 12 times, giving him a stolen base average of 80.6%. Only baseball father Julian Javier registers a better percentage in the NL; Javier steals 19 bases and is caught four times for an 82.6% mark. Vern Law pitches his way to a Cy Young Award and the Pirates to a pennant with a 20-9 season featuring 18 complete games (best in the majors, along with Warren Spahn and Lew Burdette). Baseball father Fred Green helps out by winning 8 games, losing 4, and saving 3. Bob Skinner contributes 86 RBIs to the Buccaneers' first NL championship since the 1927 season. Baseball father Dick Schofield comes off the bench in September to replace their injured shortstop (Dick Groat). Schofield responds by hitting .403

for the month.

The Series pits the Pittsburghers against the Yankees (whom they had also faced in 1927) and produces one of the most thrilling conclusions to a series ever when Bill Mazeroski slams his bottom-of-the-ninth home run in Game Seven. Law wins the first and fourth games and starts the climactic seventh. The Deacon also chips in with two hits in six at-bats, scores a run, and knocks one in. Bob Skinner appears in two games and Ducky Schofield in three. Fred Green makes 3 appearances, pitches 4 innings, and is rocked for 11 hits, 10 earned runs, and a 22.50 ERA. Yogi Berra records his usual stellar postseason performance, hitting .318 with a home run and eight RBIs.

Active Fathers/Sons: Felipe Alou, Ruben Amaro, Earl Averill, Gus Bell, Yogi Berra, Doug Camilli, Camilo Carreon, Dick Ellsworth, Tito Francona, Len Gabrielson, Freddie Green, Jim Hegan, Julian Javier, Marty Keogh, Vern Law, Don Lee, Chet Nichols, Dick Schofield, George Sisler, Bob Skinner, Haywood Sullivan, Ozzie Virgil, Sr., Maury Wills, and Bobby Wine.

1961

The American League expands to ten teams, adopts the 162-game schedule, and awards Roger Maris a home run record with an asterisk. A 36-year-old Berra puts in only 15 games behind the plate, but plays left field in 87 games as the Yankees muscle their way to a 109-53 season. The Yankee roster features six players with 20 or more home runs. Tito Francona lashes out 178 hits (fourth best in the league) for the fifth-place Indians (78-83). Marty Keogh legs out nine triples (second best on the circuit) for the ninth place Senators (61-100, tied with Kansas City). Maury Wills leads the NL with 35 steals and receives the Gold Glove for his play at shortstop.

The Yanks punish the Reds four games to one in October, as Berra adds three RBIs and another home run to his burgeoning career Series totals.

Active Fathers/Sons: Felipe Alou, Ruben Amaro, Earl Averill, Gus Bell, Yogi Berra, Fritz Brickell, Doug Camilli, Camilo Carreon, Dick Ellsworth, Tito Francona, Freddie Green, Julian Javier, Marty Keogh, Lew Krausse, Jr., Bill Kunkel, Vern Law, Don Lee, Chet Nichols, Bobo Osborne, Dick Schofield, George Sisler, Bob Skinner, Ron Stillwell, Haywood Sullivan, Ozzie Virgil, Sr., and Maury Wills.

1962

May 5—Earl Averill, Jr. goes one for two and scores a run for the Los Angeles Angels, as Bo "the screwball with a screwball" Belinsky pitches a no-hitter against the Orioles.

May 30—Maury Wills cracks home runs from both sides of the plate. The two round-trippers prove to be $1/3$ of Wills' season total.

June 24—Yogi Berra catches all 22 innings in a Detroit-Yankee game; the Yankees win 9-7, and reliever Luis Arroyo warms up 11 times, but never gets into the seven-hour marathon.

July 30—At Wrigley Field, Chicago, 28-year-old baseball father Dave Stenhouse becomes the first rookie to start an All-Star Game. Another AL rookie, Tom Tresh, doubles home a run in the fourth.

September 23—In St. Louis, Maury Wills steals two bases to tie and surpass Ty Cobb's season stolen base mark. Wills has been playing in pain for weeks as his right leg is bleeding internally from the pounding it has taken.

The NL expands to 10 teams with the addition of the New York Mets and Houston Colt 45s. The Dodgers begin play in Dodger Stadium.

Maury Wills establishes a record with 104 stolen bases on his way to becoming the runaway NL MVP. Wills scores 130 runs (second in the NL), raps 208 hits (also second), and ends the season in a four-way tie for the NL triples lead with 10. He adds a second Gold Glove to his accomplishments. Bob Skinner's .397 on-base percentage places him third in the league. Felipe Alou registers his first .300 season and leads the formidable Giants' lineup in hitting with .316. The Giants end the regular season tied with the Dodgers and prevail in a best-of-three play-off when they come from behind to score four runs in the ninth inning of Game Three.

Tom Tresh is named AL Rookie of the Year. Playing shortstop and outfield, the switch-hitting Tresh hits .286 with 93 RBIs and 20 home runs as the Yankees surge to another pennant. Dubbed the "new Mickey Mantle," Tresh will play until 1969, but never again approach this RBI total; it's also his highest season batting average.

However, that's still in the future as Tresh continues his impressive rookie performance in October, winning Game Five with a three-run homer. Tresh hits .321 (nine for 28) against the Giants and leads all performers with five runs scored. The Yanks defeat the Giants, four games to three.

Active Fathers/Sons: Felipe Alou, Ruben Amaro, Earl Averill, Gus Bell, Yogi Berra, Doug Camilli, Camilo Carreon, Dick Ellsworth, Tito Francona, Freddie Green, Julian Javier, Marty Keogh, Bill Kunkel, Vern Law, Don Lee, Manny Mota, Chet Nichols, Bobo Osborne, Dick Schofield, George Sisler, Bob Skinner, Dave Stenhouse, Ron Stillwell, Haywood Sullivan, Jose Tartabull, Tom Tresh, Ozzie Virgil, Sr., Maury Wills, and Bobby Wine.

1963

July 31—Tito Francona is one of four Indians to homer consecutively.

September 1—Tom Tresh homers from both sides of the plate.

The strike zone is enlarged. Bob Kennedy is named the Cubs' Head Coach, ending their "College of Coaches" experiment.

Maury Wills registers 40 stolen bases, best in the NL. Pete Rose is named the NL Rookie of the Year. Bobby Wine picks up a Gold Glove for his play at shortstop. Dick Ellsworth wins 22 games with 19 complete games, and pitches 291 innings to appear among the league leaders in those categories. His 2.10 ERA places him second to Sandy Koufax that year. In the AL, Jose Tartabull is caught only once in seventeen attempts to lead the majors with a 94.1% stolen base average. Tom Tresh scored 91 runs, tied for third in the AL.

If it's the postseason, we must be talking about ... Okay, how many ways can you say Yankees? This season, though, things are a bit different as the Dodgers' powerhouse pitching shuts down the Yankee machine in a sweep. None of our baseball fathers or sons distinguishes himself this October. For the victorious Dodgers, Wills manages a paltry two for 15 (.133). Tommy Tresh fares only slightly better, getting one more hit in the same number of at-bats for a .200 average. The 1963 Series also marks Yogi Berra's last as a player. He goes zero for one. However, consider the following. Between 1947 (his first full season) and 1963, Berra appeared in the World Series a record 14 times, played in a record 75 World Series games, and holds a record 71 hits. The Yankees won 10 times during those years, and that means a ring for every one of Yogi's stubby little fingers. Not bad for a working-class kid from a poor neighborhood in St. Louis.

Active Fathers/Sons: Felipe Alou, Ruben Amaro, Earl Averill, Gus Bell, Yogi Berra, Doug Camilli, Camilo Carreon, Dick Ellsworth, Tito Francona, Len Gabrielson, Julian Javier, Marty Keogh, Bill Kunkel, Vern Law, Don Lee, Manny Mota, Chet Nichols, Bobo Osborne, Dick Schofield, Bob Skinner, Dave Stenhouse, Jerry Stephenson, Haywood Sullivan, Jose Tartabull, Mike White, Maury Wills, and Bobby Wine.

1964

July 13—Tom Tresh homers from both sides of the plate for the second time in his career.

Yogi Berra is named Manager of the Yankees. Mel Stottlemyre, recalled in August, proceeds to win nine games. On September 26th, he ties an AL record for most hits in a game by a pitcher with four singles and a double. Bolstered by a 22-6 September, Berra's Yankees win the pennant on the next-to-last day of the season.

Rookie Mel Stottlemyre pitches a complete game victory to beat future Hall of Famer Bob Gibson in Game Two, only to see the tables turn in Game Seven as the Yankees drop the Series to St. Louis. The next day, Berra is fired and shortly thereafter replaced by former St. Louis manager Johnny Keane. Although few predict it at the time, history reveals that the long era of Yankee domination is now over. Maury Wills wins the NL stolen base crown with 53.

Active Fathers/Sons: Sandy Alomar, Sr., Felipe Alou, Ruben Amaro, Gus Bell, Mike Brumley, Doug Camilli, Camilo Carreon, Ed Connolly, Jr., Dick Ellsworth, Tito Francona, Len Gabrielson, Freddie Green, Mike Hegan, Julian Javier, Marty Keogh, Lew Krausse, Jr., Hal Lanier, Vern Law, Don Lee, Manny Mota, Chet Nichols, Dick Schofield, Bob Skinner, Dave Stenhouse, Mel Stottlemyre, Jose Tartabull, Tom Tresh, Mike White, Maury Wills, and Bobby Wine.

1965

June 6—For the third time in his career, Tom Tresh launches homers from both sides of the plate. This time, though, he adds a second round-tripper from the left-hand side as well.

The Houston Astrodome opens and a free-agent draft is instituted.

Maury Wills leads the majors with 94 stolen bases, as the Dodgers squeak past the Giants. Tom Tresh has a terrific year, tearing up the league for 94 runs, 168 hits, 29 doubles, and a total 287 bases. Tom's teammate Mel Stottlemyre stymies his opposition, posting a 20-9 season with 18 complete games and four shutouts. But Tom and Mel cannot prevail as the mighty Yankees fail. Minnesota wins 102 and the American League.

The Dodgers win the World Series in seven games. Maury Wills strokes 11 hits in 30 at-bats, scores 3 runs, knocks in 3 runs, and swipes 3 bases.

Active Fathers/Sons: Sandy Alomar, Sr., Felipe Alou, Ruben Amaro, Mike Brumley, Doug Camilli, Camilo Carreon, Joe Coleman, Dick Ellsworth, Tito Francona, Len Gabrielson, Julian Javier, Marty Keogh, Lew Krausse, Jr., Hal Lanier, Vern Law, Don Lee, Manny Mota, Dick Schofield, Bob Skinner, Jerry Stephenson, Mel Stottlemyre, Jose Tartabull, Tom Tresh, Ozzie Virgil, Sr., Mike White, Maury Wills, and Bobby Wine.

1966

July 12—At Busch Stadium, St. Louis, Maury Wills singles home the winning run in the bottom of the ninth to give the NL a 2-1 victory in the thirty-seventh All-Star Game.

For the first time since 1960, Wills is overshadowed on the base paths. Proof that other National Leaguers are now beginning to emulate Wills can be seen in the fact that he finishes third this season (38 steals), behind Lou Brock (74) and Sonny Jackson (49). Felipe Alou leads the majors with 218 hits and ties for the major league lead in runs with 122. Alou's 355 total bases lead the NL. Felipe loses the NL batting title to brother Matty; Matty hits .342 to Felipe's .327. Talk about your ups and downs, Dick Schofield starts the season with the Giants, then appears in 31 games for the Yankees and finishes the season in Los Angeles. The Giants end the season 93-68, 1½ games behind the Dodgers. The Yankees finish in the cellar. Third-string catcher and baseball father Larry Haney contributes to Baltimore's pennant by playing in 20 games; he does not appear in the Series as the Orioles sweep the Dodgers.

During the off-season, Maury Wills leaves the team in the middle of a Dodger tour of Japan. This provokes his trade to Pittsburgh.

Active Fathers/Sons: Sandy Alomar, Sr., Felipe Alou, Ruben Amaro, Mike Brumley, Doug Camilli, Jim Campanis, Camilo Carreon, Joe Coleman, Dick Ellsworth, Tito Francona, Len Gabrielson, Larry Haney, Mike Hegan, Julian Javier, Marty Keogh, Lew Krausse, Jr., Hal Lanier, Vern Law, Don Lee, Manny Mota, Mel Queen, Jr., Dick Schofield, Bob Skinner, Jerry Stephenson, Mel Stottlemyre, Jose Tartabull, Tom Tresh, Ozzie Virgil, Sr., Maury Wills, and Bobby Wine.

1967

In Mel Queen's first full season as a pitcher (he came up as an outfielder), he limits opponents to 7.12 hits per game, an opposition batting average of just .215 and an opposition on-base percentage of .270. Do stepfathers count in our survey? Pitching for Boston, Lee Stange (Jody Reed's stepfather) registers eight wins against 10 losses as the Red Sox win one of the most exciting AL races in baseball history.

Julian Javier homers in the seventh game of the World Series, and St. Louis triumphs, four games to Boston's three. Javier turns in a fine Series for the Redbirds, hitting .360 with three doubles and four RBIs. Baseball father Jose Tartabull plays all seven games for the losing Beantown nine, but hits only two for 13 for a .154 average.

Active Fathers/Sons: Sandy Alomar, Sr., Felipe Alou, Ruben Amaro, Doug Camilli, Jim Campanis, Joe Coleman, Ed Connolly, Jr., Dick Ellsworth, Tito Francona, Len Gabrielson, Larry Haney, Jim Hegan, Julian Javier, Lew Krausse, Jr., Hal Lanier,

Vern Law, Mel Queen, Jr., Dick Schofield, Jerry Stephenson, Mel Stottlemyre, Jose Tartabull, Tom Tresh, Maury Wills, and Bobby Wine.

1968

July 9—In the first indoor All-Star Game, as well as the first nighttime match, Mel Stottlemyre pitches the eighth inning. The only scoring in this NL victory comes from Willie Mays in the bottom of the first.

July 30-August 1—Tom Tresh plays 26 consecutive innings at shortstop without a fielding play.

Stottlemyre records a 21-12 season with 19 complete games. Dick Ellsworth, now with Boston, pitches his way to a 16-7 mark for the fourth-place Beantowners (86-76). Ellsworth's .696 winning percentage is fourth best in the AL; his 1.7 walks per game rank him third. Playing 156 games for the tenth place Senators (65-96), Del Unser wins second place in the Rookie of the Year vote.

In the NL, Felipe Alou ties Pete Rose for the major league lead with 210 hits. Alou legs out 37 doubles and touches 290 bases; his .317 average places him third behind brother Matty (.332) and Pete Rose (.335). Rose wins the batting crown on the final day of the regular season. The following season, Rose will become baseball's first "100,000 singles hitter." Maury Wills' 52 stolen bases again place him second to Brock in the NL. Do fathers-in-law count in this book? In this year of the pitcher, Juan Marichal, father-in-law to Jose Rijo, wins 26, with 30 complete games, 326 innings, and 218 strikeouts.

The Tigers claw their way past the Redbirds in a full seven game World Series. Julian Javier plays second all seven games and chips in with a nine for 27 effort at the plate with three RBIs.

Active Fathers/Sons: Sandy Alomar, Sr., Felipe Alou, Ruben Amaro, Bobby Bonds, Doug Camilli, Jim Campanis, Joe Coleman, Dick Ellsworth, Tito Francona, Len Gabrielson, Larry Haney, Julian Javier, Lew Krausse, Jr., Hal Lanier, Hal McRae, Manny Mota, Mel Queen, Jr., Dick Schofield, Ed Sprague, Jerry Stephenson, Mel Stottlemyre, Jose Tartabull, Tom Tresh, Del Unser, Maury Wills, and Bobby Wine.

1969

June 25—Bobby Bonds smashes a grand slam home run in his first major league game.

July 23—Mel Stottlemyre is the starter and loser of the fortieth All-Star Game.

Professional baseball's centennial year is celebrated with expansion and the introduction of divisional play, as both leagues are expanded to 12 teams of two divisions each. As part of the centennial observances, George Sisler is named to the Greatest Living Players Team by the Baseball Writers Association of America. Skinner later resigns as the Phillies' manager after they compile a 44-64 start.

Bobby Bonds ties Pete Rose for the NL lead in runs with 120. Bonds observes his first "30-30" season with 45 stolen bases and 32 home runs. He also establishes a major league record for strikeouts in a season with 187. Del Unser leads the AL with eight triples, a record for the fewest three-base hits for a season league leader. Mel Stottlemyre posts a 20-14 record.

Active Fathers/Sons: Sandy Alomar, Sr., Felipe Alou, Ruben Amaro, Bobby Bonds, Doug Camilli, Jim Campanis, Joe Coleman, Dick Ellsworth, Tito Francona, Len Gabrielson, Larry Haney, Johnny Hairston, Mike Hegan, Julian Javier, Lew Krausse, Jr., Hal Lanier, Manny Mota, Scott Northey, Mel Queen, Jr., Dick Schofield, Jerry Stephenson, Mel Stottlemyre, Jose Tartabull, Tom Tresh, Del Unser, Maury Wills, and Bobby Wine.

1970

Bobby Bonds breaks his own record with 189 strikeouts. Bonds counterbalances his whiffs with an offensive performance that includes 134 runs (second in the league and the majors), 36 doubles (a tie for third in the NL), 10 triples (also tied for third), 48 stolen bases (third in the league), and 334 total bases (fourth in the NL). Diego Segui of the A's limits opponents to a .222 average and records the season's lowest ERA, 2.56.

Active Fathers/Sons: Sandy Alomar, Sr., Bobby Bonds, Jim Campanis, Joe Coleman, Dick Ellsworth, Tito Francona, Len Gabrielson, Larry Haney, Mike Hegan, Julian Javier, Lew Krausse, Jr., Hal Lanier, Milt May, Hal McRae, Manny Mota, Mel Queen, Jr., Dick Schofield, Jerry Stephenson, Mel Stottlemyre, Del Unser, Maury Wills, and Bobby Wine.

1971

July 9 — Mel Queen relieves Eddie Fisher in baseball's longest night game, a 20-inning affair between the California Angels and the Oakland Athletics. A total of 43 batters struck out, 26 of them Angels, setting two major league records.

Curt Flood challenges baseball's reserve clause.

Seven of Mel Stottlemyre's 16 wins come by shutouts. Sandy Alomar pings out 179 hits, second best in the AL; his 689 at-bats were, at the time, the sixth highest single season total in baseball history. Alomar also eludes AL defensive efforts for 39 stolen bases. Mike Hegan comes to the Western Division champion Oakland A's about halfway through the season. He contri-

butes more with his glove than his bat; he appears in 47 games at first base and 65 total games, but registers only 55 at-bats. Diego Segui's contribution consists of a 10-8 season record. In the ALCS, Segui starts and loses Game Three as the Orioles sweep the A's; Hegan goes zero for one as a pinch hitter. Bobby Bonds wins a Gold Glove.

Active Fathers/Sons: Sandy Alomar, Sr., Bobby Bonds, Joe Coleman, Dick Ellsworth, Ross Grimsley, Jr., Mike Hegan, Julian Javier, Lew Krausse, Jr., Hal Lanier, Milt May, Hal McRae, Manny Mota, Mel Queen, Jr., Dick Schofield, Ed Sprague, Mel Stottlemyre, Del Unser, Maury Wills, and Bobby Wine.

1972

The first players' strike lasts 13 days and results in the cancellation of 86 games. Yogi Berra debuts as manager of the Mets, and is elected to the Hall of Fame the same year.

Mel Stottlemyre throws another seven shutouts.

Joe Coleman contributes to the Tigers' Eastern Division crown by winning 19 (losing 14). The Motor City nine clinch at home by taking two of three from Boston, who finish the season in second, ½ game out. In Game Three of the ALCS, Coleman blanks the A's and sets a play-off record by striking out fourteen. Despite Coleman's effort, the A's take the series, three games to two.

Ross Grimsley pitches effectively (14-8) in his second full season as Cincinnati waltzes through the Western Division in the National League. Grimsley manacles the Pirates in Game Four of the NLCS, restricting them to two hits in a 7-1 Red victory.

Six of the seven games in this World Series are decided by one run. Grimsley starts Game Two against the A's, but loses, 2-1. He bounces back to claim relief wins in Games Five and Six. Finishing out his career, Julian Javier makes two appearances as a pinch hitter for the Reds, but fails to connect. Despite limited action during the regular season, Hal McRae appears in 5 of the 7 games and hits 4 for 13 (.444). Mike Hegan again gives the A's a reliable late-inning glove man; he appears in five games at first and registers an equal number of at-bats as the A's prevail, four games to three.

Active Fathers/Sons: Mike Adams, Sandy Alomar, Sr., Buddy Bell, Bobby Bonds, Bob Boone, Joe Coleman, Ross Grimsley, Larry Haney, Mike Hegan, Julian Javier, Lew Krausse, Jr., Hal Lanier, Milt May, Hal McRae, Manny Mota, Mel Queen, Jr., Ed Sprague, Mel Stottlemyre, Del Unser, Maury Wills, and Bobby Wine.

1973-1991

When the American League opened play in 1973, it introduced an innovation that profoundly affected the baseball world at large—the Designated Hitter rule. Proponents say the rule adds both offense AND strategy, translating into excitement for the fans. They say it opened new opportunities and prolonged playing careers. Opponents decry the rule as a blasphemous break with tradition. In a baseball game, players are supposed to play both offense and defense, they argue. To date, the rule's proponents seem to have the upper hand as the rule has been adopted by virtually every league and level of baseball except the National League. Rumors circulate periodically that present-day Commissioner Fay Vincent secretly yearns to get rid of the rule, but, for the moment, it appears it will stand.

Several distinguished baseball names appear among the roster of players putting the rule's first season into the record books. Tommy Davis hit .306 and drove in 89 runs for the AL Eastern champs, the Baltimore Orioles. Orlando Cepeda, The Baby Bull, hefted his stick in Boston, while Frank Robinson slammed 30 homers and drove in 97 runs for the California Angels. Tony Oliva hit .291 and drove in 92 runs for the Twins. Quite a few other players, not recording such impressive numbers, nevertheless served notice that they were worth keeping in the lineup—Oscar Gamble, Carlos May, Gates Brown, and Alex Johnson to name a few. And, of course, a baseball father was on hand to usher in this profound change in baseball's conduct.

Cincinnati brought Harold Abraham McRae up to the big show as a 22-year-old second baseman in 1968. He appeared in 17 games, but mustered a meager .196 average. McRae sat out the 1969 season with a broken leg, and when he reappeared with the Reds in 1970, Sparky Anderson used him more as an outfielder than as an infielder. Hal distinguished himself in the Series, going five for 11.

Hal platooned with Bernie Carbo in the outfield in 1971 as the Reds dropped to fourth place. His playing time fell off in 1972 when Cincinnati claimed another NL championship, but he registered four hits in nine at-bats in the Reds' losing cause in the 1972 Series.

So far, McRae's career appeared good, but not outstanding. In 1973, he went over to Kansas City. He found there a home and a position, and from the inception of the DH rule and for a decade thereafter, Hal McRae became synonymous with the new position. He set the standards and established the model. He took pride in preparing himself mentally and "staying in the game." Perched up on the top step of the dugout, peering out at the playing field, McRae insisted that a successful DH followed the game intently rather than retreating to the clubhouse when not loosening up in the on-deck circle or facing opposition pitchers.

McRae played more games in the outfield than at DH in 1973. In 1974, he recorded 90 games in the designated hitter spot, and the first of six .300 seasons. McRae went back into the outfield for the 1975 season as the Royals brought in an aging Harmon Killebrew for what would prove to be his final hurrah. Despite a disappointing performance from Killebrew, the Royals, climbing from fifth to second, served notice on the rest of the division that they were a club to be contended with. In 1976, under Whitey Herzog, the Royals arrived; they finished 2½ games ahead of Oakland and claimed the AL West. McRae, appearing in 117 games as the DH and another 31 in the outfield, hit .332 and slugged .461 with 73 RBIs.

1973

July 24—In Royals Stadium, Kansas City, although not a starter, Bobby Bonds enters the All-Star Game in the fifth inning and smashes a two-run homer and a double; he is named the game's MVP.

The American League adopts the Designated Hitter rule.

Bobby Bonds wins his second Gold Glove. He also establishes a major league record with 11 home runs as a lead-off hitter during the season; this is his second season with more than 30 stolen bases and 30 home runs. Bonds leads the majors with 131 runs and 341 total bases. During his career, Bonds will go on to define the major league record of 35 round-trip blows as lead-off man.

Yogi Berra becomes the second manager in baseball history (Joe McCarthy was the first) to win pennants in both leagues, as the Mets win the NL East with an 82-79 record, just 1½ games ahead of the Cardinals. Their .509 winning percentage proves the lowest ever for a champion in major league play. The Mets defeat Cincinnati 3-2 in the NLCS, and battles hard against the A's in the World Series, but lose 4-3.

Active Fathers/Sons: Mike Adams, Sandy Alomar, Sr., Buddy Bell, Bobby Bonds, Bob Boone, Jim Campanis, Joe Coleman, Ken Griffey, Sr., Ross Grimsley, Jerry Hairston, Larry Haney, Mike Hegan, Tom Heintzelman, Lew Krausse, Jr., Hal Lanier, Milt May, Hal McRae, Manny Mota, Ed Sprague, Mel Stottlemyre, and Del Unser.

1974

Hank Aaron sets a new home run record. Bobby Bonds is awarded his third Gold Glove. Ross Grimsley posts an 18-13 record for the AL East champion Orioles. He pitches in two of the ALCS games, posting a 1.69 ERA in 5.1 innings of work; nevertheless, the A's vanquish the Orioles and go on to defeat the Dodgers 4-1 in the Series.

Active Fathers/Sons: Mike Adams, Sandy Alomar, Sr., Buddy Bell, Bobby Bonds, Bob Boone, Joe Coleman, Ken Griffey, Sr., Ross Grimsley, Jerry Hairston, Larry Haney, Mike Hegan, Tom Heintzelman, Lew Krausse, Jr., Jerry Martin, Milt May, Hal McRae, Manny Mota, Paul Siebert, Ed Sprague, Mel Stottlemyre, and Del Unser.

1975

May 4 — Baseball son Milt May's three-run homer drives in major league baseball's ONE MILLIONTH run.

June 1—Despite giving up only one run, Ross Grimsley is the losing pitcher in Nolan Ryan's fourth career no-hitter; Grimsley and the Orioles lose 1-0. Ryan's feat was later named one of baseball's most memorable moments, selected by the 24 major league clubs.

Earl Averill is named to the Hall of Fame. Bobby Bonds plays his third 30-30 season with 30 stolen bases and 32 home runs. Now playing for the Yankees, Bonds becomes the first player to have a 30-30 season in both leagues.

Cincinnati rampages through the regular season (108-54) and the NLCS (3-0), and then bests Boston 4-3 in a memorable Series, their first major league championship in 35 years. Ken Griffey, Sr. establishes himself as an important cog in the Big Red Machine, hitting .305 in the regular season, .333 in the NLCS, and .269 in the Series.

Active Fathers/Sons: Mike Adams, Sandy Alomar, Sr., Buddy Bell, Bobby Bonds, Bob Boone, Joe Coleman, Ken Griffey, Sr., Ross Grimsley, Jerry Hairston, Larry Haney, Mike Hegan, Tom Heintzelman, Jerry Martin, Milt May, Hal McRae, Manny Mota, Paul Siebert, Roy Smalley III, Ed Sprague, and Del Unser.

1976

August 28 and 29—Roy Smalley, III ties a major league record by striking out eight times in two consecutive games (26 innings).

Fred Lindstrom is elected to the Hall of Fame.

In their first season back in a refurbished Yankee Stadium, the Bronx Bombers claim their first championship since 1964. Sandy Alomar helps out by playing games at first, second, shortstop, third, DH, and the outfield.

Ken Griffey appears among the NL leaders in runs (111, fourth), average (.336, second), and on-base percentage (.403, fourth), as the Reds roll to consecutive titles (102-60). Griffey bats .385 in the play-offs versus Philadelphia but stumbles badly against the Yanks. He leads all Reds with 17 at-bats, but musters a solitary hit for a measly .059 average. Nevertheless, the Reds sweep the Series.

Active Fathers/Sons: Mike Adams, Sandy Alomar, Sr., Buddy Bell, Bobby Bonds, Bob Boone, Joe Coleman, Ken Griffey, Sr., Ross Grimsley, Jerry Hairston, Larry Haney, Mike Hegan, Tom Heintzelman, Jerry Martin, Milt May, Hal McRae, Manny Mota, Paul Siebert, Roy Smalley III, Ed Sprague, and Del Unser.

1977

Bobby Bonds steals 41 bases and wallops 37 round-trippers, the fourth time in his career that he exceeds 30 stolen bases and 30 home runs. He drives in 115 runs for good measure. Nevertheless, the Angels finish fifth in the division, 28 games behind Kansas City. Hal McRae smashes 54 doubles and drives in 92 runs for Whitey Herzog's Royals. In league championship play, he leads all hitters with a .444 average. Despite this, the Yankees prevail.

Bob Boone backstops the Phillies and bats .284. The Phillies succumb to the Dodgers in four games despite Boone's .400 play-off average. Manny Mota, now used almost exclusively as a pinch hitter by the Dodgers, registers a perfect one for one in the NLCS but fails to get a hit in three at-bats during the Series as the Dodgers drop the Series to the Yankees, four games to two.

Active Fathers/Sons: Mike Adams, Sandy Alomar, Sr., Buddy Bell, Dale Berra, Bobby Bonds, Bob Boone, Joe Coleman, Ken Griffey, Sr., Ross Grimsley, Jerry Hairston, Larry Haney, Mike Hegan, Tom Heintzelman, Matt Keogh, Jerry Martin, Milt May, Hal McRae, Manny Mota, Paul Siebert, Roy Smalley III, Del Unser, and Bump Wills.

1978

For the fifth time in his career, Bobby Bonds steals more than 30 bases and hits more than 30 home runs. Roy Smalley collects 85 walks, fifth in the AL. Bump Wills steals 52 bases, third best in the AL. Ross Grimsley, now pitching for Montreal, wins 20 with 19 complete games (both second best in the NL) in 263 innings (third in the league). Bob Boone calls the signals and collects a Gold Glove as the Phillies win another divisional title. Boone and the Phillies struggle in postseason play. Boone hits only .182 as the Phillies succumb to the Dodgers. Manny continues his NLCS pinch-hitting perfection with another one for one performance.

Active Fathers/Sons: Mike Adams, Sandy Alomar, Sr., Buddy Bell, Dale Berra, Bobby Bonds,

Bob Boone, Joe Coleman, Ken Griffey, Sr., Ross Grimsley, Jerry Hairston, Larry Haney, Tom Heintzelman, Terry Kennedy, Matt Keogh, Jerry Martin, Milt May, Hal McRae, Manny Mota, Allen Ripley, Paul Siebert, Roy Smalley III, Steve Trout, Del Unser, and Bump Wills.

1979

Managed by baseball father Chuck Tanner, the "We Are Family" Pirates dance their way to a divisional title (98-64), sweep the Reds in the NLCS, and overcome the Orioles in the World Series, four games to three. Bob Boone and Buddy Bell bring home Gold Gloves. Bell bangs out 200 hits, including 42 doubles. Buddy's teammate Bump Wills beats opposition batteries for 35 thefts.

Active Fathers/Sons: Buddy Bell, Dale Berra, Bobby Bonds, Bob Boone, Joe Coleman, Ken Griffey, Sr., Ross Grimsley, Jerry Hairston, Terry Kennedy, Matt Keogh, Jerry Martin, Milt May, Hal McRae, Manny Mota, Allen Ripley, Roy Smalley III, Steve Trout, Del Unser, and Bump Wills.

1980

July 8 — Ken Griffey's solo home run in the bottom of the fifth inning of the All-Star game opens the scoring for the NL, which goes on to defeat the AL 5-4.

Buddy Bell's sparkling defensive play at third lands him the second of what will become six consecutive Gold Gloves. Forty-two-year-old Manny Mota retires to the Dodgers' coaching box, but still claims three hits in seven at-bats.

In Game Five of the NLCS, the lead changes hands three times before Del Unser races home with the winning run in the bottom of the tenth to bring the Phillies their first pennant in 30 years.

In the World Series, Bob Boone catches all six games and goes seven for 17 at the plate for a hefty .412 average. The Phillies overcome the Royals, 4-2. Hal McRae bats a respectable .375 for the losing KC team.

Active Fathers/Sons: Charlie Beamon, Buddy Bell, Dale Berra, Bobby Bonds, Bob Boone, Ken Griffey, Sr., Ross Grimsley, Jerry Hairston, Terry Kennedy, Matt Keogh, Vance Law, Jerry Martin, Milt May, Hal McRae, Manny Mota, Allen Ripley, Roy Smalley III, Steve Trout, Del Unser, Ozzie Virgil, Jr., and Bump Wills.

1981

April 19—A minor league game played in the International League goes eight hours and seven minutes and ends in a 2-2 tie after 32 innings; the game is finished on June 23rd, with Pawtucket beating Rochester 3-2 in the 33rd inning. The box score reveals Rochester third baseman Cal Ripken going two for 13 with no RBIs.

A strike staged by the Major League Players Association results in the loss of 713 games and a split season format.

Ken Griffey finishes the season fifth in the NL in hits (123) and fourth in average (.311). Buddy Bell earns his third Gold Glove.

Active Fathers/Sons: Buddy Bell, Dale Berra, Bobby Bonds, Bob Boone, Terry Francona, Ken Griffey, Sr., Jerry Hairston, Matt Keogh, Terry Kennedy, Vance Law, Jerry Martin, Milt May, Hal McRae, Allen Ripley, Roy Smalley III, Steve Trout, Del Unser, Ozzie Virgil, Jr., and Bump Wills.

1982

Cal Ripken is named AL Rookie of the Year. In 94 games at shortstop and 71 games at third base, Ripken hits 28 home runs and 32 doubles, and drives in 93 runs. Despite Ripken's efforts, Baltimore falls one game short of Milwaukee in the AL East. In the West, Bob Boone anchors the Angels and wins his first AL Gold Glove. Terry Kennedy collects 42 doubles for the San Diego Padres, second in the NL. Remarkably, not a single baseball father or son appears in this year's World Series, which St. Louis wins against Milwaukee four games to three.

Active Fathers/Sons: Buddy Bell, Dale Berra, Bob Boone, Terry Francona, Ken Griffey, Sr., Ross Grimsley, Jerry Hairston, Terry Kennedy, Matt Keogh, Vance Law, Jerry Martin, Milt May, Hal McRae, Manny Mota, Allen Ripley, Roy Smalley III, Mike Stenhouse, Marc Sullivan, Steve Trout, Del Unser, Ozzie Virgil, Jr., and Bump Wills.

1983

Cal Ripken edges out teammate Eddie Murray to win AL MVP honors. In Ripken's second full season, he leads the league in runs (121), hits (211), and doubles (47), and is second only to Jim Rice in total bases (Ripken logs 343, one fewer than Rice); his .318 average is good enough for fifth in the AL. Terry Kennedy drives in 98 runs, fifth in the NL.

Ripken leads all hitters in the ALCS, hitting .400 against a Chicago White Sox team featuring baseball sons Vance Law and Jerry Hairston. However, Cal falters in the Series (three for eighteen, or .167) as Baltimore breezes past the Phillies, four games to one.

Active Fathers/Sons: Buddy Bell, Dale Berra, Bobby Boone, Terry Francona, Ken Griffey, Sr., Jerry Hairston, Terry Kennedy, Matt Keogh, Vance Law, Jerry Martin, Milt May, Hal McRae, Dick Schofield, Joel Skinner, Roy Smalley III, Mike Stenhouse, Steve Trout, and Ozzie Virgil, Jr.

1984

Cal Ripken produces another fine season with 195 hits, 37 doubles, and 327 total bases. He hits for the cycle in a May 6th game against Texas. Buddy Bell hits .315 (fourth in the AL) and drives in 83 runs for last place Texas (69-92) to go along with his sixth consecutive Gold Glove.

Steve Trout's 13-7 season assists the Cubs to their first NL East divisional title. Sentimental baseball fans around the country joined long-suffering Cub fanatics and cheered as the Cubby Bears won their first championship of anything since 1945. When Steve Trout won Game Two, it appeared the sentimentalists might win. But with Terry Kennedy calling the signals, the San Diego Padres prevailed in the NLCS.

In the World Series, the Padres bumped into a Detroit nine that was seemingly a team of destiny. In Game Four, Terry Kennedy launched a solo home run in the second inning, but later made the game's final out. Detroit prevails in five.

Active Fathers/Sons: Buddy Bell, Dale Berra, Bob Boone, Terry Francona, Ken Griffey, Sr., Jerry Hairston, Stan Javier, Terry Kennedy, Jeff Kunkel, Vance Law, Jerry Martin, Milt May, Hal McRae, Dick Schofield, Joel Skinner, Roy Smalley III, Randy St. Claire, Mike Stenhouse, Marc Sullivan, Danny Tartabull, Steve Trout, and Ozzie Virgil, Jr.

1985

After a 6-10 start, Yankee owner George Steinbrenner fires Yogi Berra. Berra, embarrassed, vows never to return to Yankee Stadium as long as Steinbrenner remains the owner.

Active Fathers/Sons: Buddy Bell, Dale Berra, Bob Boone, Terry Francona, Ken Griffey, Sr., Jerry Hairston, Terry Kennedy, Matt Keogh, Jeff Kunkel, Vance Law, Hal McRae, Dick Schofield, Joel Skinner, Roy Smalley III, Randy St. Claire, Mike Stenhouse, Marc Sullivan, Danny Tartabull, Steve Trout, Ozzie Virgil, Jr., and Robbie Wine.

1986

The California Angels capture the AL West with a lineup that includes baseball sons Dick Schofield at shortstop and Bob Boone behind the plate. Boone receives his second AL Gold Glove (his fourth overall) for his work. Over in the East, Marc Sullivan and Mike Stenhouse play backup roles for the Red Sox. The veteran Boone dominates Boston pitching in the ALCS, hitting a remarkable ten for twenty-two (.455). The youngster Dick Schofield hits an even .300 (nine for thirty). Their efforts aren't enough, though. Boston wins the last three games and goes on to face the Mets in one of baseball's most thrilling

World Series yet.

Active Fathers/Sons: Buddy Bell, Dale Berra, Barry Bonds, Bob Boone, Terry Francona, Gary Green, Ken Griffey, Sr., Jerry Hairston, Stan Javier, Terry Kennedy, Matt Keogh, Jeff Kunkel, Vance Law, Hal McRae, Dick Schofield, Joel Skinner, Roy Smalley III, Randy St. Claire, Kurt Stillwell, Marc Sullivan, Danny Tartabull, Steve Trout, Ozzie Virgil, Jr., and Robbie Wine.

1987

The Baltimore Orioles feature three baseball sons in their everyday lineup. Terry Kennedy anchors the club behind the plate while the Ripken brothers solidify the middle of the infield. The Orioles try a variety of players at second before giving the job to Cal's younger brother. Billy comes up in July, and the Orioles immediately enjoy an eleven-game winning streak. Over the rest of the season, Billy contributes by hitting .308 in 58 games. Cal ends his streak of 8,243 consecutive innings but keeps his consecutive game streak alive.

In his first full season with Kansas City, Danny Tartabull finishes the season with a .309 average, 34 homers, and 101 RBIs—his first 100-plus RBI season. He also leads the majors with 25 game-winning RBIs.

Roy Smalley climaxes his baseball career by DH'ing for the Twins as they surge to an AL pennant and a World Series victory. Smalley is used sparingly in the Series, but goes two for four as a pinch hitter.

Bob Boone receives another Gold Glove for his defensive prowess.

Active Fathers/Sons: Buddy Bell, Dale Berra, Barry Bonds, Bob Boone, Mike Brumley, Mark Carreon, Terry Francona, Ken Griffey, Sr., Jerry Hairston, Stan Javier, Terry Kennedy, Jeff Kunkel, Vance Law, Dick Schofield, Joel Skinner, Roy Smalley III, Randy St. Claire, Kurt Stillwell, Marc Sullivan, Danny Tartabull, Steve Trout, Ozzie Virgil, Jr., and Robbie Wine.

1988

The Ripken brothers emerge as the best double-play combination in the American League. They turn a combined total of 229. Danny Tartabull sets a Kansas City club record with three grand slams; he turns in his second consecutive 100-plus RBI season. Stan Javier proves his versatility by playing more than one position in 31 games. Bob Boone is awarded yet another Gold Glove. Young Roberto Alomar claims the regular second baseman's job in San Diego; he is only 20 years old.

Active Fathers/Sons: Roberto Alomar, Buddy Bell, Barry Bonds, Bob Boone, Mark Carreon,

Steve Ellsworth, Terry Francona, Ken Griffey, Sr., Stan Javier, Terry Kennedy, Jeff Kunkel, Bill Landrum, Vance Law, Dick Schofield, Joel Skinner, Kurt Stillwell, Marc Sullivan, Danny Tartabull, and Ozzie Virgil, Jr.

1989

Baseball sons claim the distinction of being the youngest players in both major leagues. Roberto Alomar is the youngest player in the NL, while Ken Griffey, Jr. excites AL fans. Griffey finishes third in this season's Rookie of the Year voting. Young Todd Stottlemyre shows great poise in winning five consecutive games during late August and September, a major factor in the Blue Jays' successful drive to an AL East championship. Stan Javier imitates a feat accomplished by his father as he records the highest stolen base percentage in the majors. He steals 20 bases in 21 attempts. Jeff Kunkel is this season's Mr. Versatile as he records games in all three outfield positions as well as second and third, all in the space of 10 games; he pinch-hits and pinch-runs for good measure. Within a week, he plays shortstop and pitches. Bob Boone wins a Gold Glove. Cal Ripken finishes third in the year's MVP voting.

The Griffeys become baseball's first father-son combination to play in the major leagues at the same time. Sandy Alomar, Jr. is named Minor League Player of the Year for the second consecutive year.

Active Fathers/Sons: Roberto Alomar, Buddy Bell, Barry Bonds, Bob Boone, Mark Carreon, Steve Ellsworth, Terry Francona, Ken Griffey, Sr., Ken Griffey, Jr., Stan Javier, Terry Kennedy, Jeff Kunkel, Vance Law, Dick Schofield, Joel Skinner, Kurt Stillwell, Marc Sullivan, Danny Tartabull, and Ozzie Virgil, Jr.

1990

It proves to be a banner year for baseball sons. Sandy Alomar, Jr. is voted to the starting lineup for the American League All-Star team as a rookie. His brother Roberto is on the NL team. Young Sandy goes on to win a Gold Glove as well as Rookie of the Year honors. Two other baseball sons garner both Gold Gloves and All-Star honors—Ken Griffey, Jr. and Barry Bonds. Bonds, on his way to the MVP award, records a torrid July. He hits .326 with 18 runs, 5 homers, 22 RBIs, a .450 on-base mark, and a .547 slugging percentage. The Griffeys establish a baseball legend on September 14th, when father and son smash home runs back-to-back for the Mariners.

Active Fathers/Sons: Roberto Alomar, Sandy Alomar, Jr., Moises Alou, Barry Bonds, Bob Boone, Mike Brumley, Mark Carreon, Terry Francona, Ken Griffey, Jr., Ken Griffey, Sr., Stan Javier, Terry Kennedy, Jeff Kunkel, Bill Landrum, Brian McRae, Jaime Navarro, Billy Ripken, Cal Ripken, Jr., Dick Schofield, Joel Skinner, Kurt Stillwell, Mel Stottlemyre, Jr., Todd Stottlemyre, Danny Tartabull, and Ozzie Virgil, Jr.

1991

Twenty-seven baseball sons and one baseball father appear in major league uniforms. Baseball's sons again assert themselves, continuing the trend toward seasons that overshadow the records of their fathers. Cal Ripken turns in one of the best seasons ever for a shortstop, despite Baltimore's plunge in the standings. Ken Griffey, Jr. and Roberto Alomar show once again that they must be respected as stars of the present as well as the future. Danny Tartabull reasserts himself as a possible superstar. Hal McRae, Jr. establishes himself as a potent lead-off man. After a slow start, Barry Bonds surges towards a possible second consecutive MVP, leading Pittsburgh into the National League play-offs.

Baltimore loses 95 games, and teams frequently pitch around Cal Ripken due to the absence of injured slugger Glenn Davis from the Orioles lineup. Yet Cal Ripken seems unstoppable. The iron man again plays all 162 games; Toronto's Joe Carter is the only other major leaguer to record this perfecto. This boosts Ripken's career streak to 1,572 games. Cal, Jr. observes a career high .323 average, sixth best in the AL. He also celebrates career marks with 34 home runs and 114 RBIs. He leads the league with 85 extra-base hits, and his 46 doubles prove second on the circuit. If all that isn't enough, he again leads AL shortstops in fielding percentage. In mid-October, the Associated Press overwhelmingly votes Ripken the AP Player of the Year.

Pittsburgh's Barry Bonds finishes third in the voting. He leads the league in on-base percentage, finishes one RBI behind Howard Johnson with 116, and is second in the league with 107 walks and 25 intentional walks. His .514 slugging percentage lodges him fourth place in that category.

Over in the AL, Danny Tartabull slugs .593 to lead the league. Tartabull also finds himself among the league leaders in batting average, home runs, and RBIs. His 100 RBIs tie him with Ken Griffey, Jr. for eighth place in the league. Griffey ties for third in the league's batting title race, and his 42 doubles place him in a tie for fourth place. That figure outpaces Roberto Alomar by one double. Alomar rips 11 triples, second in the league, but just two ahead of newcomer Hal McRae, Jr. McRae proves he learned a thing or two about hitting from his dad, and will undoubtedly be a force to reckon with for years to come.

Among other developments, 1991 witnesses the return from Japan of Vance Law. Law filled in at third base for an injured Carney Lansford in the Angels' organization. Appearing in the major leagues for the first time are Ruben Amaro, Jr., Chris Haney, and Andreas Mota. On a sadder note, Jimmy "Scoops" Cooney passes away on August 8th. Cooney played seven major league seasons, and will be remembered for his unassisted triple play on May 30, 1927; he was then with the Cubs.

Active Fathers/Sons: Roberto Alomar, Sandy Alomar, Jr., Ruben Amaro, Jr., Barry Bonds, Mike Brumley, Mark Carreon, Ken Griffey, Jr., Ken Griffey, Sr., Chris Haney, Todd Hundley, Stan Javier, Terry Kennedy, Bill Landrum, Vance Law, Derrick May, Hal McRae, Jr., Andy Mota, Jose Mota, Jaime Navarro, Billy Ripken, Cal Ripken, Jr., Dick Schofield, David Segui, Joel Skinner, Ed Sprague, Randy St. Claire, Kurt Stillwell, Todd Stottlemyre, and Danny Tartabull.

ON THE HORIZON

A host of other sons loom on the baseball horizon. During the 1991 preseason, baseball legend Nolan Ryan pitched against his son in an exhibition game against the University of Texas. Also garnering preseason publicity were the Mota family. The durable Manny boasted no fewer than four sons in the minors. Jose, a 26-year-old switch hitter, played for the Padres' organization. Domingo played for the Dodger organization after a college career at collegiate powerhouse Cal State Fullerton. Gary, the tallest, may also be the strongest. He reportedly possesses excellent tools, but needs some seasoning; the Astros plan to provide that to the 20-year-old outfielder. Finally, Andreas, another second baseman, actually became the first of the four to appear in a major league game when Houston brought him up for a short tour.

If the Mota family is striving to put all four sons in the majors, another race is on to see who will become baseball's first third generation family. Bret Boone displayed considerable power for a second baseman but racked up a lot of strikeouts as well while playing for the Mariners' club in Jacksonville in the AA Southern League. He teamed up with Jim Campanis, also striving to establish baseball's third generation. Meanwhile, one step down the ladder, David Bell plays for the Columbus Indians of the Class A South Atlantic League. Like his father, David plays third.

Actually, two families can already claim three generations at the major league level, although not as players. Roger Bossard succeeded his father as head groundskeeper at Comiskey Park; his grandfather tended Cleveland's Municipal Stadium lawn. The other third generation family is more renowned. Chip Caray became the third generation of Carays to broadcast at the big-league level, following his father Skip and the most famous Caray, Harry.

One baseball offspring who appears likely to make it to the majors soon is Jamie McAndrew. McAndrew's father, Jim, recorded seven seasons in the majors. Jamie played collegiately at the University of Florida and was named one of the Dodgers' top prospects in the preseason by *Baseball America*. A couple of other hurlers playing in the minors this season were Scott Carlton, Steve's son, who signed a free-agent contract with the Phillie organization, and John O'Donoghue, the son of Frederick Keys' pitching coach John O'Donoghue.

Stepping out of collegiate ball and into the minors, Eduardo Perez hopes to follow in the steps of his father Tony. Like father, like son, Eduardo is a slugging first baseman.

As yet still in high school, Ryan Luzinski booms out home runs for Holy Cross High School in Delran, New Jersey, to the delight of his father and coach, Greg. Ryan is expected to go high in the 1992 draft.

WHEN DAY IS DONE: IN THE BLUE

During the dim, foggy past of baseball's infancy, the umpire was usually an unpaid volunteer selected by the home team. As this was a gentleman's game, the gentlemanly home team captain would select a local gentleman distinguished and recognized for his integrity.

Times changed, the game got rougher, and gentlemen proved harder to find. The first professional umpires came with the creation of the National League in 1876. They received $5 a game, and one man worked the game. Some would position themselves behind the plate; others behind the pitcher. Sometime during the mid- to late-1880s, they began the practice of positioning themselves behind the plate with no one on base and then rotating out behind the pitcher with runners on base.

The records are not completely clear, but it is probable that John Henry Doscher was the first baseball father to appear as a professional umpire. Doscher, you may remember, sired the first son to appear in a major league game. We know that the National League lists a John H. Doscher as an umpire between 1879-82. We also know that John Henry (Herm) played during this same period. However, Herm played few enough games (50 in 1879, 5 in 1881, and 25 in 1882) that it is at least possible that Doscher did both. John H. Doscher umpired in the National League again in 1887. Doscher jumped to the American Association for the 1888 and 1890 seasons. The AA pioneered the development of an umpiring staff hired and assigned by the league itself.

If there's any question about whether the umpire John H. Doscher was one and the same as John Henry Doscher the player, there's no question about the next major league father to appear as a major league umpire. Orator Jim O'Rourke boomed out the balls and strikes during the 1893-94 National League seasons. However, O'Rourke's greatest contribution to baseball umpiring came in a different way. O'Rourke is credited with discovering and developing Bill Klem, ordained by many as the greatest umpire of all time. Popular legend credits Klem as the first umpire to use hand signals; others assert that "Catfish" Bill Klem was the first to use the inside chest protector. Whether true or not, Klem, the man who "never missed one" in "his heart" was elected to the Hall of Fame in 1953.

Ban Johnson opened the American League in 1901. At the time, he promised "clean baseball, beer, and plenty of 25 cent seats" — half the general admission price the National League charged. One of the steps he took to insure clean baseball was to introduce the two-man crew. By 1912 this was standard in both leagues. Thus, when Big Ed Walsh donned the blue in 1922, he would have been part of a two-man crew.

Baseball son Charles F. Berry initiated his umpiring career during the war years (1942) and spent the next 20 years as an American League arbiter. Berry enjoyed a long and varied athletic career. He gained All-American honors as an end for an undefeated Lafayette College football team in 1924. Lafayette played a punishing, grinding style of single wing football. One contemporary observer thought that they probably had fewer than 10 pass plays all season, so Berry evidently made his mark as a blocker. Berry went on to play in the NFL and became captain of the Pottsville Maroons. After he finished his NFL playing days, he became a referee. Berry entered major league baseball in 1925 and embarked upon a journeyman career that extended to the 1938 season. He coached for Connie Mack's A's 1936-40.

When Berry began umpiring, he would have been part of a three-man crew that had gained acceptance during the 1930s. In 1952, when baseball adopted the modern four-man crew, he would also have been part of that transition.

Bill Kunkel probably decided to become an umpire after taking a hard honest look at his potential as a pitcher. He called his first American League game in 1968 and stayed around until 1984; he probably would have stayed longer had it not been for his premature death by cancer in 1985. When Bill's son Jeff began attracting attention, it provoked a certain amount of speculation in the baseball world. What were the ethical implications of Bill umpiring in the league at the same time his son was playing? In fact, the Texas Rangers brought Jeff up in late July 1984, while Bill was still active. However, at the time, most of the baseball world knew Bill was fatally ill, and to their credit they were big enough to celebrate the pride and joy of a father witnessing his son make it to the major leagues rather than worry about any potential compromises.

One other father-son umpire pair needs to be mentioned. Ed P. Runge rang up balls and strikes in the American League from 1954 to 1970. His son, Paul E., has called them over in the senior circuit from 1973 through the present.

PART II

Father/Son Records and Notes

This next section shows in detail the baseball careers of all father and son combinations. For each player is given: his birthdate; birthplace; how he batted and threw and what his height and weight were during his playing days; what teams he played for and when; coaching experience; and honors and records, if any. Also included is a brief synopsis of the player and his career. Following this, complete statistics are given. These are complete career statistics for those no longer playing, but for players still active today, year-by-year statistics are given for the past few years. Completing the section is a comprehensive list of all baseball cards known to have been issued for each player, including card numbers.

In order to give the reader all of this information, many abbreviations have been used. Below is the key for all of the abbreviations. Please refer to this key when any questions arise.

Records

Players

G	=	Games
AB	=	At-bats
R	=	Runs
H	=	Hits
2B	=	Doubles
3B	=	Triples
HR	=	Home runs
RBI	=	Runs batted in
BB	=	Walks
SO	=	Strikeouts
SB	=	Stolen bases
BA	=	Batting average
SA	=	Slugging average

Pitchers

W	=	Wins
L	=	Losses
Pct.	=	Win-loss percentage
Sv.	=	Saves

G	=	Games appeared in
GS	=	Games started
CG	=	Complete games
IP	=	Innings pitched
H	=	Hits allowed
BB	=	Walks allowed
SO	=	Strikeouts
ShO	=	Shutouts
ERA	=	Earned run average

Cards

Here's an example of a card listing and what each part means.

1951B	#288R
↓	↓
Card company	Special card

Not all cards have a special status, and a very few cards have no numbers. Tobacco cards (T205, T206, and T207) were originally unnumbered. Today most collectors follow a numbering system based on the alphabetical order of the cards. These numbers have been given in the card listings.

Companies

B	=	Bowman
BBW	=	Bowman Black/White
BC	=	Bowman Color
BR	=	Berk Ross (72-card sets issued in 1951 and 1952. The 1951 set was issued in four groups and included stars from other sports.)
BU	=	Batter Up (192-card set issued by National Chicle 1934-36)
D	=	Donruss
DDK	=	Donruss Diamond Kings
DRR	=	Donruss Rated Rookie
DU	=	Donruss Update
DL	=	Delong Chewing Gum Company (24-card set issued in 1933.)
DP	=	Double Play

DS = Diamond Star
F = Fleer
FU = Fleer Update
G = Goudey (Issued 1933-36 and 1938. In numbering these, E, C, and L are arbitrary designations assigned by collectors to known variations.)
K = Kellogg's
L = Leaf
P = Post
PB = Play Ball
RH = Red Heart
RM = Red Man (Issued by Red Man Tobacco Company from 1952-55.)
S = Score
SU = Score Update
SPF = Sportsflics
SS = Sports Stars Publishing Company (690-card set. Known as the "Pure Set" because the fronts are photos with no logos, manufacturer's symbols, etc.)
T = Topps
TCMAS = Topps Connie Mack All-Stars
TBB = Topps Blue Backs (Issued in 1951 in sets of 52 cards, as were the Red Backs; they could be used for a tabletop baseball game.)
TRB = Topps Red Backs
TDE = Topps Deckle Edge (Issued in 1969 as a special insert set of 33 cards with a serrated edge.)
TDH = Topps Double Header
TE = Topps Embossed
TS = Topps Super (A 66-card set issued in 1969 and measuring 2¼ x 3¼.)
TSU = Topps Stand-Ups (77-card unnumbered set)
TT = Topps Traded
UD = Upper Deck

Special Cards
M = Manager Card
R = Rookie Card
SP = Special Card (These are cards a player appears on, but the card is not his "regular" card. These can range from a team checklist card to a commemorative card.)
USOC = United States Olympic Committee

◆ BOBBY ADAMS

Robert Henry
Born: December 14, 1921
Birthplace: Tuolumne, California
Bats: Right   **Throws:** Right
Height: 5'10"   **Weight:** 170
Played for: Cincinnati: 1946-55; Chicago (AL): 1955; Baltimore: 1956; Chicago (NL): 1957-59
Coaching Experience: Chicago (NL): 1961-64.

Bobby signed with the Reds after getting out of the Air Force in 1945. He led the NL in assists for third basemen in 1952 and in double plays in 1953. A versatile ballplayer who played first, second, third, and the outfield, Bobby prolonged his career with outstanding pinch-hitting ability. He hit .277 as a pinch hitter, 21st on the all-time ca-

reer list. Bob's brother Dick played for the 1947 Phillies.

◇ MIKE ADAMS

Robert Michael
Born: July 24, 1948
Birthplace: Cincinnati, Ohio
Bats: Right   **Throws:** Right
Height: 5'9"   **Weight:** 180
Played for: Minnesota: 1972-73; Chicago (NL): 1976-77; Oakland: 1978

Mike was two for six in his first major league go-round, and appeared in 24 games in the outfield the succeeding season. He resurfaced in the majors with the Cubs in 1976, playing the outfield, second, and third.

RECORDS

Bobby Adams (14 Years)

G	AB	R	H	2B	3B	HR	RBI	BB	SO	SB	BA	SA
1,281	4,019	591	1,082	188	49	37	303	414	447	67	.269	.368

Mike Adams (5 Years)

G	AB	R	H	2B	3B	HR	RBI	BB	SO	SB	BA	SA
100	118	27	23	5	0	3	9	32	29	2	.195	.314

Cards

Bobby Adams
1951B—#288   1952B—#166   1952T—#249   1953B—#108   1953T—#152   1954B—#108
1954T—#123   1955B—#118   1955T—#178   1956T—#287   1958T—#99   1959T—#249
Mike Adams
1974T—#573

◆ SANDY ALOMAR, SR.

Santos
Born: October 19, 1943
Birthplace: Salinas, Puerto Rico
Bats: Switch   **Throws:** Right
Height: 5'9"   **Weight:** 155
Played for: Milwaukee (NL): 1964-65; Atlanta: 1966; New York (NL): 1967; Chicago (AL): 1967-69; California: 1969-74; New York (AL): 1974-76; Texas: 1977-78
Coaching Experience: San Diego: 1986-89
Honors: American League All-Star in 1970

Sandy made his professional debut for Quad Cities in the Midwestern League when he was just 17. A journeyman utility player, Sandy led the majors in at-bats in 1971, with 689. He was an effective base-stealer; his 73.9% success rate places him 41st on the career list for players with 100 or more lifetime steals. When he finished his playing days, he became a minor league instructor for the Padres.

◇ ROBERTO ALOMAR

Born: February 5, 1968
Birthplace: Salinas, Puerto Rico
Bats: Switch   **Throws:** Right
Height: 6'   **Weight:** 184
Played for: San Diego: 1988-90; Toronto: 1991

Honors: National League All-Star in 1990, 1991

Roberto quickly established himself as one of the National League's premier second basemen. Although he is two years younger than Sandy, Jr., Roberto made it to the major leagues sooner. During his rookie season, he was second on the Padres in hitting.

◇ SANDY ALOMAR, JR.

Born: June 18, 1966
Birthplace: Salinas, Puerto Rico
Bats: Right   **Throws:** Right
Height: 6'5":   **Weight:** 200
Played for: San Diego: 1989; Cleveland (AL): 1990-91
Honors: American League All-Star and Rookie of the Year in 1990

Sandy was named *The Sporting News* minor league player of the year for two consecutive seasons. He finally got his chance to play full-time in the majors when San Diego traded him to Cleveland in exchange for Joe Carter before the start of the 1990 season. He responded with an outstanding rookie season; he was named the American League starting catcher for the 1990 All-Star game and won American League Rookie-of-the-Year honors.

RECORDS

Sandy Alomar, Sr. (15 Years)

G	AB	R	H	2B	3B	HR	RBI	BB	SO	SB	BA	SA
1,481	4,760	558	1,168	126	19	13	282	302	482	227	.245	.288

Roberto Alomar

G	AB	R	H	2B	3B	HR	RBI	BB	SO	SB	BA	SA
1988												
143	545	84	145	24	6	9	41	47	83	24	.266	.382
1989												
158	623	82	184	27	1	7	56	53	76	42	.295	.376
1990												
147	586	80	168	27	5	6	60	48	72	24	.287	.381
1991												
161	637	88	188	41	11	9	69	57	86	53	.295	.436

Sandy Alomar, Jr.

G	AB	R	H	2B	3B	HR	RBI	BB	SO	SB	BA	SA
1989												
7	19	1	4	1	0	1	6	3	3	0	.211	.421
1990												
132	445	60	129	26	2	9	66	25	46	4	.290	.418
1991												
51	184	10	40	9	0	0	7	8	24	0	.217	.266

Cards

Sandy Alomar, Sr.

1965T—#82R	1966T—#428	1967T—#561	1968T—#541	1969T—#283	1970T—#29
1971T—#745	1971T—#253	1973T—#123	1974T—#347	1975T—#266	1976T—#629
1976SS—#441	1977T—#54	1978T—#533	1979T—#144	1989B—#258	

Roberto Alomar

1988SS—#105	1988DRR—#34	1988FU—#122	1988SU—#4	1989B—#458	1989F—#630
1989D—#246	1989F—#299	1989S—#232	1989SPF—#20	1989T—#206	1989UD—#471
1990D—#111	1990F—#149	1990S—#12	1990T—#517	1990UD—#346	1991DDK—#6
1991D—#682	1991F—#523	1991S—#25	1991T—#315	1991UD—#335	

Sandy Alomar, Jr.

1989B—#454	1989D—#28	1989F—#300	1989F—#630	1989S—#30	1989SPF—#223
1989T—#648	1989UD—#5	1990D—#30	1990F—#150	1990S—#577	1990T—#353
1990UD—#655	1991DDK—#3	1991D—#489	1991F—#359	1991S—#400	1991T—#165
1991UD—#144					

◆ FELIPE ROJAS ALOU

Born: May 12, 1935
Birthplace: Haina, Dominican Republic
Bats: Right   **Throws:** Right
Height: 6′   **Weight:** 195
Played for: San Francisco: 1958-63; Milwaukee (NL): 1964-65; Atlanta: 1966-69; Oakland: 1970-71; New York (AL): 1971-73; Montreal: 1973; Milwaukee (AL): 1974

The oldest of the three Alou brothers and the first to play in the majors, Felipe made his debut June 8, 1958 and immediately established himself as one of the Giants' regular outfielders. He marked up the first of his three .300 seasons during San Francisco's 1962 National League Championship season. He also banged 98 runs across the plate that season — his career high. Yankee pitching restricted Felipe to .269 in the Series. In 1963, after the Giants brought Jesus up, the Giants could field an all-Alou outfield. Felipe's finest year came after he joined the Braves.

In 1966, the Braves' first year in Atlanta, Felipe led the National League with 122 runs, 218 hits, and 355 total bases while hitting .327. He lost the batting crown to his younger brother Matty. Felipe led the league in hits again in 1968.

◇ MOISES ALOU

Born: July 3, 1966
Birthplace: Atlanta, Georgia
Bats: Right   **Throws:** Right
Height: 6′3″   **Weight:** 185
Played for: Montreal: 1990

A lanky line drive hitter with excellent defensive tools, Moises performed well enough to get some major league exposure in 1990. Montreal brought him up for 16 games. *Baseball America* (October 10, 1990) evaluated him as one of the top 10 prospects in the AAA American Association. Unfortunately, an injured Moises had to sit out the entire 1991 season.

RECORDS

Felipe Alou (17 Years)

G	AB	R	H	2B	3B	HR	RBI	BB	SO	SB	BA	SA
2,082	7,339	985	2,101	359	49	206	852	423	706	107	.286	.433

Moises Alou

	G	AB	R	H	2B	3B	HR	RBI	BB	SO	SB	BA	SA
1990	16	20	4	4	0	1	0	0	0	3	0	.200	.300
1991 Injured													

Cards

Felipe Alou

1959T—#102	1960T—#287	1961T—#565	1962T—#133	1963T—#270	1964T—#65
1965T—#383	1966T—#96	1967T—#240	1967T—#530	1968T—#55	1969T—#2
1969T—#300	1969TDE—#17	1969TS—#35	1970T—#434	1971T—#495	1972T—#263
1973T—#650	1974T—#485	1974TT—#485	1982D—#650		

Moises Alou

1990F—#650	1990S—#592	1991D—#38	1991S—#813	1991T—#526	1991UD—#665

◆ RUBEN AMARO, SR.

Born: January 14, 1936
Birthplace: Vera Cruz, Mexico
Bats: Right   **Throws:** Right
Height: 5'11"   **Weight:** 175
Played for: St. Louis (NL): 1958; Philadelphia (NL): 1960-65; New York (AL): 1966-68; California: 1969

Ruben came up as a shortstop, but probably prolonged his career by proving his ability to handle every position in the infield (except catching) and even an occasional trip to the outfield. In 1964 with the Phillies, he recorded games at every infield position while hitting .264 and driving in 34 runs.

◇ RUBEN AMARO, JR.

Born: February 12, 1965
Birthplace: Philadelphia, Pennsylvania
Bats: Switch   **Throws:** Right
Height: 5'10"   **Weight:** 170
Played for: California: 1991

Ruben converted from the infield to the outfield in the California minor league system. The Angels brought him up for 10 games in 1991. His hitting will be the key to whether or not he can successfully establish himself at the major league level. He hit .326 at the AAA level (Edmonton).

RECORDS

Ruben Amaro (11 years)

G	AB	R	H	2B	3B	HR	RBI	BB	SO	SB	BA	SA
940	2,155	211	505	75	13	8	156	227	280	11	.234	.280

Ruben Amaro, Jr.

G	AB	R	H	2B	3B	HR	RBI	BB	SO	SB	BA	SA
10	23	0	5	1	0	0	2	3	3	0	.217	.261

Cards

Ruben Amaro, Sr.
1959T—#178   1961T—#103   1962T—#284   1963T—#455   1963F—#50   1964T—#432
1965T—#419   1966T—#186   1967T—#358   1968T—#138   1969T—#598

Ruben Amaro, Jr.
None (as of 1991)

◆ ANGEL ARAGON

Angel Valdez, Sr.
Nicknames: Bing, Pete
Born: August 2, 1893
Birthplace: Havana, Cuba
Died: January 24, 1952
Bats: Right   **Throws:** Right
Height: 5'5"   **Weight:** 150
Played for: New York (AL): 1914, 1916-17

During the 1913 season, Angel played for the Class D Long Branch team in the New York-New Jersey League. The team owner, Cuban-born Dr. Carlos Henriquez, recruited an all-Cuban team. They posted a 65-29 record and finished the season 20½ games ahead of the league's second-place team. In his short major league career, An-gel logged games at shortstop, third, and the out-field.

◇ JACK ARAGON

Angel Valdez, Jr.
Born: November 20, 1915
Birthplace: Havana, Cuba
Died: April 4, 1988
Bats: Right   **Throws:** Right
Height: 5'10"   **Weight:** 176
Played for: New York (NL): 1941; Military Service: 1942-44

Jack's only major league appearance came on August 13, 1941, when he was inserted into the game as a pinch runner.

RECORDS												
Angel Aragon (3 Years)												
G	AB	R	H	2B	3B	HR	RBI	BB	SO	SB	BA	SA
33	79	4	9	1	0	0	5	5	6	2	.114	.127
Jack Aragon												
G	AB	R	H	2B	3B	HR	RBI	BB	SO	SB	BA	SA
1	0	0	*	*	*	*	*	*	*	0	*	*
										* No plate appearances.		

Cards
None

◆ EARL AVERILL

Howard Earl
Born: March 5, 1903
Birthplace: Snohomish, Washington
Died: August 16, 1983
Bats: Left   **Throws:** Right
Height: 5'10"   **Weight:** 172
Played for: Cleveland (AL): 1929-39; Detroit: 1939-40; Boston (NL): 1941
Honors: *Sporting News* All-Star in 1931, 1932, 1934, and 1936. American League All-Star in 1933, 1934, 1936, 1937, and 1938. Most Valuable Player Placement: fourth in 1931; third in 1932; and third in 1936.
Records: American League Leader in at-bats, with 627, in 1931; hits, with 232, in 1936; and triples, with 15, in 1936.
Hall of Fame: Elected in 1975, by the Committee on Veterans (Election to the Hall of Fame can come in two ways: a panel of baseball writers or the Committee on Veterans.)

This Hall of Famer homered in his very first major league at-bat, on April 16, 1929. Earl is one of seven Cleveland Indians to hit 30 or more homers in at least two seasons. (Trosky, Calavito, Thornton, Doby, Rosen, and Carter are the others.) Averill drove in 143 runs and scored 140 runs in 1931. He hit .378 and had 385 total bases in 1936. One of the best centerfielders of his day, you won't find Earl's name often while examining the single season marks. However, Earl's lifetime batting average places him 48th on the all-time list; his .534 career slugging mark is good enough to make him 20th on that lifetime list.

◇ EARL AVERILL

Earl Douglass
Born: September 9, 1931
Birthplace: Cleveland, Ohio
Bats: Right   **Throws:** Right
Height: 5'10"   **Weight:** 200
Played for: Cleveland (AL): 1956, 1958; Chicago (NL): 1959-60; Chicago (AL): 1960; Los Angeles (AL): 1961-62; Philadelphia (NL): 1963

Earl first came up as a backup to Jim Hegan, hitting .287 for the second-place Indians. (Thirty-four games behind the plate; 42 overall.) When he came back up, it was as a third baseman, but again returned to the minors. Chicago brought him back up in 1960, when he mustered a 3 for 14 batting average. Earl's only season as a regular was with the expansion Los Angeles team in 1961, when he recorded a .266 batting average with a .489 slugging percentage.

RECORDS

Howard Earl Averill (13 Years)

G	AB	R	H	2B	3B	HR	RBI	BB	SO	SB	BA	SA
1,669	6,358	1,224	2,020	401	128	238	1,165	775	518	69	.318	.533

Earl Douglass Averill (7 Years)

G	AB	R	H	2B	3B	HR	RBI	BB	SO	SB	BA	SA
449	1,031	137	249	41	0	44	159	162	220	3	.242	.409

Cards

Earl Averill

1933G—#194	1934DS—#35	1934DS—#100	1935G—#1L	1935G—#2E	1935G—#6E
1935G—#7E	1935BU—#24	1935BU—#113	1939PB—#143	1940PB—#46	1960F—#71
1961F—#5					

Earl Averill

1959T—#301	1960T—#39	1960L—#110	1961T—#358	1962T—#452	1962P—#80
1963T—#139					

◆ JIM BAGBY, SR.

James Charles Jacob, Sr.
Nickname: Sarge
Born: October 5, 1889
Birthplace: Barnett, Georgia
Died: July 28, 1954
Bats: Switch   **Throws:** Right
Height: 6'1"   **Weight:** 180
Played for: Cincinnati: 1912; Cleveland (AL): 1916-22; Pittsburgh: 1923
Records: American League Leader in Wins (31), Complete Games (30), Innings (340), and Games (48) in 1920.

In *Total Baseball*, baseball historian and sabremetician Bill Deane chooses Bagby as the Hypothetical 1916 Rookie of the Year. Through the 1920 season, Sarge was one of only nine pitchers in the 20th century to win 30 games or more. In addition to leading the majors in wins during his remarkable 1920 season, the elder Bagby led the American League with 30 complete games and 340 innings. Cleveland went on to defeat the Brooklyn Robins 5 games to 2 in the World Series. Sarge lost the second game, but came back to win the fifth, a game in which he became the first pitcher in history to hit a World Series home run. However, that game is best remembered for Bill Wambsganss' unassisted triple play in the fifth inning.

◇ JIM BAGBY, JR.

James Charles Jacob, Jr.
Born: September 18, 1916
Birthplace: Cleveland, Ohio
Died: September 2, 1988
Bats: Right   **Throws:** Right
Height: 6'2"   **Weight:** 170
Played for: Boston (AL): 1938-40; Cleveland (AL): 1941-45; Boston (AL): 1946; Pittsburgh: 1947

During his rookie season, Junior won 15 and lost 11 while appearing in 43 games (third highest in the American League). Jim was the final pitcher faced by Joe DiMaggio when the Yankee Clipper's 56-game hitting streak ended on July 17, 1941. Bagby's best season came in 1942 when he recorded 17 wins against 9 losses. The following season, he again won 17 and led the American League with 273 innings pitched, while losing 14. His career subsequently went into a decline as he posted records of 4-5, 8-11, 7-6, and 5-4.

RECORDS													
Jim Bagby, Sr. (9 Years)													
W	L	Pct.	Sv.	G	GS	CG	IP	H	BB	SO	ShO	ERA	
127	87	.593	28	316	209	132	1,828	1,884	458	450	15	3.10	
Jim Bagby, Jr. (11 Years)													
W	L	Pct.	Sv.	G	GS	CG	IP	H	BB	SO	ShO	ERA	
97	96	.503	9	303	198	84	1,666	1,815	608	431	13	3.96	

Cards
James Bagby, Sr.
1961F—#92
James Bagby, Jr.
1939PB—#40   1940PB—#32

◆ CLYDE BARNHART

Clyde Lee
Nickname: Pooch
Born: December 29, 1895
Birthplace: Buck Valley, Pennsylvania
Died: January 21, 1980
Bats: Right   **Throws:** Right
Height: 5'10"   **Weight:** 155
Played for: Pittsburgh: 1920-28

Pooch showed a lot of promise when he broke in with the Pirates, hitting .326 and playing third base in 12 games. He became their regular third baseman the following year, but gave way to the legendary Pie Traynor in 1922. He moved into the outfield as a regular for the 1923 campaign; thereafter he remained an outfielder. Pooch played all seven games in Pittsburgh's 1925 Series victory, hitting .250.

◇ VIC BARNHART

Victor Dee
Born: September 1, 1922
Birthplace: Hagerstown, Maryland
Bats: Right   **Throws:** Right
Height: 6'   **Weight:** 188
Played for: Pittsburgh: 1944-46

Vic was a shortstop and third baseman. He logged 60 games at short and 4 at third for the 1945 Pirates.

RECORDS												
Clyde Barnhart (9 Years)												
G	AB	R	H	2B	3B	HR	RBI	BB	SO	SB	BA	SA
814	2,673	404	788	121	62	27	436	265	149	35	.295	.418
Vic Barnhart (3 Years)												
G	AB	R	H	2B	3B	HR	RBI	BB	SO	SB	BA	SA
74	204	21	55	7	0	0	19	10	12	2	.270	.304

Cards
None

◆ CHARLIE BEAMON, SR.

Charles Alfonzo
Born: December 25, 1934
Birthplace: Oakland, California
Bats: Right   **Throws:** Right
Height: 5'11"   **Weight:** 195
Played for: Baltimore: 1956-58

Charlie must have excited the Orioles' management when he went 2-0 after being called up in 1956. Neverthless, he was sent back down, and only appeared in four games during the 1957 season. Beamon evened up his major league record the next year with a 1-3 record, and never appeared in another major league game.

◇ CHARLIE BEAMON, JR.

Charles Alfonzo
Born: December 4, 1953
Birthplace: Oakland, California
Bats: Left   **Throws:** Left
Height: 6'1"   **Weight:** 185
Played for: Seattle: 1978-79; Toronto: 1981

Charlie's short major league career was spent in limited action as a first baseman, a designated hitter, and an outfielder. His last shot at the majors came in 1981 when Toronto summoned him up; he only registered a .200 average (3 for 15). Like his father, his major league career was brief.

RECORDS

Charlie Beamon, Sr. (3 Years)

W	L	Pct.	Sv.	G	GS	CG	IP	H	BB	SO	ShO	ERA
3	3	.500	0	27	5	1	72	64	36	45	1	3.88

Charlie Beamon, Jr. (3 Years)

G	AB	R	H	2B	3B	HR	RBI	BB	SO	SB	BA	SA
45	51	8	10	2	0	0	0	3	8	1	.196	.235

Cards

Charlie Beamon, Sr.
1959T—#192

Charlie Beamon, Jr.
1980T—#672

◆ GUS BELL

David Russell
Born: November 15, 1928
Birthplace: Louisville, Kentucky
Bats: Left   **Throws:** Right
Height: 6'1"   **Weight:** 196
Played for: Pittsburgh: 1950-52; Cincinnati: 1953-61; New York (NL): 1962; Milwaukee (NL): 1962-64
Honors: National League All-Star: 1953, 1954, 1956, 1957, 1960.
Records: Led National League in 1951 in triples, with 12 (tied with Musial).

Gus was first named to the All-Star team in 1953 as an outfielder from the eighth-place Reds, who finished 37 games out of first. That year he stroked an even .300 in 151 games. Gus followed that up with a .299 season (153 games, 619 at-bats). A .308 season followed, and another two All-Star seasons after that. He garnered one more All-Star appearance in 1960, subsequently ending his career with Milwaukee. Gus was a journeyman, but one in the very best sense of the word; if your team was one trade away from a pennant, this might be the man you wanted.

◇ BUDDY BELL

David Gus
Born: August 27, 1951
Birthplace: Pittsburgh, Pennsylvania
Bats: Right   **Throws:** Right
Height: 6'2"   **Weight:** 190
Played for: Cleveland (AL): 1972-78; Texas: 1979-85; Cincinnati: 1985-88; Houston: 1988; Texas: 1989
Honors: American League All-Star: 1973, 1980, 1984; American League Gold Glove: 1979-84.

Buddy's career stats are such that he has to be considered a serious candidate for the Hall of Fame. He ranks 50th on the lifetime games played roster and 44th in at-bats. Baseball historian Peter Palmer developed a measure he calls the "Total Player Rating." According to this, Bell ranks 108th lifetime, ahead of players such as George Sisler, Duke Snider, Ernie Banks, Graig Nettles, and Brooks Robinson. A decent but not great hitter, Buddy's career really shines in the fielding statistics. He ranks 5th in games played at third, 4th in assists (4,913), and 2nd in assists per game (2.27 to Mike Schmidt's 2.30). In the category he designated "Fielding Wins," Peter Palmer placed Bell 11th on the all-time list.

RECORDS

Gus Bell (15 Years)

G	AB	R	H	2B	3B	HR	RBI	BB	SO	SB	BA	SA
1,741	6,478	865	1,823	311	66	206	942	470	636	30	.281	.445

Buddy Bell (18 Years)

G	AB	R	H	2B	3B	HR	RBI	BB	SO	SB	BA	SA
2,405	8,995	1,120	2,514	425	56	201	1,106	836	776	55	.279	.406

Cards

Gus Bell

1951TRB—#17	1951B—#40	1952T—#170	1953T—#118	1953BBW—#1	1954B—#124
1954RH—#3	1954RM—#NL19	1955RM—#NL23	1955B—#243	1956T—#162	1957T—#180
1958T—#75	1959T—#365	1960T—#235	1960T—#352SP	1961T—#25SP	1961T—#215
1961P—#186	1962T—#408	1962P—#120	1963T—#547	1964T—#534	1976T—#66SP
1985T—#131SP					

Buddy Bell

1973T—#31	1974T—#257	1974K—#10	1975T—#38	1976T—#66SP	1976T—#358
1976SS—#517	1977T—#590	1978T—#280	1979T—#690	1980T—#190	1981D—#145
1981F—#625	1981T—#475	1982D—#23	1982D—#368	1982F—#313	1982T—#50
1983D—#215	1983F—#562	1983T—#330	1983F—#632SP	1983T—#412SP	1984D—#56
1984F—#413	1984T—#665	1984T—#37SP	1985D—#56	1985F—#556	1985T—#745
1985T—#131SP	1986D—#447	1986F—#172	1986SPF—#151	1986T—#285	1987D—#556
1987F—#193	1987SPF—#141	1987T—#545	1988D—#206	1988F—#227	1988S—#99
1988SPF—#147	1988T—#130	1988TT—#13	1989B—#229	1989F—#352	1989S—#610
1989T—#461	1989UD—#112				

◆ YOGI BERRA

Lawrence Peter
Born: May 12, 1925
Birthplace: St. Louis, Missouri
Bats: Left   **Throws:** Right
Height: 5'8"   **Weight:** 195
Played for: New York (AL): 1946-63
Coaching Experience: New York (AL): 1964 (Manager); New York (NL): 1965-71; 1972-75 (Manager); New York (AL): 1976-83; 1984-85 (Manager); Houston: 1986-88.
Honors: Most Valuable Player in 1951, 1954, 1955; voted third in 1950; fourth in 1952; second in 1953 and 1956. *Sporting News All-Star* in 1950, 1952, 1954, 1956, 1957. American League All-Star from 1949 through 1962.
Hall Of Fame: Elected in 1972, by the Baseball Writers of America.

A three-time Most Valuable Player, there is little doubt that Yogi must be considered one of the game's greatest catchers. His home run total places him 36th on the all-time list and 10th during his era (1942-60). However, Yogi was also one of baseball's toughest hitters to strike out. His at-bats per strikeout ratio (18.2) ranks him 78th on that lifetime list. Yogi retired from baseball at the end of the 1989 season.

◇ DALE BERRA

Dale Anthony
Born: December 13, 1956
Birthplace: Ridgewood, New Jersey
Bats: Right   **Throws:** Right
Height: 6'   **Weight:** 190
Played for: Pittsburgh: 1977-84; New York (AL): 1985-86; Houston: 1987

Dale played shortstop for his father during the 1985 season. Although not as gifted a ballplayer as his father, the youngest of Yogi's four sons proved he was good enough to stick around for 11 seasons. Yogi's influence indisputably shone through when Dale, asked to compare himself with his father, replied, "Our similarities are different."

Records

Yogi Berra (19 Years)

G	AB	R	H	2B	3B	HR	RBI	BB	SO	SB	BA	SA
2,120	7,555	1,175	2,150	321	49	358	1,430	704	414	30	.285	.482

Dale Berra (11 Years)

G	AB	R	H	2B	3B	HR	RBI	BB	SO	SB	BA	SA
853	2,553	236	603	109	9	49	278	210	422	32	.236	.344

Cards

Yogi Berra

1948B—#6	1949B—#60	1950B—#46	1951TRB—#1	1951B—#2	1951TCMAS
1951BR—#B4	1952BR—#3	1952T—#191	1952B—#1	1952RM—#AL3	1953RM—#AL3
1953T—#104	1953BC—#44SP	1953BC—#121	1954RM—#AL20	1954T—#50	1954B—#161
1955RM—#AL16	1955T—#198	1955B—#168	1956T—#110	1957T—#2	1957T—#407SP
1958T—#370	1959T—#180	1960T—#480	1961T—#425	1961T—#75SP	1961P—#1
1962T—#360	1962P—#7	1963T—#340	1963P—#17	1964T—#21	1965T—#470
1973T—#257M	1974T—#179M	1975T—#189SP	1975T—#192SP	1975T—#193SP	1975T—#421M
1981D—#351	1982D—#387	1984TT—#13	1985T—#132SP	1985T—#155SP	

Dale Berra

1979T—#723R	1980T—#292	1981D—#253	1981F—#369	1981T—#147	1982D—#250
1982F—#476	1982T—#588	1983D—#185	1983F—#303	1983T—#433	1984D—#430
1984F—#245	1984T—#18	1985D—#444	1985F—#461	1985T—#305	1985T—#132SP
1985FU—#4	1985TT—#6	1986D—#295	1986F—#100	1986T—#692	

◆ CHARLIE BERRY

Charles Joseph
Born: September 16, 1860
Birthplace: Elizabeth, New Jersey
Died: January 22, 1940
Bats: Right   **Throws:** Right
Height: 5'11"   **Weight:** 175
Played for: Altoona, Kansas City, and Chicago-Pittsburgh (Union Association): 1884

In the fall of 1883, the Union Association of Base Ball Clubs organized itself in Pittsburgh. It announced its opposition to the reserve clause, but attracted few legitimate big-leaguers. The eight-team league commenced play in 1884 with a 128-game schedule. Charlie was one of the aspiring ballplayers who got a chance when the new league was formed. Charlie was a second and third baseman who bounced around the Union Association during its only season. He made his debut for Altoona on April 30, 1884, staying with them for seven games before going to Kansas City. He played 29 games there before ending his major league career as part of the combined Chicago-Pittsburgh team.

◇ CHARLIE BERRY

Charles Francis
Born: October 18, 1902
Birthplace: Phillisburg, New Jersey
Died: September 6, 1972
Bats: Right   **Throws:** Right
Height: 6'   **Weight:** 185
Played for: Philadelphia (AL): 1925; Boston (AL): 1928-32; Chicago (AL): 1932-33; Philadelphia (AL): 1934-36, 1938

Charlie earned All-American honors as an end on the Lafayette College football team in 1924. The Athletics signed him to a contract, and he caught four games for the Mack men in 1925. This season and the next, he divided his time between baseball and the National Football League, playing for the Pottsville Maroons. Charlie gave up football after the 1926 season. He became the Bosox regular catcher in 1929, and hit .289 in 85 games in 1930. In 1932, after being traded to the White Sox, he hit .305 and caught 70 games. Charlie coached for the Athletics between 1936 and 1940. In 1942, he became an American League umpire, a position he filled until 1962. He also served as a referee in the NFL.

Records

Charlie Berry

G	AB	R	H	2B	3B	HR	RBI	BB	SO	SB	BA	SA
43	170	21	38	8	1	1	*	1	*	*	.224	.300

*Not available

Charlie Berry

G	AB	R	H	2B	3B	HR	RBI	BB	SO	SB	BA	SA
709	2,018	196	539	88	29	23	256	160	196	13	.267	.374

Cards

Charlie Berry
None

Charlie Berry
1933G—#184   1940PB—#190   1955B—#281 (Umpire)

◆ JOE BERRY, SR.

Joseph Howard
Nickname: Hodge
Born: September 10, 1872
Birthplace: Wheeling, West Virginia
Died: March 13, 1961
Bats: Switch   **Throws:** Right
Height: 5'9"   **Weight:** 172
Played for: Philadelphia (NL): 1902

Hodge caught his only major league game on September 4, 1902.

◇ JOE BERRY, JR.

Joseph Howard
Nickname: Nig
Born: December 31, 1894
Birthplace: Philadelphia, Pennsylvania

Died: April 29, 1976
Bats: Switch   **Throws:** Right
Height: 5'11"   **Weight:** 165
Played for: New York (NL): 1921-22

Nig played seven games at second and was used as pinch runner by John McGraw's 1921 Giants. The Giants beat the Yankees 5 games to 3 in that season's World Series, but Joe did not appear, perhaps because he played for the Rochester Jeffersons in the NFL that season. The Jeffersons didn't complete their full schedule, but went 2-3-0 to place 10th in a 21-team league. Joe, Jr. was a halfback and played his college ball at the University of Illinois. Nig played both sports again in 1922. He appeared in six games as a pinch runner; the Jeffersons posted a record of 0-4-1 as the Canton Bulldogs won the NFL with a 10-0-2 record.

RECORDS												

Joe Berry, Sr.

G	AB	R	H	2B	3B	HR	RBI	BB	SO	SB	BA	SA
1	4	0	1	0	0	0	1	1	*	1	.250	.250

*Not available

Joe Berry, Jr.

G	AB	R	H	2B	3B	HR	RBI	BB	SO	SB	BA	SA
15	6	0	2	0	1	0	2	1	1	0	.333	.667

Cards
None

◆ BOBBY BONDS

Bobby Lee
Born: March 15, 1946
Birthplace: Riverside, California
Bats: Right   **Throws:** Right
Height: 6'1"   **Weight:** 195
Played for: San Francisco: 1968-74; New York (AL): 1975; California: 1976-77; Chicago (AL): 1978; Texas: 1978; Cleveland (AL): 1979; St. Louis (NL): 1980; Chicago (NL): 1981
Coaching Experience: Cleveland (AL): 1984-87.
Honors: National League All-Star in 1971 and 1973. American League All-Star in 1975.
Records: 1969 NL Leader in strikeouts, with 187. 1970 NL Leader in strikeouts, with 189. 1973 NL Leader in strikeouts, with 148. National League Gold Glove Award in 1971, 1973, and 1974.

Bobby broke the mold for leadoff hitters, or, perhaps, simply created a new model. Like most leadoff hitters, Bonds scored lots of runs and had good speed. He ranks within the top 100 in lifetime runs, and his stolen base average qualifies for 47th lifetime. However, unlike the typical leadoff hitter, Bobby struck out a lot, sixth all-time, but he was also capable of quickly disrupting a game with a leadoff home run. He established records for most home runs as a leadoff hitter in both the season (11 of his 39 clouts during the 1973 campaign) and career categories (35 career leadoff homers; 30 in the National League and 5 in the American League).

◇ BARRY BONDS

Barry Lamar
Born: July 24, 1964
Birthplace: Riverside, California
Bats: Left   **Throws:** Left
Height: 6'1"   **Weight:** 185
Played for: Pittsburgh: 1986-91
Honors: National League Most Valuable Player in 1990; National League All-Star in 1991.

Prior to the 1990 season, the knock on Barry was that he didn't play up to his potential. He lost a case in arbitration during the off-season, and that, combined with the motivation provided by his father and Pirates' conditioning coach Warren Sipe, resulted in an awesome season. Barry began playing up to his potential. He joined his father in the esteemed "30-30" club, making them the first father-son combination both to hit more than 30 homers and steal more than 30 bases in a season. He became the Pirates' first 30-30 player. He was the first player ever to hit .300 with 30 homers, have 100 or more RBIs, and have 50 stolen bases. Regardless, he believed that his habitual feuding with the press would probably prevent his receiving any postseason accolades. He was wrong. Bobby was just one vote shy of being a unanimous selection for the National League Most Valuable Player; an honor that eluded his father throughout his career.

RECORDS

Bobby Bonds (14 Years)

G	AB	R	H	2B	3B	HR	RBI	BB	SO	SB	BA	SA
1,849	7,043	1,258	1,886	302	66	332	1,024	914	1,757	461	.268	.471

Barry Bonds

G	AB	R	H	2B	3B	HR	RBI	BB	SO	SB	BA	SA
1986-87												
263	964	171	236	60	12	41	107	119	190	68	.245	.460
1988												
144	538	97	152	30	5	24	58	72	82	17	.283	.491
1989												
159	580	96	144	34	6	19	58	93	93	32	.248	.426
1990												
151	519	104	156	32	3	33	114	93	83	52	.301	.565
1991												
153	510	95	149	28	5	25	116	107	73	43	.292	.468

Cards					
Bobby Bonds					
1969T—#630	1970T—#425	1971T—#295	1972T—#711	1972T—#712SP	1973T—#145
1973K—#B	1974T—#30	1974K—#39	1975T—#55	1976T—#2SP	1976T—#380
1976TT—#380	1976SS—#439	1977T—#570	1978T—#150	1979T—#285	1980T—#410
1981D—#71	1981F—#548	1981T—#635	1982F—#588	1982T—#580	
Barry Bonds					
1986DU—#11	1986FU—#14	1986TT—#11	1987D—#361	1987F—#604	1987T—#320
1988D—#326	1988F—#322	1988S—#265	1988SPF—#119	1988T—#450	1989B—#426
1989D—#92	1989F—#202	1989S—#127	1989SPF—#146	1989T—#620	1989UD—#440
1990D—#126	1990F—#461	1990S—#4	1990T—#220	1990UD—#227	1991DDK—#14
1991D—#495	1991F—#33	1991S—#330	1991T—#570	1991UD—#152	

NICKNAMES

JoJo White earned his nickname from the way he pronounced his native state (Georgia). Baseball players have always developed nicknames, and baseball's fathers and sons are no exception. While several monikers fall into the predictable category (there are three "Lefty's," for example), there are also some great baseball *nom de diamonds*. How on earth do you suppose Ralph Austin became "The Human Whipcord"? Clyde Barnhart had to go through life as "Pooch." Why do you suppose Joe Berry, Jr. was called "Nig," or Merrill May, "Pinkie"? Was Eddie Collins truly "Cocky," and who do you suppose first dubbed Connie Mack "The Tall Tactician"? Do you suppose he liked it better than "Slats" McGillicuddy, the name he was called as a player? Were "Wee Willie" Mills or Jerry Hairston's "Popeye" descriptive appellations, like Ron "The Round Man" Northey? How did Eugene Moore become "Blue Goose"; Guy Morton, "The Alabama Blossom"; or George Cyril Methodius Susce,

"The Good Kid"?

"Orator Jim" O'Rourke gained his nickname through his speech-making. George Frederick Graham became "Peaches" and Don Mueller earned "Mandrake the Magician" for their prowess in the field. Some say "Smokey Joe" Wood originated with the speed of his fastball, others say it came from his dark good looks. Similarly, some say "Gorgeous George" Sisler evolved from his looks, while others maintain it was his fielding.

"Dixie" Walker also patrolled Brooklyn's outfield as "The People's Cherce," and his brother Harry became "The Hat" because he fidgeted with hats so frequently. As far as nicknames for both the father and the son are concerned, two pairs stand out. First, there is "Tiny" and "Bobo" Osborne. However, the all-time father and son great nicknames must belong, indisputably, to "Dizzy" and "Rainbow" Trout.

◆ RAY BOONE

Raymond Otis
Born: July 27, 1923
Birthplace: San Diego, California
Bats: Right   **Throws:** Right
Height: 6'1"   **Weight:** 180
Played for: Cleveland (AL): 1948-53; Detroit: 1953-58; Chicago (AL): 1958-59; Kansas City: 1959
Records: 1955 AL Leader in RBIs, with 116 (tied with Jackie Jensen).

In 1953, Ray hit four grand slams. While Ray came up as a shortstop, he prolonged his career with a move to third and finished the 1960 season at first. Ray scouted his grandson for the Red Sox. Bret (Bob's son) won All-American recognition as a second baseman at USC. He signed with the Seattle organization, putting the Boones in serious contention to become the first three generation major league family.

◇ BOB BOONE

Raymond Robert
Born: November 19, 1947
Birthplace: San Diego, California
Bats: Right   **Throws:** Right
Height: 6'2"   **Weight:** 200
Played for: Philadelphia (NL): 1972-81; California: 1982-88; Kansas City: 1989-90
Honors: National League All-Star in 1976, 1978, and 1979. National League Gold Glove Award in 1978 and 1979. American League Gold Glove Award in 1982, 1986, 1987, and 1989.

Bob has logged more games behind the plate (2,264, and the number's still climbing) than any other catcher in the history of the game. Bob's bid to sustain his career long enough to become the second father-son combination to play together came to an end when he failed to catch on with the Seattle Mariners. He was released just prior to the opening of the 1991 season.

RECORDS

Ray Boone (12 Years)

G	AB	R	H	2B	3B	HR	RBI	BB	SO	SB	BA	SA
1,373	4,589	645	1,260	162	46	151	737	608	463	21	.275	.429

Bob Boone

G	AB	R	H	2B	3B	HR	RBI	BB	SO	SB	BA	SA
1972-87												
1,971	6,371	597	1,595	270	24	99	735	568	533	32	.250	.347
1988												
122	352	38	104	17	0	5	39	29	26	2	.295	.386
1989												
131	405	33	111	12	2	1	43	49	37	3	.274	.323
1990												
40	117	11	28	3	0	0	9	17	12	1	.239	.265

Cards

Ray Boone

1951TRB—#23	1952T—#55	1952B—#214	1953T—#25	1953BC—#79	1954T—#77
1955T—#65	1955RM—#AL1	1955TDH—#113	1956T—#6	1957T—#102	1958T—#185
1959T—#252	1960T—#281	1976T—#67SP	1985T—#133SP		

Bob Boone

1973T—#613R	1974T—#131	1975T—#351	1976T—#67SP	1976T—#318	1976SS—#471
1977T—#545	1978T—#161	1979T—#90	1980T—#470	1981D—#262	1981F—#4
1981T—#290	1982D—#471	1982F—#240	1982T—#615	1982TT—#9	1983D—#192
1983F—#79	1983T—#765	1984D—#158	1984F—#509	1984T—#520	1984F—#637
1985D—#230	1985F—#295	1985T—#348	1985T—#133SP	1986D—#230	1986F—#149
1986T—#62	1987D—#233	1987F—#73	1987T—#166	1988D—#305	1988F—#485
1988S—#63	1988SPF—#212	1988T—#498	1989B—#119	1989D—#170	1989F—#469
1989S—#233	1989SPF—#40	1989T—#243	1989UD—#119	1990D—#326	1990F—#102
1990S—#60	1990T—#671	1990UD—#271	1991D—#356	1991F—#551	1991UD—#502

◆ FRED BRICKELL

George Frederick
Born: November 9, 1906
Birthplace: Saffordville, Kansas
Died: April 8, 1961
Bats: Left   **Throws:** Right
Height: 5'7"   **Weight:** 160
Played for: Pittsburgh: 1926-30; Philadelphia (NL): 1930-33

When he got a chance during the 1926 season, 19-year-old Fred appeared in the outfield for 14 games and hit an impressive 19 for 55 with a .436 slugging mark. However, the 1927 Pirate outfield boasted the two Waners and Pooch Barnhart (another baseball father), who hit .319 and platooned with Kiki Cuyler, who hit .309. So Fred was limited to three games in the outfield, but he was a valued pinch hitter who hit .286 in 21 at-bats; he made two pinch-hitting appearances in that year's series, going 0 for 2, but scoring a run. The following season, he appeared in enough games (81—50 of them in the outfield) to be considered a regular and hit .302 in 202 at-bats. But

Lloyd Waner returned to full-time service the next year, and Fred was again relegated to a backup role. He was traded to the Phillies during the 1930 season, became a regular again in 1931, but slowly faded from baseball after that.

◇ FRITZIE BRICKELL

Fritz Darrell
Born: March 19, 1935
Birthplace: Wichita, Kansas
Died: October 15, 1965
Bats: Right   **Throws:** Right
Height: 5'7"   **Weight:** 157
Played for: New York (AL): 1958-59; Los Angeles (AL): 1961

Fritzie got a "cup of coffee" during 1958, then appeared in 15 games at shortstop and 3 at second the following year. (A player brought up at the end of a season for only a few games is said to have had a "cup of coffee.") His last shot came in 17 games at shortstop for the Los Angeles Angels, an American League expansion team.

RECORDS												
Fred Brickell (8 Years)												
G	AB	R	H	2B	3B	HR	RBI	BB	SO	SB	BA	SA
501	1,448	221	407	54	23	6	131	106	121	19	.281	.363
Fritzie Brickell (3 Years)												
G	AB	R	H	2B	3B	HR	RBI	BB	SO	SB	BA	SA
41	88	7	16	1	0	1	7	7	19	0	.182	.227

Cards				
Fred Brickell				
1933G—#38	1935G—#1E	1935G—#3C	1935G—#5C	1935G—#6C
Fritzie Brickell				
1961T—#333				

◆ EARLE BRUCKER, SR.

Earle Francis
Born: May 6, 1901
Birthplace: Albany, New York
Died: May 8, 1981
Bats: Right   **Throws:** Right
Height: 5'11"   **Weight:** 195
Played for: Philadelphia (AL): 1937-40, 1943
Coaching Experience: Philadelphia (AL): 1941-49; St. Louis (AL): 1950-51; Cincinnati: 1952 (Manager)

Earle was a catcher who didn't appear in a major league game until he cracked the A's lineup as a 36-year-old rookie. He broke a bone in his hand, limiting him to 92 games, and spent the remainder of his playing career as a backup catcher. He managed the Reds for five games in 1952, turning in a 3-2 record.

◇ EARLE BRUCKER, JR.

Earle Francis
Born: August 29, 1925
Birthplace: Los Angeles, California
Bats: Left   **Throws:** Right
Height: 6'2"   **Weight:** 210
Played for: Philadelphia (AL): 1948

Earle made his major league debut October 2, 1948. He was also a catcher.

RECORDS												
Earle Brucker (4 Years)												
G	AB	R	H	2B	3B	HR	RBI	BB	SO	SB	BA	SA
241	707	87	205	53	8	12	105	97	65	2	.290	.438
Earle Brucker												
G	AB	R	H	2B	3B	HR	RBI	BB	SO	SB	BA	SA
2	6	0	1	1	0	0	0	1	1	0	.167	.333

Cards
None

◆ **MIKE BRUMLEY**

Tony Mike
Born: July 10, 1938
Birthplace: Granite, Oklahoma
Bats: Left   **Throws:** Right
Height: 5'10"   **Weight:** 195
Played for: Washington (AL): 1964-66

Mike caught 132 games his rookie season and hit .244 for the ninth-place Senators. In 1965, he shared catching duties with baseball son Doug Camilli.

◇ **MIKE BRUMLEY**

Anthony Michael
Born: April 9, 1963
Birthplace: Oklahoma City, Oklahoma
Bats: Switch   **Throws:** Right
Height: 5'10"   **Weight:** 165
Played for: Chicago (NL): 1987; Detroit: 1989; Seattle: 1990; Boston (AL): 1991

Mike played college ball at the University of Texas. His light hitting keeps him out of a regular lineup, but he contributes as a slick-fielding utility player.

RECORDS

Mike Brumley (3 Years)

G	AB	R	H	2B	3B	HR	RBI	BB	SO	SB	BA	SA
224	660	52	151	24	2	5	50	60	89	2	.229	.294

Mike Brumley

	G	AB	R	H	2B	3B	HR	RBI	BB	SO	SB	BA	SA
1987	39	104	8	21	2	2	1	9	10	30	7	.202	.288
1989	92	212	33	42	5	2	1	11	14	45	8	.198	.255
1990	62	147	19	33	5	4	0	7	10	22	0	.224	.313
1991	63	118	16	25	5	0	0	5	10	22	2	.212	.254

Cards

Mike Brumley
1964T—#167R   1965T—#523   1966T—#29

Mike Brumley
1988D—#609   1989D—#302   1989F—#302   1990D—#533   1990T—#471   1990UD—#312
1991F—#445   1991S—#624

◆ DOLPH CAMILLI

Adolph Louis
Born: April 23, 1907
Birthplace: San Francisco, California
Bats: Left   **Throws:** Left
Height: 5'10"   **Weight:** 185
Played for: Chicago (NL): 1933-34; Philadelphia (NL): 1934-37; Brooklyn (NL): 1938-43; Military Service in 1944; Boston (AL): 1945
Honors: National League All-Star in 1939; National League Most Valuable Player in 1941.
Records: 1941 NL leader in home runs, with 34; strikeouts, with 94; RBIs, with 120. 1934 NL leader in strikeouts, with 94. 1935 NL leader in strikeouts, with 113. 1938 NL leader in walks, with 119. 1939 NL leader in walks, with 110.

In his major league debut on September 9, 1933, Dolph won a game for the Cubs with a home run, after coming up from Sacramento in the Pacific Coast League. He subsequently became one of the top power hitters and premier RBI men of his day. From 1935-42 he never hit fewer than 23 home runs. Dolph drove in at least 100 runs five times during his career; he led the Phillies in RBIs in 1936 and 1937, then paced the Dodgers for five consecutive seasons. Dolph ran away with Most Valuable Player honors in 1941, outpolling teammates Pete Reiser and Whit Wyatt. This marked the first time in major league history that three teammates ranked first, second, and third in the Most Valuable Player voting. After his playing days, Dolph served as a scout for the Yankees. He signed two of his sons to Yankee minor league contracts. Although neither of them played in the majors, his son Doug spent nine seasons with the Dodgers and Senators.

◇ DOUG CAMILLI

Douglas Joseph
Born: September 22, 1936
Birthplace: Philadelphia, Pennsylvania
Bats: Right   **Throws:** Right
Height: 5'11"   **Weight:** 195
Played for: Los Angeles (NL): 1960-64; Washington (AL): 1965-67, 1969
Coaching Experience: Washington (AL): 1968-69; Boston (AL): 1970-73.

Doug spent his career as a backup catcher. He recorded his career high in games and at-bats during the 1965 season when he appeared in 75 games with 193 at-bats for Washington.

RECORDS

Dolph Camilli (12 Years)

G	AB	R	H	2B	3B	HR	RBI	BB	SO	SB	BA	SA
1,490	5,353	936	1,482	261	86	239	950	947	961	60	.277	.492

Doug Camilli (9 Years)

G	AB	R	H	2B	3B	HR	RBI	BB	SO	SB	BA	SA
313	767	56	153	22	4	18	80	56	146	0	.199	.309

Cards

Dolph Camilli

1934G—#594R	1935BU—#150	1936G—#5	1939PB—#86	1940PB—#68	1941PB—#51
1941DP—#20	1961F—#97				

Doug Camilli

1962T—#594R	1963T—#196	1964T—#249	1965T—#77	1966T—#593	1967T—#551
1973T—#131C					

◆ AL CAMPANIS

Alexander Sebastian
Born: November 2, 1916
Birthplace: Kos, Greece
Bats: Switch   **Throws:** Right
Height: 6'   **Weight:** 185
Played for: Brooklyn (NL): 1943; Military Service in 1944-45

During his short playing career, Al was a second baseman. Later, as Dodger general manager, Al got himself into trouble with remarks he made about black ballplayers. During an ABC-TV "Nightline" segment on April 6, 1987, Al responded to host Ted Koppel's query about prejudice in baseball's front offices by saying, "No, I don't believe it's prejudice. I truly believe that they may not have some of the necessities to be, let's say, a field manager, or perhaps a general manager." Campanis' remarks created a furor and cost him his job. Campanis, who had been a friend of Jackie Robinson in Montreal in 1946, seemed genuinely puzzled by the fuss his remarks created. To his credit, he made an effort to understand and within a few months was lecturing at a UC Berkeley class on Sports Sociology given by African-American activist Dr. Harry Edwards. Al established a reputation as one of the game's best judges of talent as a scout; he signed both Sandy Koufax and Roberto Clemente.

◇ JIM CAMPANIS

James Alexander
Born: February 9, 1944
Birthplace: New York, New York
Bats: Right   **Throws:** Right
Height: 6'   **Weight:** 195
Played for: Los Angeles (NL): 1966-68; Kansas City: 1969-70; Pittsburgh: 1973

Jim was signed to a Dodger contract by his father, Los Angeles' director of scouting in 1962. Jim's son (Jimmy) played at USC with Bret Boone. Seattle signed both Boone and Jimmy Campanis to minor league contracts.

RECORDS

Al Campanis

G	AB	R	H	2B	3B	HR	RBI	BB	SO	SB	BA	SA
7	20	3	2	0	0	0	0	4	5	0	.100	.100

Jim Campanis (6 Years)

G	AB	R	H	2B	3B	HR	RBI	BB	SO	SB	BA	SA
113	217	13	32	6	0	4	9	19	49	0	.147	.230

Cards

Al Campanis
None

Jim Campanis

1967T—#12R	1968T—#281	1969T—#396	1970T—#671	1974T—#513	1988T—#23 (USOC)

◆ CAM CARREON

Camilo
Born: August 6, 1937
Birthplace: Colton, California
Died: September 2, 1987
Bats: Right   **Throws:** Right
Height: 6'1"   **Weight:** 198
Played for: Chicago (AL): 1959-64; Cleveland (AL): 1965; Baltimore: 1966

Cam made his debut on September 27 for the 1959 "Go-Go Sox." When regular catcher Sherm Lollar went on the disabled list in 1962, Cam stepped in and caught 93 games.

◇ MARK CARREON

Mark Steven
Born: July 19, 1963
Birthplace: Chicago, Illinois
Bats: Right   **Throws:** Left
Height: 6'   **Weight:** 170
Played for: New York (NL): 1987-91

Mark tore a ligament in his knee during the 1990 season. Personal problems compounded his rehabilitation; he checked into an alcohol rehabilitation center for a month towards the end of September.

RECORDS

Cam Carreon (8 Years)

G	AB	R	H	2B	3B	HR	RBI	BB	SO	SB	BA	SA
354	986	113	260	43	4	11	114	97	117	3	.264	.349

Mark Carreon

	G	AB	R	H	2B	3B	HR	RBI	BB	SO	SB	BA	SA
1987	9	12	0	3	0	0	0	1	1	1	0	.250	.250
1988	7	9	5	5	2	0	1	1	2	1	0	.381	.619
1989	68	133	20	41	6	0	6	16	12	17	2	.308	.489
1990	82	188	30	47	12	0	10	26	15	29	1	.250	.473
1991	106	254	18	66	6	0	4	21	12	26	2	.260	.331

Cards

Camilo Carreon

1960T—#121	1960L—#88	1961T—#509	1962T—#178	1963T—#308	1964T—#421
1965T—#578	1966T—#513				

Mark Carreon

1988T—#129	1989B—#389	1989F—#29	1990D—#454	1990F—#198	1990S—#363
1990T—#434	1990UD—#135	1991D—#731	1991F—#142	1991S—#165	1991T—#764

◆ JOE COLEMAN

Joseph Patrick
Born: July 3, 1922
Bats: Right   **Throws:** Right
Height: 6'2"   **Weight:** 200
Played for: Philadelphia (AL): 1942; Military Service in 1943-45; Philadelphia (AL): 1946-51, 1953; Baltimore: 1954-55; Detroit: 1955
Honors: American League All-Star in 1948

As a 20-year-old rookie, Joe didn't start but he pitched six innings and took the loss in his September 19, 1942 debut. He went 0-2 his first year back after military service and became part of the Athletics starting rotation in 1947, going 6-12 in 21 starts. Joe's best season proved to be 1948, when he registered a 14-13 record with three shutouts and pitched three perfect innings in the All-Star game. A sore arm sidelined him most of 1950 and 1951.

◇ JOE COLEMAN

Joseph Howard
Born: February 3, 1947
Bats: Right   **Throws:** Right
Height: 6'3"   **Weight:** 195
Played for: Washington (AL): 1965-70; Detroit: 1971-76; Chicago (NL): 1976; Oakland: 1977-78; Toronto: 1978; San Francisco: 1979; Pittsburgh: 1979
Coaching Experience: California: 1988.

As an 18-year-old rookie, Joe pitched and won two complete games for the 1965 Senators, a team that finished in eighth place, 32 games out of first place. In 1971, he won 20 games and his 236 strikeouts placed him third in the American League. In 1972, Joe (along with staff ace Mickey Lolich) helped pitch Detroit into the American League play-offs. During the third game, he set an ALCS record with 14 strikeouts in a 3-0 shutout of the A's. In 1973, he won 23 games.

RECORDS

Joe P. Coleman (10 Years)

W	L	Pct.	Sv.	G	GS	CG	IP	H	BB	SO	ShO	ERA
52	76	.406	6	223	140	60	1,133	1,172	566	444	11	4.38

Joe H. Coleman (15 Years)

W	L	Pct.	Sv.	G	GS	CG	IP	H	BB	SO	ShO	ERA
142	135	.513	7	484	340	94	2,571	2,416	1,003	1,728	18	3.69

Cards

Joe P. Coleman
1950B—#141	1951B—#120	1953T—#279	1954T—#156	1955T—#162	1955B—#3
1955RM—#AL17	1976T—#68SP				

Joe H. Coleman
1966T—#333R	1967T—#167R	1968T—#573	1969T—#246	1970T—#127	1971T—#403
1972T—#96SP	1972T—#640	1972K—#18	1973T—#120	1973K—#48	1974T—#240
1974K—#3	1975T—#42	1976T—#68SP	1976T—#456	1976SS—#358	1977T—#219
1978T—#554	1979T—#329				

◆ EDDIE COLLINS, SR.

Edward Trowbridge
Nickname: Cocky
Born: May 2, 1887
Birthplace: Millerton, New York
Died: March 25, 1951
Bats: Left   **Throws:** Right
Height: 5'9"   **Weight:** 175
Played for: Philadelphia (AL): 1906-14; Chicago (AL): 1915-26; Philadelphia (AL): 1927-30 (Played as Eddie Sullivan in 1906.)
Coaching Experience: Chicago (AL): 1925-26 (Manager); Philadelphia (AL): 1932-33.
Hall of Fame: Elected in 1939 by Baseball Writers of America.
Honors: Chalmers Award (Most Valuable Player) in 1914; Most Valuable Player Placement: third in 1911; third in 1913; fifth in 1922; second in 1923; second in 1924. Projected as Most Valuable Player by Bill Deane for 1915.

One of the game's all-time greats, Collins ranks eighth in career hits and 11th in triples. He posted an on-base percentage over .400 13 times and batted over .300 during 17 full seasons. He ranks fifth on the all-time stolen base list. During a playing career that spanned 25 years, this Columbia University product established 48 American League, major league, and World Series records. After more than half a century, 16 of those records still stand, including most games played at second (2,650), most putouts for a second baseman (6,526), and most total chances (14,591). Cocky was one of the game's most difficult men to strike out. In 1915, for example, when he recorded 521 at-bats, he led the league with 119 walks and struck out only 27 times. In 1920, with 601 at-bats, he fanned a mere 19 times. A member of the 1919 "Black Sox," Eddie emerged from baseball's greatest scandal with a clean reputation.

◇ EDDIE COLLINS, JR.

Edward Trowbridge
Born: November 23, 1916
Birthplace: Lansdowne, Pennsylvania
Bats: Left   **Throws:** Right
Height: 5'10"   **Weight:** 175
Played for: Philadelphia (AL): 1939, 1941-42; Military Service in 1943-45

Eddie made his major league debut on July 4, 1939. During that season he appeared in 32 games but registered only 21 at-bats. He played six games in the outfield and one at second. Including 50 games in the outfield, he appeared in 80 games in 1941 before his career was interrupted by military service.

RECORDS												
Eddie Collins (25 Years)												
G	AB	R	H	2B	3B	HR	RBI	BB	SO	SB	BA	SA
2,826	9,949	1,818	3,311	437	186	47	1,299	1,503	286	743	.333	.428
Eddie Collins (3 Years)												
G	AB	R	H	2B	3B	HR	RBI	BB	SO	SB	BA	SA
132	274	41	66	9	3	0	16	24	29	4	.241	.296

Cards

Eddie Collins, Sr.
T205—#4   T205—#5   T206—#72   T207—#34   1933G—#42   1951TCMAS
1960F—#20

Eddie Collins, Jr.
None

◆ ED CONNOLLY, SR.

Edward Joseph
Born: July 17, 1908
Birthplace: Brooklyn, New York
Died: November 12, 1963
Bats: Right   **Throws:** Right
Height: 5′9″   **Weight:** 180
Played for: Boston (AL) 1929-32

Ed's first major league game came on September 20, 1929. A catcher, Ed plied his trade for the hapless Boston teams of the early 1930s. He was baseball son Charlie Berry's backup in 1930 on a team that also featured baseball father Bill Narleski. The light-hitting backstop, perhaps recognizing his own limitations, apparently encouraged Junior to try his luck from the other side of the plate. The Connollys constitute one of baseball's father-son batteries.

◇ ED CONNOLLY, JR.

Edward Joseph
Born: December 2, 1939
Birthplace: Brooklyn, New York
Bats: Left   **Throws:** Left
Height: 6′1″   **Weight:** 190
Played for: Boston (AL): 1964; Cleveland (AL): 1967

Unfortunately, little Ed's ability as a major league pitcher seems to reflect his father's success as a hitter. Working as a spot starter and middle reliever, Ed compiled a dismal 4-11 record during his rookie campaign.

RECORDS

Ed Connolly, Sr. (4 Years)

G	AB	R	H	2B	3B	HR	RBI	BB	SO	SB	BA	SA
149	371	13	66	11	4	0	31	29	50	0	.178	.220

Ed Connolly, Jr. (2 Years)

W	L	Pct.	Sv.	G	GS	CG	IP	H	BB	SO	ShO	ERA
6	12	.333	0	42	19	1	130	143	91	118	1	5.88

Cards

Ed Connolly, Sr.
None

Ed Connolly, Jr.
1965T—#543

◆ JIMMY COONEY

James Joseph
Born: July 9, 1865
Birthplace: Cranston, Rhode Island
Died: July 1, 1903
Bats: Right   **Throws:** Right
Height: 5'9"   **Weight:** 155
Played for: Chicago (NL): 1890-92; Washington (NL): 1892

During the rough-and-tumble baseball of the 1890s, Jimmy made his big league debut April 19, 1890. The term "big league" was just coming into common use; it originally referred to the 12-team National League, but shortly became synonymous with "major league." Jimmy played most of his games at shortstop, but in an unusual display of versatility filled in as catcher as well.

◇ JIMMY COONEY

James Edward
Nickname: Scoops
Born: August 24, 1894
Birthplace: Cranston, Rhode Island
Bats: Right   **Throws:** Right
Height: 5'11"   **Weight:** 160
Played for: Boston (AL): 1917; Military Service in 1918; New York (NL): 1919; St. Louis (NL): 1924-25; Chicago (NL): 1926-27; Philadelphia (NL): 1927; Boston (NL): 1928

Scoops made his American League debut on September 22, 1917 and played 10 games at second base and one at shortstop before the end of the season. He went into military service in 1918 and returned to the majors in 1919. However, he disappeared from the majors until 1924 when he became the Cardinals' regular shortstop and hit .294 in 110 games. He also smacked one of his two career homers during this "career" year. Jimmy is the only player in major league history to participate in two unassisted triple plays. Cooney was on second when Pirate shortstop Glenn Wright grabbed a line drive off Jim Bottomley's bat, doubled out Cooney who was off second base, and tagged Honus Wagner. Almost exactly two years later, Cooney himself turned an unassisted triple play.

◇ JOHNNY COONEY

John Walter
Born: March 18, 1901
Birthplace: Cranston, Rhode Island
Died: July 8, 1986
Bats: Right   **Throws:** Left
Height: 5'10"   **Weight:** 165
Played for: Boston (NL): 1921-30, 1938-42; Brooklyn (NL): 1935-37, 1943-44; New York (AL): 1944
Coaching Experience: Boston (NL): 1940-42, 1946-49, 1950, 1952; Milwaukee (NL): 1953-55; Chicago (AL): 1957-64

Johnny broke in with the Boston Braves as a pitcher on April 19, 1921. However, he didn't stick with the club until he appeared as a pitcher, an outfielder, and a first baseman during the 1923 season. Johnny gave up pitching after the 1930 season and fought his way back into the National League as an outfielder for Brooklyn in 1935, when he was 34 years old. By the next year, he had established himself as a regular and hit .282 in 130 games for Casey Stengel's Dodgers. He did even better in 1937, hitting .293. He must have been Stengel's type of ballplayer because in 1938 when Stengel left Brooklyn to manage Boston, Cooney also went to the Braves. His last season as a regular proved to be 1941, when he hit .319 as a 40 year old in 123 games.

RECORDS

Jimmy Cooney (4 Years)

G	AB	R	H	2B	3B	HR	RBI	BB	SO	SB	BA	SA
324	1,302	221	315	35	14	4	118	148	48	77	.242	.300

Jimmy Cooney (7 Years)

G	AB	R	H	2B	3B	HR	RBI	BB	SO	SB	BA	SA
448	1,575	181	413	64	16	2	150	76	58	30	.262	.327

Johnny Cooney

G	AB	R	H	2B	3B	HR	RBI	BB	SO	SB	BA	SA
1,172	3,372	408	965	130	26	2	219	208	107	30	.286	.342

Pitching Record

W	L	Pct.	Sv.	G	GS	CG	IP	H	BB	SO	ShO	ERA
34	44	.436	6	159	76	44	796	858	223	224	7	3.72

Cards
Jimmy Cooney None
Jimmy Cooney None
Johnny Cooney 1939PB—#85   1940PB—#60   1941PB—#50   1960T—#458 (Coach)

WHEN DAY IS DONE: IN THE BOX

Some love the game. Others stick around because it's all they know; baseball was their first full-time job. There are doubtlessly dozens of other explanations. Whatever the reason, a lot of baseball players seek baseball-related jobs when their days on the diamond expire, and this includes baseball's fathers and sons. Baseball fathers and sons have prolonged their connection with the game by becoming scouts, coaches, managers, umpires, and owners. It's difficult to know how many became scouts, but we can count the others with pretty reliable accuracy.

The first baseball father to take up a position in the coaching box was Big Ed Walsh, who coached for the White Sox from 1923-25 and again between 1928 and 1930. Walsh's first year in the coaching box came the year after he tried and abandoned umpiring—we'll say more about this later. The latter period parallels the years that Big Ed's son (Ed also) pitched for the White Sox. Those were lean years for the White Sox, and neither Big Ed's presence nor little Ed's pitching could do much to help.

One year after Big Ed's coaching debut, Connie Mack brought his son Earle onto the A's as a coach. Earle thus became the first baseball son to coach and the only son to coach for his father. He stayed until Connie retired in 1950. Later, the Macks became one of only two father-son combinations to have both managed. Earle performed a variety of duties for the A's and was one of the only people associated with baseball not to refer to The Tall Tactician as "Mr. Mack." He was simply "Daddy." Since Mr. Mack did not wear a uniform, baseball rules stated he had to remain in the dugout. Consequently, one of Earle's duties often was to notify pitchers when Mack had decided their turn on the mound was finished. It must have been occasionally disconcerting for a player when Earle approached the mound to relieve a pitcher and announced, "Daddy says you can come out now."

Counting Ed, Connie, and Earle, a total of 23 baseball fathers and 15 sons have coached in the major leagues. Several of them, like George Susce, established coaching careers that exceeded their playing careers. George Susce appeared for five different teams in eight major league seasons between 1929 and 1944. His major league career totalled 146 games; he hit .228 with two home runs. But George was a catcher, and that probably kept him around the game. Whatever George did, he did it well enough as a coach that he found regular work. Between 1941 and 1972, six teams kept him steadily employed. George is also one of the few baseball fathers who scouted and signed his own son to a professional contract.

One of baseball's most unusual experiments occurred between 1961 and 1965 when P.K. Wrigley embarked upon a "College of Coaches" for the Cubs. A staff of eight coaches shared various duties and responsibilities including field manager. Baseball father Bob Kennedy spent 1962, 1963, and 1964 working under this arrangement. In fact, one of his baseball cards issued at the time lists him as "Head Coach." Some say P.K. Wrigley was ahead of his time, and that his idea might still work if a team has better personnel. The more popular opinion seems to be that P.K. swallowed too much of his family's product and that it went to his brain. The idea was abandoned and has never been tried again.

◆ RED CORRIDEN

John Michael, Sr.
Born: September 4, 1887
Birthplace: Logansport, Indiana
Died: September 28, 1959
Bats: Right   **Throws:** Right
Height: 5'9"   **Weight:** 165
Played for: St. Louis (AL): 1910; Detroit: 1912; Chicago (NL): 1913-15
Coaching Experience: Chicago (NL): 1932-40; Brooklyn (NL): 1941-46; New York (AL): 1947-48; Chicago (AL): 1950 (Manager)

John's major league career began September 8, 1910. He appeared in two games as a shortstop and third baseman that season, but hit only .155. He came back up in 1912 as a utility infielder for the Tigers, a role he repeated the following year as a Cub. His only season as a regular came in 1914, the year that the Federal League opened. Al Bridwell, previously the Cubs' regular shortstop, jumped to the St. Louis Terriers in the breakaway league, thus opening up a spot for Red. Red appeared in 107 games (96 at shortstop) and hit .230. The Cubs finished fourth and manager Henry Day was history. Roger Bresnehan came in to manage the Cubs in 1915. Whether Red was injured or he somehow landed in Bresnehan's doghouse is unclear, but the records indicate that he appeared in only six games during the 1915 season, his last as a player.

In 1950, after the White Sox got off to a dismal 8-22 start, Red replaced Jack Onslow as manager and guided the Pale Hose to a 52-72 mark for the remainder of the season.

◇ JOHN CORRIDEN

John Michael, Jr.
Born: October 16, 1918
Birthplace: Logansport, Indiana
Bats: Switch   **Throws:** Right
Height: 5'6"   **Weight:** 160
Played for: Brooklyn (NL): 1946

John's only major league appearance came as a pinch runner on April 20, 1946. He scored a run.

RECORDS												

Red Corriden (5 Years)

G	AB	R	H	2B	3B	HR	RBI	BB	SO	SB	BA	SA
222	640	97	131	21	5	6	47	74	NA	26	.205	.281

John Corriden

G	AB	R	H	2B	3B	HR	RBI	BB	SO	SB	BA	SA
1	0	1	*	*	*	*	*	*	*	0	*	*

* No plate appearances.

Cards
None

◆ BILL CROUCH

William Henry
Nickname: Skip
Born: December 3, 1886
Birthplace: Marshallton, Delaware
Died: December 22, 1945
Bats: Left   **Throws:** Left
Height: 6'1"   **Weight:** 210
Played for: St. Louis (AL): 1910

Skip pitched his one and only major league game on July 12, 1910. The record books credit him with a complete game, but no decision.

◇ BILL CROUCH

William Elmar
Born: August 20, 1910
Birthplace: Wilmington, Delaware
Died: December 26, 1980
Bats: Switch   **Throws:** Right
Height: 6'1"   **Weight:** 180
Played for: Brooklyn (NL): 1939; Philadelphia (NL): 1941; St. Louis (NL): 1941, 1945

Bill got his first crack at the National League as a 28-year-old rookie. He made the most of his opportunity, logging a 4-0 record. Despite this, he didn't get another shot until the 1941 season, when he went 2-3 with the Phillies and 1-2 for the Cardinals.

RECORDS

Bill Crouch

W	L	Pct.	Sv.	G	GS	CG	IP	H	BB	SO	ShO	ERA
0	0	NA	0	1	1	1	8	6	7	2	0	3.38

Bill Crouch

W	L	Pct.	Sv.	G	GS	CG	IP	H	BB	SO	ShO	ERA
8	5	.615	7	50	12	4	155	159	52	55	0	3.48

Cards

Bill Crouch
None

Bill Crouch
1941G—#27

◆ HERM DOSCHER

John Henry, Sr.
Born: December 20, 1852
Birthplace: New York, New York
Died: March 20, 1934
Bats: Right   **Throws:** Right
Height: 5'10"   **Weight:** 182
Played for: Atlantic (National Association): 1872-73; Nationals (National Association): 1875; Troy (NL): 1879 Chicago (NL): 1879; Cleveland (NL): 1881-82

Herm played the outfield, third, and short-stop, although it seems he didn't play any of them really well. The distinguishing feature of Herm's playing career seems to be his joining a series of clubs in dramatic decline. He began his playing career in the National Association with Atlantic of Brooklyn, once one of baseball's greatest clubs. But by the time Herm joined them, they were only capable of 8-27 and 17-37 seasons. Herm did get out before the Atlantics completely bottomed out; in 1875, the year Herm joined the Washington Nationals, the Atlantics won two games while losing 42, for a winning percentage of .045! Herm's new team, the Nationals, fared only slightly better, going 4-23 on the season. Herm must have really loved the game. In 1879, he trekked to Troy for the Trojans' inaugural sea-son; he appeared in 47 games, they went 19-56 and were expelled from the National League four years later. Herm joined the Chicago White Stockings for three games in 1879. These Chicago White Stockings became the Cubs; the White Stockings that became the White Sox didn't come along for several more years. Herm finished his major league playing career with the Cleveland Blues, a club that lasted only five seasons.

◇ JACK DOSCHER

John Henry, Jr.
Born: July 27, 1880
Birthplace: Troy, New York
Died: May 27, 1971
Bats: Left   **Throws:** Left
Height: 6'1"   **Weight:** 170
Played for: Chicago (NL): 1903; Brooklyn (NL): 1903-06; Cincinnati: 1908

Sometime in 1903—the Society of American Baseball Research has yet to determine exactly when—young Jack Doscher took the mound and became the very first son of a major league ballplayer also to play at the major league level. Jack didn't win his first major league game until 1905 and didn't get his second (and final) win until the 1908 season.

RECORDS												

Herm Doscher (6 Years)

G	AB	R	H	2B	3B	HR	RBI	BB	SO	SB	BA	SA
80	325	26	73	10	0	0	29	2	26	*	.225	.255

* Not available

Jack Doscher (5 Years)

W	L	Pct.	Sv.	G	GS	CG	IP	H	BB	SO	ShO	ERA
2	11	.154	0	27	13	10	145	118	68	61	0	2.86

Cards
None

◆ DICK ELLSWORTH

Richard Clark
Born: March 22, 1940
Birthplace: Lusk, Wyoming
Bats: Left   **Throws:** Right
Height: 6'1"   **Weight:** 195
Played for: Chicago (NL): 1958, 1960-66; Philadelphia (NL): 1967; Boston (AL): 1968-69; Cleveland (AL): 1969-70; Milwaukee (AL): 1970-71

A strong showing at Houston (2-0, 0.86 ERA in 21 innings), then in the American Association, resulted in Dick's 1960 promotion to the parent Cubs. He quickly established himself in the Cubs' rotation. Dick pitched a one-hitter against the Phillies in June 1963. That season he became the first Cubs pitcher in 43 years to post 20 or more victories in a season; he recorded a 22-10 mark. That was Dick's first winning season; he didn't have another one until 1968, when he went 16-7 for Boston. In 1966, Dick Ellsworth led the National League in losses, with 22.

◇ STEVE ELLSWORTH

Steven Clark
Born: July 30, 1960
Birthplace: Chicago, Illinois
Bats: Right   **Throws:** Right
Height: 6'8"   **Weight:** 220
Played for: Boston (AL): 1988

Steve was the Red Sox' #1 selection in the June 1981 Special Draft. He never developed into the major league pitcher the Red Sox hoped for.

RECORDS

Dick Ellsworth (13 Years)

W	L	Pct.	Sv.	G	GS	CG	IP	H	BB	SO	ShO	ERA
115	137	.456	5	407	310	87	2,156	2,274	595	1,140	9	3.72

Steve Ellsworth

W	L	Pct.	Sv.	G	GS	CG	IP	H	BB	SO	ShO	ERA
1	6	.142	0	8	7	0	36	47	16	16	0	6.75

Cards

Dick Ellsworth

1960T—#125	1961T—#427	1962T—#264	1963T—#399	1964T—#1SP	1964T—#220
1964TS—#17	1964TSU	1965TE—#67	1965T—#165	1966T—#447	1967T—#359
1968T—#406	1969T—#605	1970T—#59	1971T—#309		

Steve Ellsworth

1988DU—#54	1988SU—#83	1989T—#299

◆ JIM ESCHEN

James Godrich
Born: August 21, 1891
Birthplace: Brooklyn, New York
Died: September 27, 1960
Bats: Right   **Throws:** Right
Height: 5'10"   **Weight:** 160
Played for: Cleveland (AL): 1915

Jim's big league debut came July 10, 1915. He was an outfielder.

◇ LARRY ESCHEN

Lawrence Edward
Born: September 22, 1920
Birthplace: Suffern, New York
Bats: Right   **Throws:** Right
Height: 6'   **Weight:** 180
Played for: Philadelphia (AL): 1942

Larry's brief career included games at second and shortstop. It would seem that even during the World War II manpower shortage, Larry didn't quite possess big league tools. Note that in his 11 American League at-bats, he struck out six times.

RECORDS												

Jim Eschen

G	AB	R	H	2B	3B	HR	RBI	BB	SO	SB	BA	SA
15	42	11	10	1	0	0	2	5	9	0	.238	.262

Larry Eschen

G	AB	R	H	2B	3B	HR	RBI	BB	SO	SB	BA	SA
12	11	0	0	0	0	0	0	4	6	0	.000	.000

Cards
None

◆ TITO FRANCONA

John Patsy
Born: November 4, 1933
Birthplace: Aliquippa, Pennsylvania
Bats: Left   **Throws:** Left
Height: 5′11″   **Weight:** 190
Played for: Baltimore: 1956-57; Chicago (AL): 1958; Detroit: 1958; Cleveland (AL): 1959-64; St. Louis (NL): 1965-66; Philadelphia (NL): 1967; Atlanta: 1967-69; Oakland: 1969-70; Milwaukee (AL): 1970
Honors: Most Valuable Player Placement: fifth in 1959.

Playing outfield and first base, Tito established himself as a regular during his first full season. However, Luis Aparicio overshadowed him in the Rookie of the Year balloting. He enjoyed his best season in 1959 when he hit .363 and slugged .566. Unfortunately for him, he ended the season with too few plate appearances to qualify for the batting title. Tito finished fifth in that season's Most Valuable Player tally.

◇ TERRY FRANCONA

Terry Jon
Born: April 22, 1959
Birthplace: Aberdeen, South Dakota
Bats: Left   **Throws:** Left
Height: 6′1″   **Weight:** 182
Played for: Montreal: 1981-85; Chicago (NL): 1986; Cincinnati: 1987; Cleveland (AL): 1988; Milwaukee (AL): 1989-90

Terry was an All-American at the University of Arizona and the Most Valuable Player in the 1980 College World Series.

RECORDS

Tito Francona (15 Years)

G	AB	R	H	2B	3B	HR	RBI	BB	SO	SB	BA	SA
1,719	5,121	650	1,395	224	34	125	656	544	694	46	.272	.403

Terry Francona

	G	AB	R	H	2B	3B	HR	RBI	BB	SO	SB	BA	SA
1981-87	552	1,282	112	354	56	5	12	108	52	81	10	.276	.356
1988	62	212	24	66	8	0	1	12	5	18	0	.311	.363
1989	90	233	26	54	10	1	3	23	8	20	2	.232	.322
1990	3	4	1	0	0	0	0	0	0	0	0	0	0

Cards

Tito Francona

1957T—#184	1958T—#316	1959T—#268	1960T—#30	1960T—#260SP	1961T—#503
1961P—#64	1962T—#97	1962P—#40	1963T—#248	1963P—#392SP	1963F—#12
1963P—#64	1964T—#583	1965T—#256	1966T—#163	1967T—#443	1968T—#527
1969T—#398	1970T—#663	1985T—#134SP			

Terry Francona

1982D—#627	1982F—#188	1982T—#118	1983D—#592	1983F—#281	1983T—#267
1984D—#463	1984F—#275	1984T—#496	1985D—#132	1985F—#398	1985T—#578
1985T—#134SP	1986D—#401	1986F—#248	1986T—#374	1986FU—#43	1986TT—#38
1987F—#564	1987T—#785	1987TT—#34	1988S—#297	1988T—#686	1989S—#597
1989T—#31	1989UD—#536	1990S—#216	1990T—#214	1990UD—#180	

◆ **LEN GABRIELSON**

Leonard Hilborne
Born: September 8, 1915
Birthplace: Oakland, California
Bats: Left   **Throws:** Left
Height: 6'3"   **Weight:** 210
Played for: Philadelphia (NL): 1939

Len played first base. He made his debut on April 21, 1939, went on the injured list shortly thereafter, and never returned to the majors.

◇ **LEN GABRIELSON**

Leonard Gary
Born: February 14, 1940
Birthplace: Oakland, California
Bats: Left   **Throws:** Right

Height: 6'4"   **Weight:** 215
Played for: Milwaukee (NL): 1960, 1963-64; Chicago (NL): 1964-65; San Francisco: 1965-66; California: 1967; Los Angeles (NL): 1967-70

Len was an outfielder and first baseman who occasionally filled in at third base. He went 0 for 3 the first time he faced major league pitching in 1960. It was 1963 before he found himself back in a major league uniform. He recorded 22 games in the outfield, 16 at first, and 3 at second for the Braves. Traded to the Cubs during the 1964 season, he emerged as a regular. Traded again during the 1965 season, he arrived in San Francisco and contributed with a .301 average in 269 at-bats. Len's 1965 Topps baseball card informs us that he was second on the Cubs with 10 stolen bases in 1964.

RECORDS

Len Gabrielson

G	AB	R	H	2B	3B	HR	RBI	BB	SO	SB	BA	SA
5	18	3	4	0	0	0	1	2	3	0	.222	.222

Len Gabrielson (9 Years)

G	AB	R	H	2B	3B	HR	RBI	BB	SO	SB	BA	SA
708	1,764	178	446	64	12	37	176	145	315	21	.253	.366

Cards

Len Gabrielson
None

Len Gabrielson

1963T—#253R	1964T—#198	1965T—#14	1966T—#395	1967T—#469	1968T—#357
1969T—#615	1970T—#204				

◆ JOHN GANZEL

John Henry
Born: April 7, 1874
Birthplace: Kalamazoo, Michigan
Died: January 14, 1959
Bats: Right   **Throws:** Right
Height: 6'   **Weight:** 195
Played for: Pittsburgh: 1898; Chicago (NL): 1900; New York (AL): 1903-04; Held out in 1905-06; Cincinnati: 1907-08
Coaching Experience: Cincinnati: 1908 (Player-Manager); Brooklyn (Federal): 1915 (Manager)

John established himself as the New York Highlander's regular first baseman during their first American League season (they later became the Yankees). However, he was a hold-out during the 1905 and 1906 campaigns. He returned to baseball in 1907 for the Cincinnati Red Stockings and slugged 16 triples to lead the National League. John spent the 1908 campaign as a player-manager; Cincinnati finished fifth (73-81). John's brother Charlie played major league ball between 1884 and 1897. In 1888, Charlie recorded games at every position.

◇ BABE GANZEL

Foster Pirie
Born: May 22, 1901
Birthplace: Malden, Massachusetts
Died: February 6, 1978
Bats: Right   **Throws:** Right
Height: 5'10"   **Weight:** 172
Played for: Washington (AL): 1927-28

When Babe broke in as an outfielder, he showed a lot of promise. In 13 games with 48 at-bats, he bashed 21 hits for an impressive .438 average and a hefty .667 slugging record. However, the following year he could only muster two hits in 26 at-bats over seven games and was out of major league baseball after that.

RECORDS

John Ganzel (8 Years)

G	AB	R	H	2B	3B	HR	RBI	BB	SO	SB	BA	SA
747	2,718	281	682	104	50	18	336	136	*	46	.251	.346

* Not available

Babe Ganzel

G	AB	R	H	2B	3B	HR	RBI	BB	SO	SB	BA	SA
23	74	9	23	5	2	1	17	8	7	0	.311	.473

Cards

John Ganzel
T206—#446

Babe Ganzel
None

◆ LARRY GILBERT

Lawrence William
Born: December 3, 1891
Birthplace: New Orleans, Louisiana
Died: February 17, 1965
Bats: Left   **Throws:** Left
Height: 5'9"   **Weight:** 158
Played for: Boston (NL): 1914-15

After his April 14, 1914 debut, Larry logged 60 games in the outfield during his rookie year for the pennant-winning Boston Braves. He appeared in the World Series as a pinch hitter, but failed to connect.

◇ CHARLIE GILBERT

Charles Mader
Born: July 8, 1919
Birthplace: New Orleans, Louisiana
Died: August 13, 1983
Bats: Left   **Throws:** Left
Height: 5'9"   **Weight:** 165
Played for: Brooklyn (NL): 1940; Chicago (NL): 1941-43; Military Service in 1944-45; Chicago (NL): 1946; Philadelphia (NL): 1946-47

Charlie appeared in 43 games as a 20-year-old outfielder. He never really established himself as a regular. His debut came April 16, 1940.

◇ TOOKIE GILBERT

Harold Joseph
Born: April 4, 1929
Birthplace: New Orleans, Louisiana
Died: June 23, 1967
Bats: Left   **Throws:** Right
Height: 6'2"   **Weight:** 185
Played for: New York (NL): 1950, 1953

Tookie cracked a home run in his major league debut on May 5, 1950 and played 111 games at first during his rookie season. Despite this, he didn't return to the majors until 1953, when he struggled at the plate and could only manage to hit .169 in 160 at-bats. Light hitting seems to have been a family trait.

RECORDS												

Larry Gilbert (2 years)

G	AB	R	H	2B	3B	HR	RBI	BB	SO	SB	BA	SA
117	330	43	76	10	1	5	29	37	47	7	.230	.312

Charlie Gilbert (6 years)

G	AB	R	H	2B	3B	HR	RBI	BB	SO	SB	BA	SA
364	852	109	195	27	9	5	55	86	82	7	.229	.299

Tookie Gilbert (2 years)

G	AB	R	H	2B	3B	HR	RBI	BB	SO	SB	BA	SA
183	482	52	98	15	2	7	48	65	57	4	.203	.286

Cards

Larry Gilbert
None

Charlie Gilbert
None

Tookie Gilbert
1950B—#235   1952T—#61

◆ PEACHES GRAHAM

George Frederick
Born: February 23, 1877
Birthplace: Aledo, Illinois
Died: July 25, 1939
Bats: Right   **Throws:** Right
Height: 5'9"   **Weight:** 180
Played for: Cleveland (AL): 1902; Chicago (NL): 1903; Boston (NL): 1908-11; Chicago (NL): 1911; Philadelphia (NL): 1912

Peaches appeared in one game during the 1902 season as a 25-year-old second baseman. The following year, he again got into only one game, this time as a pitcher. He lost a no-hitter. He returned to the majors five years later as a 31-year-old catcher. He also played first, third, the outfield, and even a game at shortstop. Graham remains something of a mystery man. The author of *Eight Men Out*, the definitive study of the 1919 "Black Sox" scandal tentatively identified Graham as Billy Maharg (Graham spelled backwards), one of the gamblers involved in paying off the Sox. Maharg was a former professional boxer. To make matters even more confusing, there is a Billy Maharg recorded as playing one game for Detroit in 1912 and one game for the Phillies in 1916.

◇ JACK GRAHAM

Jack Bernard
Born: December 24, 1916
Birthplace: Minneapolis, Minnesota
Bats: Left   **Throws:** Left
Height: 6'2"   **Weight:** 200
Played for: Brooklyn: 1946; New York (NL): 1946; St. Louis (AL): 1949

Jack was an outfielder and first baseman. He spent 1943-45 in the Army Air Force. Jack's 1950 Bowman baseball card tells us that Jack "holds a private pilot's license." When the folks at Bowman use some of their precious space on the back of their tiny cards to relate this sort of information, it doesn't take a rocket scientist to figure out that the player in question probably doesn't have a great future in professional baseball. It was certainly true in this case, as Jack didn't even play in the majors in 1950.

RECORDS

Peaches Graham (7 years)

G	AB	R	H	2B	3B	HR	RBI	BB	SO	SB	BA	SA
373	999	99	265	34	6	1	85	114	*	21	.265	.314

W	L	Pct	Sv	G	GS	CG	IP	H	BB	SO	ShO	ERA
0	1	.000	0	1	1	0	5	9	3	4	0	5.4

* Not available

Jack Graham (2 years)

G	AB	R	H	2B	3B	HR	RBI	BB	SO	SB	BA	SA
239	775	105	179	28	5	38	126	84	99	1	.231	.427

Cards

Peaches Graham
T205—#38   T206—#144   T207—#69
Jack Graham
1950B—#145

◆ FREDDIE GREEN

Fred Allan
Born: September 14, 1933
Birthplace: Titusville, New Jersey
Bats: Right   **Throws:** Left
Height: 6'4   **Weight:** 190
Played for: Pittsburgh: 1959-61; Washington (AL): 1962; Pittsburgh: 1964

Freddie posted an 8-4 record during Pittsburgh's 1960 National League Championship season. During the World Series, he appeared in 4 innings over 3 games and was rocked for 11 hits and a staggering 22.50 ERA!

◇ GARY GREEN

Gary Allan
Born: January 14, 1962
Birthplace: Pittsburgh, Pennsylvania
Bats: Right   **Throws:** Right
Height: 6'3"   **Weight:** 175
Played for: San Diego: 1986, 1989; Texas: 1990

Gary was a member of the 1984 U.S. Olympic team.

RECORDS												

Freddie Green (5 years)

W	L	Pct.	Sv.	G	GS	CG	IP	H	BB	SO	ShO	ERA
9	7	.563	4	88	1	0	142	142	63	77	0	3.49

Gary Green (3 years)

G	AB	R	H	2B	3B	HR	RBI	BB	SO	SB	BA	SA
90	148	16	33	7	0	0	10	8	30	1	.223	.270

Cards

Fred Green
1960T—#272   1961T—#181

Gary Green
1985T—#396 (USOC)

◆ KEN GRIFFEY, SR.

George Kenneth
Born: April 10, 1950
Birthplace: Donora, Pennsylvania
Bats: Left   **Throws:** Left
Height: 6'   **Weight:** 190
Played for: Cincinnati: 1973-81; New York (AL): 1982-86; Atlanta: 1986-88; Cincinnati: 1988-90; Seattle: 1990-91
Honors: National League All-Star in 1976.

The Griffeys are the only father-son combination to be active as players at the same time at the major league level. As a regular, Ken has hit over .300 seven times. During the 1990 season, Ken, Sr. was released by Cincinnati to be claimed on waivers by Seattle, thus enabling him to join his son's team. His Reds' teammates showed their respect for the Senior Griffey when they voluntarily stenciled his number onto their hats during the 1990 World Series.

◇ KEN GRIFFEY, JR.

George Kenneth
Born: November 21, 1969

Birthplace: Charleroi, Pennsylvania
Bats: Left   **Throws:** Left
Height: 6'3"   **Weight:** 195
Played for: Seattle: 1989-91
Honors: American League All-Star in 1991.

Ken was the #1 player taken in the June 1987 draft. Recognizing his superior athletic ability, baseball pundits tagged him "The Natural," and he graced the covers of publications such as *Baseball America* and *Sports Illustrated*. He handled the publicity and pressure with such an easy grace that he immediately became a fan favorite; he had a chocolate bar named for him his rookie season. Ken's baseball legend began in little league. He played a full season BEFORE HE MADE AN OUT. He cried when he made his first out at age eleven. He hammered the ball so hard in high school that he provoked actual fear in his coach when he had to throw Ken, Jr. batting practice. Ken played so well in the spring of 1989 that he virtually gave the Mariners no choice but make him the youngest player in the major leagues that season. In 1990, when he hit .300, he was still only 20 years old.

RECORDS

Ken Griffey, Sr.

G	AB	R	H	2B	3B	HR	RBI	BB	SO	SB	BA	SA
1973-86												
1,800	6,525	1,048	1,953	339	74	135	771	646	804	193	.299	.436
1988												
94	243	26	62	6	0	4	23	19	31	1	.255	.329
1989												
106	236	26	62	8	3	8	30	29	47	4	.263	.424
1990 (Cincinnati)												
46	63	6	13	2	0	1	8	2	5	2	.206	.286
1990 (Seattle)												
21	77	13	29	2	0	3	18	10	3	0	.377	.519
1991												
30	85	10	24	7	0	1	9	13	13	0	.282	.400

Ken Griffey, Jr.

G	AB	R	H	2B	3B	HR	RBI	BB	SO	SB	BA	SA
1989												
127	455	61	120	23	0	16	61	44	83	16	.264	.420
1990												
155	597	91	179	28	7	22	80	63	81	16	.300	.481
1991												
154	548	76	179	42	1	22	100	71	82	18	.327	.527

Cards

Ken Griffey, Sr.

1974T—#598R	1975T—#284	1976T—#128	1976SS—#40	1976K—#44	1977T—#320
1977K—#49	1978K—#4	1978T—#80	1979T—#420	1980T—#550	1981D—#184
1981F—#199	1981T—#280	1982D—#634	1982F—#67	1982T—#620	1982T—#621
1982T—#756SP	1982TT—#40	1982D—#486	1983F—#382	1983T—#110	1984D—#613
1984F—#126	1984T—#770	1985D—#347	1985F—#128	1985T—#380	1986D—#126
1986F—#105	1986T—#40	1986TT—#42	1987D—#513	1987F—#516	1987T—#711
1988D—#202	1988F—#540	1988S—#390	1988SPF—#178	1988T—#443	1989B—#259
1989S—#609	1990D—#469	1990F—#420	1990S—#338	1990T—#581	1990UD—#682
1991D—#452	1991S—#835	1991T—#465	1991UD—#572		

Ken Griffey, Jr.

1989B—#220	1989D—#33	1989F—#548	1989UD—#1	1990D—#4DK	1990D—#365
1990F—#513	1990S—#560	1990T—#336	1990UD—#24SP	1990UD—#156	1991D—#77
1991D—#49	1991F—#450	1991S—#2	1991T—#465	1991UD—#572	

◆ RAY GRIMES

Oscar Ray, Sr.
Born: September 11, 1893
Birthplace: Bergholz, Ohio
Died: May 25, 1953
Bats: Right   **Throws:** Right
Height: 6'   **Weight:** 175
Played for: Boston (AL): 1920; Chicago (NL): 1921-24; Philadelphia (NL): 1926

Playing for the Cubs in 1922, Ray established a major league record when he drove in at least one run in 17 consecutive games in which he played. This promising slugger placed second to Rogers Hornsby in the National League that season in doubles (45), batting average (.354), on-base percentage (.442), and slugging (.572). However, this young first baseman sustained a back injury during the 1923 season, saw limited action in 1924, and didn't play in 1925. He attempted a comeback with the Phillies in 1926, hit a respectable .297 in 32 games and 101 at-bats, but hung up his cleats anyway. Ray's twin brother Roy played in 1920.

◇ OSCAR GRIMES

Oscar Ray, Jr.
Born: April 13, 1915
Birthplace: Minerva, Ohio
Bats: Right   **Throws:** Right
Height: 5'11"   **Weight:** 178
Played for: Cleveland (AL): 1938-42; New York (AL): 1943-46; Philadelphia (AL): 1946

Oscar established himself as a valuable utility player, playing 48 games at second, 43 at first, and 37 at shortstop during the 1939 campaign. A broken cheekbone limited his action in 1940. He won a position as a regular at third base for the 1944 and 1945 Yankees.

RECORDS												

Ray Grimes (6 Years)

G	AB	R	H	2B	3B	HR	RBI	BB	SO	SB	BA	SA
433	1,537	269	505	101	25	27	263	204	133	21	.329	.480

Oscar Grimes (9 Years)

G	AB	R	H	2B	3B	HR	RBI	BB	SO	SB	BA	SA
602	1,832	235	469	73	24	18	200	297	303	30	.256	.352

Cards

Ray Grimes
Ray appears on a 1922 American Caramel Card, #157.
Oscar Grimes
None

◆ ROSS GRIMSLEY, SR.

Ross Albert
Nickname: Lefty
Born: June 4, 1922
Birthplace: Americus, Kansas
Bats: Left   **Throws:** Left
Height: 6'   **Weight:** 175
Played for: Chicago (AL): 1951

Ross pitched in the American League for the first time on September 3, 1951. He appeared in seven games for the White Sox, but registered no decisions.

◇ ROSS GRIMSLEY, JR.

Ross Albert
Born: January 7, 1950
Birthplace: Topeka, Kansas
Bats: Left   **Throws:** Left
Height: 6'3"   **Weight:** 200
Played for: Cincinnati: 1971-73; Baltimore: 1974-77; Montreal: 1978-80; Cleveland (AL): 1980; Rib injury in 1981; Baltimore: 1982

Ross won two and lost one for Cincinatti in the 1972 World Series (2.57 ERA). He appeared in two games during Baltimore's 1974 League Championship Series with Oakland and recorded a 1.69 ERA. Ross' finest season came in 1978, when he posted a 20-11 mark and a 3.05 ERA.

RECORDS

Ross Grimsley, Sr.

W	L	Pct.	Sv.	G	GS	CG	IP	H	BB	SO	ShO	ERA
0	0	NA	0	7	0	0	14	12	10	8	0	3.86

Ross Grimsley, Jr. (11 years)

W	L	Pct.	Sv.	G	GS	CG	IP	H	BB	SO	ShO	ERA
124	99	.556	3	345	295	79	2,039	2,105	559	750	15	3.81

Cards

Ross Grimsley, Sr.
None

Ross Grimsley, Jr.

1972T—#99	1973T—#357	1974T—#59	1974TT—#59	1975K—#2	1975T—#458
1976T—#257	1976SS—#377	1977T—#572	1978T—#691	1979T—#15	1980T—#375
1981F—#406	1981T—#170				

◆SAM HAIRSTON

Samuel
Born: January 28, 1920
Birthplace: Crawford, Mississippi
Bats: Right   **Throws:** Right
Height: 5'10   **Weight:** 187
Played for: Chicago (AL): 1951
Coaching Experience: Chicago (AL): 1978.

Sam was a catcher who made his major league debut with the White Sox on July 21, 1951.

◇ JOHNNY HAIRSTON

John Louis
Born: August 29, 1945
Birthplace: Birmingham, Alabama
Bats: Right   **Throws:** Right
Height: 6'2"   **Weight:** 200
Played for: Chicago (NL): 1969

When Johnny first appeared for the Cubs on September 6, 1969, the Hairstons became major league baseball's first black father-son combination.

◇ JERRY HAIRSTON

Jerry Wayne
Nickname: Popeye
Born: February 16, 1952
Birthplace: Birmingham, Alabama
Bats: Switch   **Throws:** Right
Height: 5'10"   **Weight:** 185
Played for: Chicago (AL): 1973-77; Pittsburgh: 1977; Chicago (AL): 1981-89

Jerry came up as an outfielder and spent most of his career there and as a designated hitter. He sometimes filled in at first and even at second. With the exception of 51 games for the Pirates in 1977, Jerry's entire career was with the White Sox.

RECORDS

Sam Hairston

G	AB	R	H	2B	3B	HR	RBI	BB	SO	SB	BA	SA
4	5	1	2	1	0	0	1	2	0	0	.400	.800

John Hairston

G	AB	R	H	2B	3B	HR	RBI	BB	SO	SB	BA	SA
3	4	0	1	0	0	0	0	0	2	0	.250	.250

Jerry Hairston (14 Years)

G	AB	R	H	2B	3B	HR	RBI	BB	SO	SB	BA	SA
859	1,699	216	438	91	6	30	205	282	240	4	.258	.371

Cards

Sam Hairston
None

Johnny Hairston
None

Jerry Hairston

1974T—#96	1975T—#327	1976T—#391	1976SS—#153	1983D—#616	1983F—#236
1983T—#487	1984D—#86	1984F—#60	1984T—#177	1985D—#135	1985F—#515
1985T—#596	1986D—#424	1986F—#207	1986T—#778	1987D—#285	1987F—#498
1987T—#685	1988D—#285	1988T—#281			

Bobby Adams

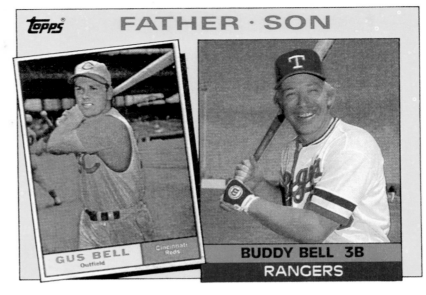

FATHER · SON

GUS BELL
Outfield
Cincinnati Reds

BUDDY BELL 3B
RANGERS

DONRUSS
DIAMOND KINGS

ROBERTO ALOMAR

1989 ROOKIE

PADRES
C
SANDY ALOMAR

PIRATES ▾ MOISES ALOU

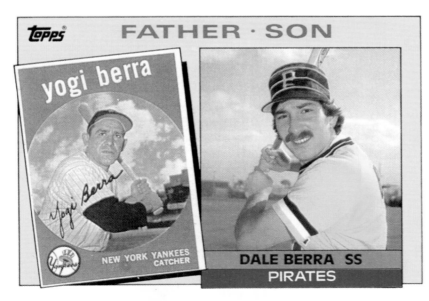

FATHER · SON

yogi berra

NEW YORK YANKEES CATCHER

DALE BERRA SS
PIRATES

EARL AVERILL

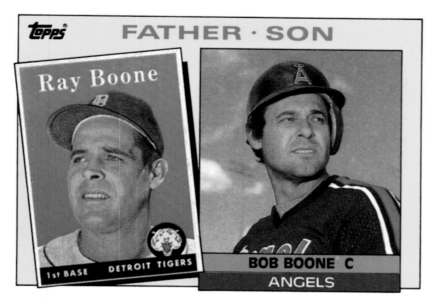

FATHER · SON

Ray Boone

1st BASE   DETROIT TIGERS

BOB BOONE C
ANGELS

charley beamon

BALTIMORE ORIOLES
PITCHER

BOBBY BONDS
IN ACTION

BARRY BONDS

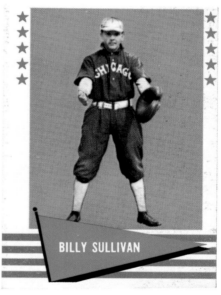

BILLY SULLIVAN

EDDIE COLLINS

FATHER & SON — Big Leaguers

JOE COLEMAN
pitcher BALTIMORE ORIOLES

JOE COLEMAN, JR.
P DETROIT TIGERS

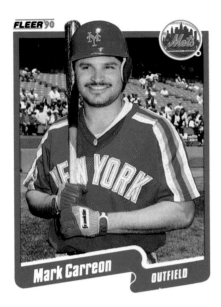

Mark Carreon — OUTFIELD

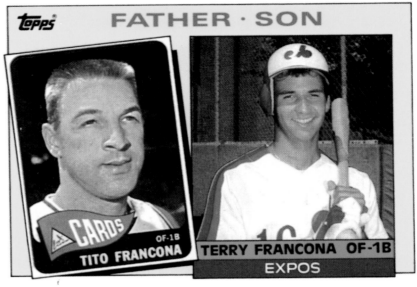

FATHER · SON

Tito Francona — OF-1B

Terry Francona OF-1B — EXPOS

1961 ROOKIE

CAMILO CARREON — Catcher — Chicago White Sox

CUBS

DICK ELLSWORTH — pitcher

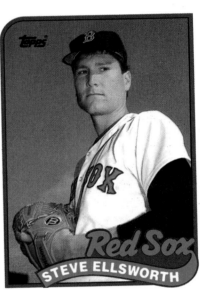

Red Sox — STEVE ELLSWORTH

FATHER & SON — Big Leaguers

JIM HEGAN — catcher CLEVELAND INDIANS

MIKE HEGAN
1B-OF MILWAUKEE BREWERS

REDS

TOPPS 1971 ALL-STAR ROOKIE

ROSS GRIMSLEY

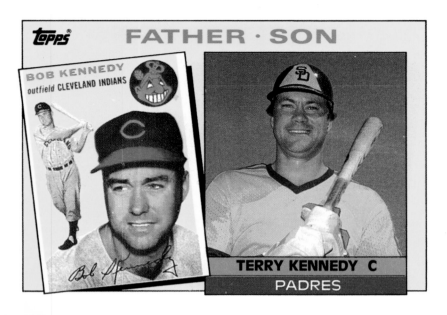

FATHER · SON

Topps

BOB KENNEDY
outfield CLEVELAND INDIANS

TERRY KENNEDY C
PADRES

Ebbie St Claire

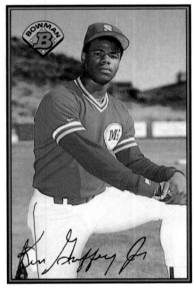

BOWMAN

Ken Griffey Jr

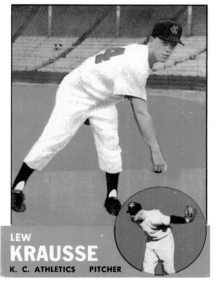

LEW
KRAUSSE
K. C. ATHLETICS   PITCHER

expos

Topps

RANDY
ST. CLAIRE

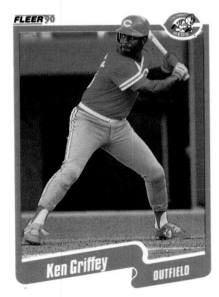

FLEER '90

Ken Griffey
OUTFIELD

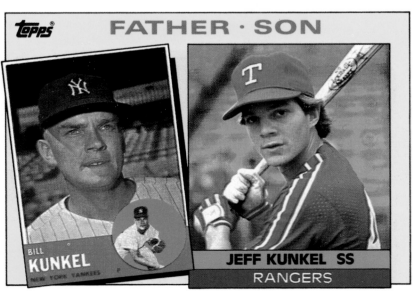

Topps   FATHER · SON

BILL
KUNKEL
NEW YORK YANKEES   P

JEFF KUNKEL SS
RANGERS

BOBBY
WINE

SHORTSTOP
PHILLIES

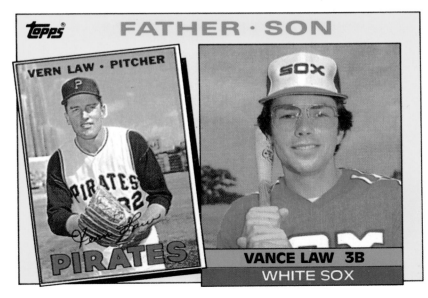

FATHER · SON

VERN LAW · PITCHER

PIRATES

VANCE LAW 3B
WHITE SOX

ASTROS

ROBBIE Wine

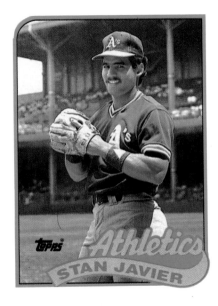

Athletics
STAN JAVIER

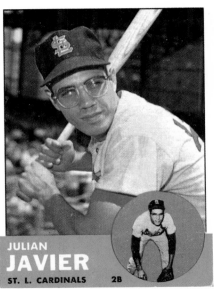

JULIAN
JAVIER
ST. L. CARDINALS 2B

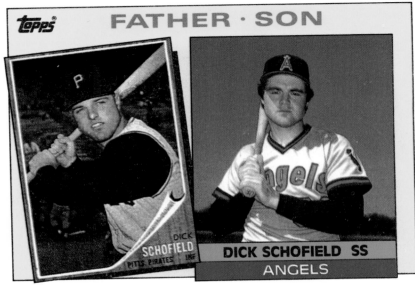

FATHER · SON

DICK
SCHOFIELD
PITTS. PIRATES INF

DICK SCHOFIELD SS
ANGELS

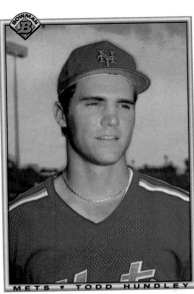

METS · TODD HUNDLEY

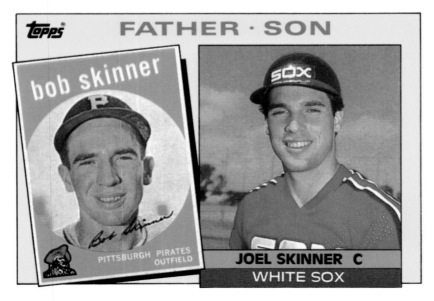

FATHER · SON

bob skinner
PITTSBURGH PIRATES
OUTFIELD

JOEL SKINNER C
WHITE SOX

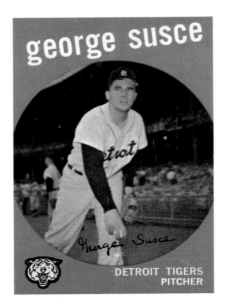

george susce
DETROIT TIGERS
PITCHER

OUTFIELD
MARTY KEOUGH

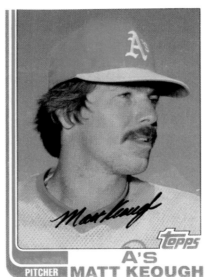

PITCHER
A'S MATT KEOUGH

DON LEE
Los Angeles Angels—Pitcher

YANKEES

FLEER

TOM TRESH outfield

THE "O's" BROTHERS
Bill Ripken—Cal Ripken, Jr.

DUANE PILLETTE
pitcher BALTIMORE ORIOLES

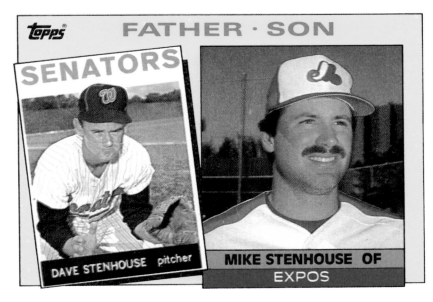

Topps   FATHER · SON

SENATORS

DAVE STENHOUSE pitcher

MIKE STENHOUSE OF
EXPOS

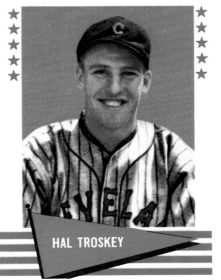

HAL TROSKEY

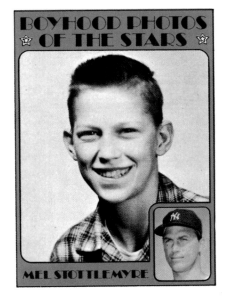

BOYHOOD PHOTOS
OF THE STARS

MEL STOTTLEMYRE

ROYALS   Topps

Royals
52

MEL STOTTLEMYRE, JR.

Topps   FATHER · SON

DIZZY TROUT
pitcher BOSTON RED SOX

STEVE TROUT P
CUBS

FATHER · SON

ROY SMALLEY SS-3B-1B
WHITE SOX

KURT STILLWELL

JOSE
TARTABULL
K. C. ATHLETICS OF

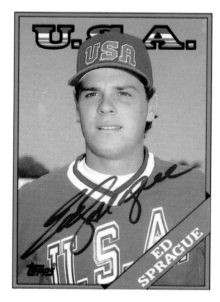

ED SPRAGUE

DEL UNSER OF
EXPOS

DANNY
TARTABULL

FATHER · SON

OSSIE VIRGIL

OZZIE VIRGIL C
PHILLIES

◆ LARRY HANEY

Wallace Larry
Born: November 19, 1942
Birthplace: Charlottesville, Virginia
Bats: Right   **Throws:** Right
Height: 6′2″   **Weight:** 195
Played for: Baltimore: 1966-68; Seattle: 1969; Oakland: 1969-70, 1972-73; St. Louis: 1973; Oakland: 1974-76; Milwaukee (AL): 1977-78

Larry had the tools to stay 12 seasons in the majors as a backup catcher and the luck to play for three world champions — Baltimore in 1966 and Oakland in 1972 and 1974.

◇ CHRIS HANEY

Born: November 16, 1968
Birthplace: Baltimore, Maryland
Bats: Left   **Throws:** Left
Height: 6′3″   **Weight:** 185
Played for: Montreal: 1991

Chris broke into the Expos starting rotation after just over a year of professional baseball. He threw nine wild pitches, the most on the Expos staff, but the Expos believe this was more a matter of his relative youth and inexperience at the major league level.

RECORDS

Larry Haney (12 years)

G	AB	R	H	2B	3B	HR	RBI	BB	SO	SB	BA	SA
480	919	68	198	30	1	12	73	44	175	3	.215	.289

Chris Haney

W	L	Pct.	Sv.	G	GS	CG	IP	H	BB	SO	ShO	ERA
1991												
3	7	.300	0	16	16	0	85	94	43	51	0	4.04

Cards

Larry Haney
1967T—#507   1968T—#42   1969T—#209   1970T—#648   1973T—#563   1975T—#626
1976T—#446   1977T—#12   1978T—#391

Chris Haney
None (as of 1991)

◆ JIM HEGAN

James Edward
Born: August 3, 1920
Birthplace: Lynn, Massachusetts
Died: June 17, 1984
Bats: Right   **Throws:** Right
Height: 6'2"   **Weight:** 195
Played for: Cleveland (AL): 1941-42; Military Service in 1943-45; Cleveland (AL): 1946-57; Detroit: 1958; Philadelphia (NL): 1958-59; San Francisco: 1959; Cincinnati: 1960
Honors: American League All-Star in 1950 and 1951.

One of baseball's premier defensive catchers of his era, Jim established an American League record in 1949 when he allowed only four passed balls in 152 games. He caught a record three no-hitters: in 1947 (Don Black), 1948 (Bob Lemon), and 1951 (Bob Feller).

◇ MIKE HEGAN

James Michael
Born: July 21, 1942
Birthplace: Cleveland, Ohio
Bats: Left   **Throws:** Left
Height: 6'1"   **Weight:** 188
Played for: New York (AL): 1964, 1966-67; Seattle: 1969; Milwaukee (AL): 1970-71; Oakland: 1971-73; New York (AL): 1973-74; Milwaukee (AL): 1974-77

An original member of the Seattle Pilots (a franchise that went bankrupt after only one year and reestablished itself in Milwaukee), Mike hit .292 playing 64 games in the outfield and 19 at first. Mike played in six of the seven games during Oakland's 1972 World Series victory over Cincinnati, primarily as a late-inning defensive replacement.

RECORDS

Jim Hegan (17 Years)

G	AB	R	H	2B	3B	HR	RBI	BB	SO	SB	BA	SA
1,666	4,772	550	1,087	187	46	92	525	456	742	15	.228	.344

Mike Hegan (12 Years)

G	AB	R	H	2B	3B	HR	RBI	BB	SO	SB	BA	SA
965	2,080	281	504	73	18	53	229	311	489	28	.242	.371

Cards

Jim Hegan

1948L—#28	1950B—#7	1951TRB—#12	1951B—#79	1952T—#17	1952B—#187
1952RM—#AL11	1953T—#80	1953BC—#102	1954T—#29	1954RH—#11	1955RM—#AL7
1955TDH—#67	1955T—#7	1956T—#48	1957T—#136	1958T—#345	1959T—#372
1973T—#116C	1976T—#69SP				

Mike Hegan

1967T—#553SP	1968T—#402	1969T—#577	1970T—#111	1971T—#415	1972T—#632
1973T—#382	1974T—#517	1975T—#99	1976T—#69SP	1976T—#377	1976SS—#235
1977T—#507					

◆ KEN HEINTZELMAN

Kenneth Alphonse
Born: October 14, 1915
Birthplace: Peruque, Missouri
Bats: Right   **Throws:** Left
Height: 5'11"   **Weight:** 185
Played for: Pittsburgh: 1937-42; Military Service in 1943-45; Pittsburgh: 1946-47; Philadelphia (NL): 1947-52

Ken's major league career began with a complete game victory on October 3, 1937. He pitched two more big league innings in 1938, then went 1-1 in 17 games in 1939. By 1940, the Pirates were utilizing him regularly. Ken's finest season came in 1949, when he hurled his way to a 17-10 record for the Phillies and was named club Most Valuable Player. His five shutouts tied him for the National League lead. He dropped to a disappointing 3-9 for the 1950 "Whiz Kid" Phillies, but still drew the starting assignment for Game Three of the World Series. He pitched a fine game, going seven and two-thirds innings and giving up only four hits and one earned run before giving way to Jim Konstanty. The Phils lost the game with two outs in the bottom of the ninth and were subsequently swept by the Yankees.

◇ TOM HEINTZELMAN

Thomas Kenneth
Born: November 3, 1946
Birthplace: St. Charles, Missouri
Bats: Right   **Throws:** Right
Height: 6'   **Weight:** 185
Played for: St. Louis (NL): 1973-74; San Francisco: 1977-78

In his short career, Tom recorded games at all infield positions.

RECORDS

Ken Heintzelman (13 years)

W	L	Pct.	Sv.	G	GS	CG	IP	H	BB	SO	ShO	ERA
77	98	.440	10	319	183	66	1,502	1,540	630	564	18	3.93

Tom Heintzelman (4 years)

G	AB	R	H	2B	3B	HR	RBI	BB	SO	SB	BA	SA
90	140	17	34	5	0	3	12	14	22	0	.243	.343

Cards

Ken Heintzelman
1949B—#108   1950B—#85   1951B—#147   1951BR—#C10   1952T—#362   1952B—#148
1953T—#136

Tom Heintzelman
1974T—#607R

◆ WALLY HOOD, SR.

Wallace James
Born: February 9, 1895
Birthplace: Whittier, California
Died: May 2, 1965
Bats: Right   **Throws:** Right
Height: 5'11"   **Weight:** 160
Played for: Brooklyn (NL): 1920; Pittsburgh: 1920; Brooklyn (NL): 1921-2

Wally made his debut with Brooklyn on April 15, 1920. The young outfielder appeared in seven games with the Dodgers before being traded to the Pirates. There, he was used in two games as a pinch hitter. He returned to Brooklyn in 1921.

◇ WALLY HOOD, JR.

Wallace James
Born: September 24, 1925
Birthplace: Los Angeles, California
Bats: Right   **Throws:** Right
Height: 6'1"   **Weight:** 190
Played for: New York (AL): 1949

Wally made his professional debut on September 23, 1949.

RECORDS												

Wally Hood, Sr. (3 years)

G	AB	R	H	2B	3B	HR	RBI	BB	SO	SB	BA	SA
67	80	23	19	2	2	1	5	14	18	5	.238	.350

Wally Hood, Jr.

W	L	Pct.	Sv.	G	GS	CG	IP	H	BB	SO	ShO	ERA
0	0	NA	0	2	0	0	2	0	1	2	0	0.00

Cards
None

◆ RANDY HUNDLEY

Cecil Randolph
Born: June 1, 1942
Birthplace: Martinsville, Virginia
Bats: Right   **Throws:** Right
Height: 5'11"   **Weight:** 180
Played for: San Francisco: 1964-65, Chicago (NL): 1966-73; Minnesota: 1974, San Diego: 1975, Chicago (NL): 1976-77

Randy spent his entire career as a catcher. He made his major league debut with the Giants (September 27, 1964) and became the Cubs' regular backstop in 1966. Randy's best years came 1966-69, when he drove in more than 60 runs in each of those seasons. A knee injury limited his playing time to 73 games in 1970, a year when the Cubs finished second to the Pirates, only five games out of first. The injury lingered, and Randy missed virtually the entire 1971 season. He returned to the Cubs' starting lineup for 1972, but never hit above .226 (in 1973) during the remainder of his career.

◇ TODD HUNDLEY

Born: May 27, 1969
Birthplace: Martinsville, Virginia
Bats: Switch   **Throws:** Right
Height: 5'11"   **Weight:** 170
Played for: New York (NL): 1990-91

When dad Randy began operating "fantasy" baseball camps, youngster Todd used to go along and pick up pointers on hitting from former major leaguers like Billy Williams, Ron Santo, and Jimmy Piersall. The Mets drafted Todd in the second round of the 1987 draft, and he quickly acquired the label of their catcher of the future.

RECORDS

Randy Hundley (14 Years)

G	AB	R	H	2B	3B	HR	RBI	BB	SO	SB	BA	SA
1,061	3,442	311	813	118	13	82	381	271	565	12	.236	.350

Todd Hundley

	G	AB	R	H	2B	3B	HR	RBI	BB	SO	SB	BA	SA
1990	36	67	8	14	6	0	0	2	6	18	0	.209	.299
1991	21	60	5	8	0	1	1	7	6	14	0	.133	.217

Cards

Randy Hundley
1966T—#392   1967T—#106   1968T—#136   1969T—#347   1970T—#265   1971T—#592
1972T—#258   1973T—#021   1974T—#319   1974TT—#T319   1976T—#351   1977T—#502

Todd Hundley
1991D—#641   1991F—#150   1991S—#340   1991T—#457   1991UD—#440

◆ JULIAN JAVIER

Manuel Julian (Liranzo)
Nicknames: Hoolie, The Phantom
Born: August 9, 1936
Birthplace: San Francisco De Marcoris, Dominican Republic
Bats: Right   **Throws:** Right
Height: 6'1"   **Weight:** 175
Played for: St. Louis (NL): 1960-71; Cincinnati: 1972
Honors: National League All-Star in 1963 and 1968.

In the 1967 World Series, this slick-fielding second baseman contributed with his bat as well, hitting .360 and knocking in four runs. In a losing cause in the 1968 Series, he hit .333 and had three RBIs. Julian possessed good speed; in 1960 his 82.6% success rate led the National League.

◇ STAN JAVIER

Stanley Julian Antonio
Born: January 9, 1964
Birthplace: San Francisco De Marcoris, Dominican Republic
Bats: Switch   **Throws:** Right
Height: 6'   **Weight:** 185
Played for: New York (AL): 1984; Oakland: 1986-89; Los Angeles (NL): 1990-91

Stan might be baseball's best "fourth" outfielder. Adept at all three outfield positions, Stan started at least ten games at each station during 1988. He replaced Jose Canseco when he was injured in early 1989 and impressed fans with his range, arm, and speed. The A's traded him to the Dodgers on May 13, 1990 in the deal that sent veteran Willie Randolph to the A's. In 1988, he stole 20 bases and was only caught once for a league-leading 95.2% stolen base average.

RECORDS

Julian Javier (13 Years)

G	AB	R	H	2B	3B	HR	RBI	BB	SO	SB	BA	SA
1,622	5,722	722	1,469	216	55	78	506	314	812	135	.257	.355

Stan Javier

G	AB	R	H	2B	3B	HR	RBI	BB	SO	SB	BA	SA
1984-87												
147	272	36	52	11	1	2	17	35	61	11	.191	.261
1988												
125	397	49	102	13	3	2	35	32	63	20	.257	.320
1989												
112	310	42	77	12	3	1	28	31	45	12	.248	.316
1990												
104	276	56	84	9	4	3	24	37	44	15	.304	.399
1991												
121	176	21	36	5	3	1	11	13	36	7	.205	.284

Cards

Julian Javier

1960T—#133	1961T—#148	1962T—#118	1963T—#226	1963P—#159	1964T—#446
1965T—#447	1966T—#436	1967T—#226	1968T—#25	1969T—#497	1970T—#415
1971T—#185	1972T—#745	1978MA—#288			

Stan Javier

1986D—#584	1986FU—#56	1987D—#590	1987FU—#52	1987T—#263	1988S—#367
1989D—#185	1989F—#13	1989S—#322	1989T—#622	1989UD—#581	1990D—#568
1990F—#12	1990S—#394	1990T—#102	1990UD—#209	1991D—#239	1991F—#211
1991S—#281	1991T—#61	1991UD—#688			

◆ ADAM JOHNSON, SR.

Adam Rankin
Born: February 4, 1888
Birthplace: Burnett, Texas
Died: July 2, 1972
Bats: Right   **Throws:** Right
Height: 6'1"   **Weight:** 185
Played for: Boston (AL): 1914; Chicago (Federal League): 1914-15; Baltimore (Federal League): 1915; St. Louis (NL): 1918

Rankin took a chance and jumped to the Chicago franchise in the Federal League in 1914. It paid off as he went 9-5. Unfortunately, it was also the only winning mark he posted in his brief career. Looking at his record, and at things like his ratio of hits to innings pitched, and strikeouts to walks, he looks like one of those pitchers who should have done better.

◇ ADAM JOHNSON, JR.

Adam Rankin
Born: March 1, 1917
Birthplace: Hayden, Arizona
Bats: Right   **Throws:** Right
Height: 6'3"   **Weight:** 177
Played for: Philadelphia (AL): 1941

Adam appeared in seven games for the hapless 1941 Philadephia A's, a team that finished 64-90 and 37 games out of first. Nevertheless, he left behind a perfect 1-0 record.

RECORDS

Adam Johnson, Sr.

W	L	Pct.	Sv.	G	GS	CG	IP	H	BB	SO	ShO	ERA
23	30	.434	2	72	53	31	450	401	151	169	6	2.92

Adam Johnson, Jr.

W	L	Pct.	Sv.	G	GS	CG	IP	H	BB	SO	ShO	ERA
1	0	1.000	0	7	0	0	10	14	3	0	0	3.60

Cards

None

◆ ERNIE JOHNSON

Ernest Rudolph
Born: April 29, 1888
Birthplace: Chicago, Illinois
Died: May 1, 1952
Bats: Left   **Throws:** Right
Height: 5'9"   **Weight:** 151
Played for: Chicago (AL): 1912; St. Louis (Federal League): 1915; St. Louis (AL): 1916-18; Chicago (AL): 1921-23; New York (AL): 1923-25

Ernie played second, shortstop, and third. When he got a chance to play regularly, he responded with a .294 average in 141 games for the 1921 White Sox. He was traded to the 1923 Yankees and appeared in two games during the 1923 World Series.

◇ DON JOHNSON

Donald Spore
Nickname: Pep
Born: December 7, 1911
Birthplace: Chicago, Illinois
Bats: Right   **Throws:** Right
Height: 6'   **Weight:** 170
Played for: Chicago (NL): 1943-48

Don won the regular second base job during his first full season. His best season was Chicago's pennant-winning 1945 campaign, when he notched a .302 average in 138 games. He played in all seven Series games, but was held to a .172 average (5 for 29).

RECORDS

Ernie Johnson (10 Years)

G	AB	R	H	2B	3B	HR	RBI	BB	SO	SB	BA	SA
813	2,619	372	697	91	36	19	256	181	153	114	.266	.350

Don Johnson (6 Years)

G	AB	R	H	2B	3B	HR	RBI	BB	SO	SB	BA	SA
511	1,935	219	528	89	6	8	175	112	171	26	.273	.337

Cards

None

◆ BOB KENNEDY

Robert Daniel
Born: August 18, 1920
Birthplace: Chicago, Illinois
Bats: Right   **Throws:** Right
Height: 6'2"   **Weight:** 193
Played for: Chicago (AL): 1939-42; Military Service in 1943-45; Chicago (AL): 1946-48; Cleveland (AL): 1948-54; Baltimore: 1954-55; Chicago (AL): 1955-56; Detroit: 1956; Chicago (AL): 1957; Brooklyn (NL): 1957
Coaching Experience: Chicago (NL): 1963-65 (Manager); Oakland: 1968 (Manager)

Bob arrived in Cleveland in time to contribute to their 1948 pennant by hitting .301 and playing 50 games in the outfield. Bob was also a competent third baseman. His career was twice interrupted by military service—1943-45 and 1952. Bob played for the 1951 Indians, a team that featured three big-league fathers—Ray Boone and Jim Hegan were the other two.

◇ TERRY KENNEDY

Terrence Edward
Born: June 4, 1956
Birthplace: Euclid, Ohio
Bats: Left   **Throws:** Right
Height: 6'4"   **Weight:** 220
Played for: St. Louis (NL): 1978-80; San Diego: 1981-86; Baltimore (AL): 1987-88; San Francisco: 1989-91
Honors: National League All-Star in 1981, 1983, and 1985; American League All-Star in 1987.

The Sporting News named Terry collegiate player of the year in 1977 (Florida State). Terry hit .301 his first season playing full-time (1981, San Diego). His offensive production slumped during the 1984 World Series, when he hit only .211. Still, he managed to drive in three of the Padres' 14 runs during that five-game series. Terry established Padres' club records for home runs (21 in 1982) and RBIs (98 in 1983) by a catcher.

RECORDS

Bob Kennedy (16 Years)

G	AB	R	H	2B	3B	HR	RBI	BB	SO	SB	BA	SA
1,483	4,624	514	1,176	196	41	63	514	364	443	45	.254	.355

Terry Kennedy

	G	AB	R	H	2B	3B	HR	RBI	BB	SO	SB	BA	SA
1978-88	1,190	4,150	418	1,104	200	11	103	555	288	730	4	.266	.400
1989	125	355	19	85	15	0	5	34	35	56	1	.239	.324
1990	107	303	25	84	22	0	2	26	31	38	1	.277	.370
1991	69	171	12	40	7	1	3	13	11	31	0	.234	.339

Cards

Bob Kennedy

1951TRB—#29	1951B—#296	1952T—#77	1953T—#33	1954T—#155	1955T—#48
1955TDH—#87	1956T—#38	1957T—#149	1964T—#486	1965T—#457	1968T—#183
1985T—#135SP					

Terry Kennedy

1979T—#724R	1980T—#569	1981D—#428	1981F—#541	1981T—#353	1981T—#780
1982D—#121	1982F—#574	1982T—#65	1983D—#26	1983D—#220	1983F—#362
1983T—#274	1983T—#742SP	1984D—#112	1984F—#304	1984T—#455	1984T—#366SP
1985D—#429	1985F—#37	1985T—#635	1985T—#135SP	1986D—#356	1986F—#327
1986T—#230	1986T—#306	1987D—#205	1987F—#419	1987T—#540	1987FU—#56
1987TT—#57	1988D—#150	1988F—#563	1988S—#123	1988SPF—#94	1988T—#180
1989B—#470	1989D—#141	1989F—#610	1989S—#123	1989T—#705	1989UD—#469
1990D—#602	1990F—#58	1990S—#7	1990T—#372	1990UD—#397	1991D—#94
1991F—#263	1991S—#548	1991T—#66	1991UD—#404		

◆ MARTY KEOGH

Richard Martin
Born: April 14, 1935
Birthplace: Oakland, California
Bats: Left   **Throws:** Left
Height: 6'   **Weight:** 180
Played for: Boston (AL): 1956-60; Cleveland: 1960; Washington (AL): 1961; Cincinnati: 1962-65; Atlanta: 1966; Chicago (NL): 1966

Boston first used Marty as a pinch hitter on April 21, 1956, but he didn't stick with the parent club until 1958, when he appeared in 68 games, 25 of them in the outfield. Marty's only season as a regular came with the 1961 Washington Senators, a team that finished the season in last place, 61-100, and 47.5 games off the pace. He could also fill in at first. When he completed his career in the U.S., Marty played for a year in Japan for Osaka's Nankai Hawks. Marty's brother Joe played outfield and first base in 1968-73.

◇ MATT KEOGH

Matthew Lon
Born: July 3, 1955
Birthplace: Pomona, California
Bats: Right   **Throws:** Right
Height: 6'3"   **Weight:** 185
Played for: Oakland: 1977-83; New York (AL): 1983; St. Louis (NL): 1985; Chicago (NL): 1986; Houston: 1986
Honors: American League All-Star in 1978

Matt was originally signed as an infielder but converted to a pitcher in the minors. His first big league appearance came on September 3, 1977 for Oakland. In 1979, Matt tied a major league record by losing his first 14 starts. He redeemed himself by winning 16 (losing 13) the next season and being named Comeback Player of the Year by *The Sporting News*. When Matt journeyed to Japan to pitch for Hanshin, the Keoghs became the first American father-son combination to play in both the American and Japanese major leagues.

RECORDS

Marty Keogh (11 years)

G	AB	R	H	2B	3B	HR	RBI	BB	SO	SB	BA	SA
841	1,796	256	434	71	23	43	176	164	318	26	.242	.379

Matt Keogh (9 years)

W	L	Pct.	Sv.	G	GS	CG	IP	H	BB	SO	ShO	ERA
58	84	.408	0	215	175	53	1,190	1,190	510	590	7	4.17

Cards

Marty Keogh

1958T—#371	1959T—#303	1960T—#71	1961T—#146	1962T—#258	1962P—#69
1963T—#21	1963P—#135	1964T—#166	1965T—#263		

Matt Keogh

1978T—#709R	1979T—#554	1980T—#134	1981D—#358	1981F—#588	1981T—#301
1982D—#71	1982F—#95	1982T—#87	1983D—#239	1983F—#521	1983T—#413
1983TT—#54	1984D—#627	1984F—#130	1984T—#203		

◆ LEW KRAUSSE, SR.

Lewis Bernard
Born: June 8, 1912
Birthplace: Media, Pennsylvania
Died: September 6, 1988
Bats: Right   **Throws:** Right
Height: 6′   **Weight:** 167
Played for: Philadelphia (AL): 1931-32

Lew was only 19 years old when he got into three games and posted a 1-0 record for the 1931 American League champion Philadelphia Athletics.

◇ LEW KRAUSSE, JR.

Lewis Bernard
Born: April 25, 1943
Birthplace: Media, Pennsylvania
Bats: Right   **Throws:** Right
Height: 6′1″   **Weight:** 185
Played for: Kansas City: 1961, 1964-67; Oakland: 1968-69; Milwaukee (AL): 1970-71; Boston (AL): 1972; St. Louis (NL): 1973; Atlanta: 1974

Lew was even younger than his father when he made his major league debut. On June 16, 1961, at the tender age of 18 years and six weeks, he threw a three-hit shutout against the Angels.

RECORDS

Lew Krausse, Sr. (2 years)

W	L	Pct.	Sv.	G	GS	CG	IP	H	BB	SO	ShO	ERA
5	1	.833	0	23	4	3	68	70	30	17	1	4.50

Lew Krausse, Jr. (12 years)

W	L	Pct.	Sv.	G	GS	CG	IP	H	BB	SO	ShO	ERA
68	91	.428	21	321	167	21	1,284	1,205	493	721	5	4.00

Cards

Lew Krausse, Sr.
None

Lew Krausse, Jr.

1963T—#104	1964T—#334	1965T—#462	1966T—#256	1967T—#565	1968T—#458
1969T—#23	1970T—#233	1971T—#372	1973T—#566	1975T—#603	

◆ BILL KUNKEL

William Gustave James
Born: July 7, 1936
Birthplace: Hoboken, New Jersey
Died: May 4, 1985
Bats: Right   **Throws:** Right
Height: 6'1"   **Weight:** 185
Played for: Kansas City: 1961-62; New York (AL): 1963
Umpire: 1968-84

After serious reflection on his future as a major league pitcher, Bill became an American League umpire in 1968. It was probably a wise decision. Bill began his umpiring career in the Florida State League in 1966 and quickly worked his way into the majors, eventually becoming a crew chief. He worked League championships in 1971, 1975, 1978, and 1982; All-Star Games in 1972 and 1977; and the World Series in 1974 and 1980. Bill also worked as a referee in the NBA and ABA. When doctors diagnosed Bill's cancer, he fought back hard and returned to the diamond even after having 18" of his intestine removed. While re-covering, he spent time watching his sons play college ball—Jeff at Rider and Kevin at Stanford. Prior to his death, Bill made a film, *Safe at Home*, for the American Cancer Society.

◇ JEFF KUNKEL

Jeffry William
Born: March 25, 1962
Birthplace: West Palm Beach, Florida
Bats: Right   **Throws:** Right
Height: 6'2"   **Weight:** 175
Played for: Texas: 1984-90

Injuries plagued this versatile player almost from the start of his career. A muscle pull sustained during the final days of spring training slowed him down in 1984; he tore a ligament in his knee in 1985; a sore knee and strained throwing wrist hampered his 1986 season; and he separated a shoulder and had an appendectomy during 1987. Jeff has played all outfield positions, second, third, and shortstop, and has even pitched.

RECORDS

Bill Kunkel (3 years)

W	L	Pct.	Sv.	G	GS	CG	IP	H	BB	SO	ShO	ERA
6	6	.500	4	89	2	0	143	153	49	83	0	4.28

Jeff Kunkel (7 years)

G	AB	R	H	2B	3B	HR	RBI	BB	SO	SB	BA	SA
337	838	88	188	42	9	18	72	37	226	7	.224	.360

Cards

Bill Kunkel
| 1961T—#322 | 1962T—#147 | 1963T—#523 | 1985T—#136 | | |

Jeff Kunkel
1985D—#587	1985F—#561	1985T—#288	1985T—#136	1988S—#407	1989B—#231
1989D—#496	1989F—#527	1989S—#484	1989T—#092	1989UD—#463	1990D—#496
1990F—#304	1990S—#431	1990T—#174	1990UD—#394	1991F—#292	1991S—#783
1991T—#562					

◆ JOE LANDRUM

Joseph Butler
Born: December 13, 1928
Birthplace: Columbia, South Carolina
Bats: Right   **Throws:** Right
Height: 5'11"   **Weight:** 180
Played for: Brooklyn: 1950, 1952

Joe made his major league pitching debut on August 31, 1950. He pitched seven innings in seven games and saved one game for Brooklyn that year. In 1952, the National League champion Dodgers employed Joe as both a starter and a reliever. The Dodgers used 17 pitchers to win the pennant that season and carried two more on their roster in military service.

◇ BILL LANDRUM

Thomas William
Born: August 17, 1957
Birthplace: Columbia, South Carolina
Bats: Right   **Throws:** Right
Height: 6'2"   **Weight:** 205
Played for: Cincinnati: 1986-87; Chicago (NL): 1988; Pittsburgh: 1989-91

A knee injury hampered Bill in 1988. The Cubs released him, and the Pirates signed him as a free agent. This apparently gave Bill a new lease on his baseball life and he responded by saving 26 games for the Pirates; this included a stretch of 30 2/3 shutout innings.

RECORDS

Joe Landrum (2 years)

W	L	Pct.	Sv.	G	GS	CG	IP	H	BB	SO	ShO	ERA
1	3	.250	1	16	5	2	45	58	11	22	0	5.64

Bill Landrum

	W	L	Pct.	Sv.	G	GS	CG	IP	H	BB	SO	ShO	ERA
1986	0	0	NA	0	10	0	0	13	23	4	14	0	6.75
1987	3	2	.600	2	44	0	0	65	68	34	42	0	4.71
1988	1	0	1.000	0	7	0	0	12	19	3	6	0	5.84
1989	2	3	.400	26	56	0	0	81	60	28	51	0	1.67
1990	7	3	.700	13	54	0	0	72	69	21	39	0	2.13
1991	4	4	.500	17	61	0	0	76	76	19	45	0	3.18

Cards

Joe Landrum
None

Bill Landrum

1988F—#238	1988T—#42	1990D—#668	1990F—#472	1990S—#456	1990T—#425
1990UD—#442	1991D—#350	1991F—#41	1991S—#98	1991T—#595	1991UD—#614

◆ MAX LANIER

Hubert Max
Born: August 18, 1915
Birthplace: Denton, North Carolina
Bats: Right   **Throws:** Left
Height: 5′11″   **Weight:** 190
Played for: St. Louis (NL): 1938-46, 1949-51; Suspended: 1947-48; New York (NL): 1952-53; St. Louis (AL): 1953

Max pitched in two games during the 1942 World Series, recording one win. In the 1943 Series, he lost a game, but showed fine form in establishing a 1.76 ERA in three games and 15.1 innings of work. He won another game during the 1944 Series. He played in the Mexican League from 1946 to 1948, and was suspended for doing so. Despite this, author Peter Palmer, in his book *Total Baseball*, rates Max 116th on his career Total Pitching Index. His 3.01 ERA is good enough to place him fifth during the 1942-60 era.

◇ HAL LANIER

Harold Clifton
Born: July 4, 1942
Birthplace: Denton, North Carolina
Bats: Right   **Throws:** Right
Height: 6′2″   **Weight:** 186
Played for: San Francisco: 1964-71; New York (AL): 1972-73
Coaching Experience: St. Louis (NL): 1981-85; Houston: 1986-88 (Manager); Philadelphia (NL): 1990

Primarily a shortstop, Hal also filled in at second and third. Hal turned his hand to managing in 1986 when he guided Houston to a 96-66 first place finish in the National League West. His managerial record skidded downhill after that, finishing third the next year and fifth the season after that. His career managerial record stands at 254-232.

RECORDS

Max Lanier (14 years)

W	L	Pct.	Sv.	G	GS	CG	IP	H	BB	SO	ShO	ERA
108	82	.568	17	327	204	91	1,619	1,490	611	821	21	3.01

Hal Lanier (10 years)

G	AB	R	H	2B	3B	HR	RBI	BB	SO	SB	BA	SA
1,196	3,703	297	843	111	20	8	273	136	436	11	.228	.275

Cards

Max Lanier

1950B—#207	1951B—#230	1952T—#101	1952B—#110		

Hal Lanier

1965T—#118	1966T—#156SP	1966T—#271	1967T—#4	1968T—#436	1969T—#316
1970T—#583	1971T—#181	1972T—#589	1973T—#479	1974T—#588	1986TT—#60
1987T—#343	1988T—#684	1989T—#164			

◆ VERN LAW

Vernon Sanders
Nickname: Deacon
Born: March 12, 1930
Birthplace: Meridian, Idaho
Bats: Right   **Throws:** Right
Height: 6'2"   **Weight:** 200
Played for: Pittsburgh: 1950-51; Military Service in 1952-53; Pittsburgh: 1954-67
Coaching Experience: Pittsburgh: 1968-69.
Honors: Cy Young Award in 1960. National League All-Star in 1960.

Deacon gained his nickname because he was an ordained minister in the Mormon Church. Vern won 20 and lost 9 during his Cy Young season. In that year's Series, he won the first and fourth games for Pittsburgh. In the fourth game, he doubled in a run and scored the Pirate's third (and decisive) run as well. He started the dramatic seventh game, giving way to ace reliever Elroy Face in the sixth inning.

◇ VANCE LAW

Vance Aaron
Born: October 1, 1956
Birthplace: Boise, Idaho
Bats: Right   **Throws:** Right
Height: 6'2"   **Weight:** 185
Played for: Pittsburgh 1980-81; Chicago (AL): 1982-84; Montreal: 1985-87; Chicago (NL): 1988-89; Japan: 1990; Oakland: 1991

A versatile infielder capable of covering all infield positions, he played third base in all four games of the 1983 AL Championship Series for the White Sox. He hit only .182. The Cubs released Vance in 1990. With Japan's Chunichi Dragons, he finished the 1990 season fourth in hitting in Japan's Central Division with a .313 average; he also had 29 home runs and collected 78 RBIs. While he was with the Expos, Vance pitched 7 innings in 6 games (3 in 1986 and 3 in 1987), walked 2, struck out 2, and can boast of a career ERA (3.86) just slightly higher than his father's.

RECORDS

Vern Law (16 Years)

W	L	Pct.	Sv.	G	GS	CG	IP	H	BB	SO	ShO	ERA
162	147	.524	13	483	364	119	2,672	2,833	597	1,092	28	3.77

Vance Law

	G	AB	R	H	2B	3B	HR	RBI	BB	SO	SB	BA	SA
1980-87	857	2704	331	685	135	20	53	513	297	423	31	.253	.377
1988	151	556	73	163	29	2	11	78	55	79	1	.293	.412
1989	130	408	38	96	22	3	7	42	38	73	2	.235	.355
1991	74	134	11	28	7	1	0	9	18	27	0	.209	.276

Cards

Vernon Law

1951B—#203	1952T—#81	1952B—#71	1954T—#235	1954B—#187	1955B—#199
1956T—#252	1957T—#199	1958T—#132	1959T—#12	1959T—#428SP	1960T—#453
1961T—#47SP	1961T—#250SP	1961T—#400	1961P—#126	1962T—#295	1962P—#179
1963T—#184	1963P—#58	1964T—#472	1965T—#515	1966T—#15	1966T—#221SP
1967T—#351	1978MA—#239	1985T—#137SP			

Vance Law

1981T—#551	1982D—#582	1982F—#484	1982T—#291	1983D—#117	1983F—#245
1983T—#98	1984D—#546	1984F—#68	1984T—#667	1985D—#122	1985F—#520
1985T—#413	1985T—#137SP	1985FU—#70	1985TT—#73	1986D—#132	1986F—#252
1986T—#787	1987D—#212	1987F—#323	1987T—#127	1988D—#212	1988F—#187
1988S—#85	1988SPF—#41	1988T—#346	1988DU—#79	1988SU—#16	1988TT—#60
1989B—#293	1989D—#276	1989F—#430	1989S—#102	1989SPF—#162	1989T—#501
1989UD—#473	1990D—#629	1990F—#36			

◆ THORNTON LEE

Thornton Starr
Nickname: Lefty
Born: September 13, 1906
Birthplace: Sonoma, California
Bats: Left   **Throws:** Left
Height: 6'3"   **Weight:** 205
Played for: Cleveland (AL): 1933-36; Chicago (AL): 1937-47; New York (NL): 1948
Honors: Most Valuable Player Placement: fourth in 1941. American League All-Star in 1941.

Thornton recorded his 22-11 mark in 1941 for a team that went 77-77. Lefty also led the American League that year, with 30 complete games and a 2.37 ERA. He ranks 103rd on Peter Palmer's career Total Pitcher Index and seems to have been one of those pitchers cursed to spend his career toiling for mediocre clubs.

◇ DON LEE

Donald Edward
Born: February 26, 1934
Birthplace: Globe, Arizona
Bats: Right   **Throws:** Right
Height: 6'4"   **Weight:** 205
Played for: Detroit: 1957-58; Washington (AL): 1960; Minnesota (NL): 1961-62; Los Angeles (AL): 1962-64; California: 1965; Houston: 1965-66; Chicago (NL): 1966

Ted Williams is the only major leaguer to hit a home run off both a father and his son. Williams hit one off Thornton during "Teddy Ballgame's" rookie season, and got one off Don in 1960, the last year of Williams' career.

RECORDS

Thornton Lee (16 years)

W	L	Pct.	Sv.	G	GS	CG	IP	H	BB	SO	ShO	ERA
117	124	.485	10	374	272	155	2,331	2,327	838	937	14	3.56

Don Lee (9 years)

W	L	Pct.	Sv.	G	GS	CG	IP	H	BB	SO	ShO	ERA
40	44	.476	11	244	97	13	828	827	281	467	4	3.61

Cards

Thornton Lee
1935BU—#109   1941DP—#103

Don Lee
1957T—#379   1959T—#132   1960T—#503   1961T—#153   1962T—#166   1963T—#372
1963F—#18   1964T—#493   1965T—#595

◆ DUTCH LERCHEN

Bertram Roe
Born: April 4, 1889
Birthplace: Detroit, Michigan
Died: January 7, 1962
Bats: Right   **Throws:** Right
Height: 5'9"   **Weight:** 165
Played for: Boston (AL): 1910

Dutch made his major league debut on August 14, 1910. He was a shortstop.

◇ GEORGE LERCHEN

George Edward
Born: December 1, 1922
Birthplace: Detroit, Michigan
Bats: Switch   **Throws:** Right
Height: 5'11"   **Weight:** 175
Played for: Detroit: 1952; Cincinnati: 1953

George was a 29-year-old rookie. In 1953, he was used almost exclusively as a pinch hitter, going 5 for 17 for a .294 average. He is recorded as playing one game in the outfield that year.

RECORDS												

Dutch Lerchen

G	AB	R	H	2B	3B	HR	RBI	BB	SO	SB	BA	SA
6	15	1	0	0	0	0	0	1	*	0	.000	.000

* Not available

George Lerchen (2 years)

G	AB	R	H	2B	3B	HR	RBI	BB	SO	SB	BA	SA
36	49	3	10	2	0	1	5	12	16	1	.204	.306

Cards
None

◆ GLENN LIEBHARDT

Glenn John
Born: March 10, 1883
Birthplace: Milton, Indiana
Died: July 13, 1956
Bats: Right   **Throws:** Right
Height: 5'10"   **Weight:** 175
Played for: Cleveland (AL): 1906-09

After going 2-0 when he was called up in 1906, Glenn won 18 games and lost 14 in 1907 for a Cleveland team managed by the great Nap Lajoie. Hall-of-Famer Addie Joss was the staff's ace that year, with a 27-11 record. However, Glenn fell to 15-16 the following year, as Cleveland lost a heartbreaking race to Detroit. Cleveland's 90-64 record put them four percentage points and half a game behind Detroit at the season's end.

◇ GLENN LIEBHARDT

Glenn Ignatius
Nickname: Sandy
Born: July 31, 1910
Birthplace: Cleveland, Ohio
Bats: Right   **Throws:** Right
Height: 5'10"   **Weight:** 170
Played for: Philadelphia (AL): 1930; St. Louis (AL): 1936, 1938

Glenn appeared in five games for the World Champion 1930 Philadelphia Athletics. In those games, he pitched a total of 9 innings, gave up 14 hits, including 2 home runs, and finished the season with an ERA of 11.00. He made his debut on April 22, 1930. After the 1930 season, he did not appear in the major leagues again until 1936, when he appeared in 24 games without recording a decision for the St. Louis Browns.

RECORDS												
Glenn Liebhardt (4 years)												
W	L	Pct.	Sv.	G	GS	CG	IP	H	BB	SO	ShO	ERA
37	34	.521	1	91	66	49	612	543	183	280	7	2.18
Glenn Liebhardt (3 years)												
W	L	Pct.	Sv.	G	GS	CG	IP	H	BB	SO	ShO	ERA
0	1	.000	0	31	0	0	67	116	35	23	0	8.96

Cards
Glenn Liebhardt
T206—#212
Glenn Liebhardt
None

◆ FRED LINDSTROM

Frederick Charles
Nickname: Lindy
Born: November 21, 1905
Birthplace: Chicago, Illinois
Died: October 4, 1981
Bats: Right   **Throws:** Right
Height: 5'11"   **Weight:** 170
Played for: New York (NL): 1924-32; Pittsburgh: 1933-34; Chicago (NL): 1935; Brooklyn (NL): 1936
Hall of Fame: Elected in 1976, by the Committee on Veterans
Honors: Most Valuable Player Placement: second in 1928.

Lindstrom made an immediate impact as an 18-year-old rookie in 1924. He played third base all seven games in that year's World Series, going 10 for 30. However, the youngster was twice victimized by bad hops during the climactic seventh game. In the eighth inning, he allowed in the tying run when the ball hit a pebble; in the 12th inning, he surrendered the winning run as a result of a similar miscue. Lindy hit .358 and drove in 107 runs in 1928, as well as leading the National League with 231 hits. Lindstrom began playing the outfield during the 1931 season. He played both third and the outfield for the Cubs in the 1935 World Series. Lindstrom is, to some, a controversial Hall of Fame choice even though his .311 lifetime batting average places him 73rd among all-time leaders. Lindy batted over .300 seven seasons, including six consecutive seasons. An extremely tough man to strike out, he fanned only once for every 20.3 at-bats, 57th on the career list.

◇ CHUCK LINDSTROM

Charles William
Born: September 7, 1936
Birthplace: Chicago, Illinois
Bats: Right   **Throws:** Right
Height: 5'11"   **Weight:** 175
Played for: Chicago (AL): 1958

Chuck tripled in his only major league at-bat, on September 28, 1958.

RECORDS												

Fred Lindstrom (13 years)

G	AB	R	H	2B	3B	HR	RBI	BB	SO	SB	BA	SA
1,438	5,611	895	1,747	301	81	103	779	334	276	84	.311	.449

Chuck Lindstrom

G	AB	R	H	2B	3B	HR	RBI	BB	SO	SB	BA	SA
1	1	1	1	0	1	0	1	1	0	0	1.000	1.0

Cards

Fred Lindstrom
1933G—#133   1933DL—#11   1935BU—#122

Chuck Lindstrom
None

◆ **JACK LIVELY**

Henry Everett
Born: February 29, 1885
Birthplace: Joppa, Alabama
Died: December 5, 1967
Bats: Left   **Throws:** Right
Height: 5'9"   **Weight:** 185
Played for: Detroit: 1911

Jack made his debut on April 16, 1911.

◇ **BUD LIVELY**

Everett Adrian
Nickname: Red
Born: February 14, 1925
Birthplace: Birmingham, Alabama
Bats: Right   **Throws:** Right
Height: 6'   **Weight:** 200
Played for: Cincinnati: 1947-49

Buddy pitched his first game on April 17, 1947.

RECORDS												

Jack Lively

W	L	Pct.	Sv.	G	GS	CG	IP	H	BB	SO	ShO	ERA
7	5	.583	0	18	14	10	114	143	34	45	0	4.58

Bud Lively (3 years)

W	L	Pct.	Sv.	G	GS	CG	IP	H	BB	SO	ShO	ERA
8	13	.381	1	79	27	6	249	230	127	94	2	4.16

Cards

Jack Lively
T207—#106

Bud Lively
None

◆ CONNIE MACK

Cornelius McGillicuddy
Nickname: The Tall Tactician
Born: December 22, 1862
Birthplace: East Brookfield, Massachusetts
Died: February 8, 1956
Bats: Right   **Throws:** Right
Height: 6'1"   **Weight:** 150
Played for: Washington (NL) 1886-89; Buffalo (Players Association): 1890; Pittsburgh: 1891-96
Coaching Experience: Pittsburgh: 1894-96 (Player/Manager); Philadelphia (AL): 1901-50 (Manager)
Hall of Fame: Elected in 1937

"Slats" McGillicuddy began his playing career as a 6'1", 150-pound catcher for the Washington Senators in the National League. This spindly catcher was one of the first to adopt the practice of playing directly behind the hitter. He established a reputation as a chatty catcher with a knack for saying exactly the right thing to distract a hitter. He also perfected the trick of using his glove to imitate the sound of a foul tip and convinced more than one umpire to call an out on a "caught" foul third strike. In 1887, his 15 double plays established a rookie fielding record for catchers, which remains unbroken to this day. A founder of the American League after his playing days, Mack became a living legend as his patrician visage gazed out of the A's dugout for half a century. Mack never wore a baseball uniform while managing, preferring somber business suits with starched collars. The Tall Tactician guided the A's to nine pennants and five world championships. His "White Elephants" were a dominant force in the American League twice during his tenure. First, during the period between 1910 and 1914, they won four pennants and three World Series; this included his famous "$100,000 infield," which Mack later disbanded and traded away when pressed financially. Then, after years of frustration and rebuilding, the A's recorded back-to-back World Series championships in 1929 and 1930. Mack built this team around Mickey Cochrane, Jimmy Foxx, Jimmy Dykes, Al Simmons, and Lefty Grove. Mack's final record as a manager was 3,731-3,948—career records for games, wins, and losses.

◇ EARLE MACK

Earle Thaddeus
Nickname: McGillicuddy
Born: February 1, 1890
Birthplace: Philadelphia, Pennsylvania
Died: February 5, 1967
Bats: Left   **Throws:** Right
Height: 5'8"   **Weight:** 140
Played for: Philadelphia (AL): 1910-11, 1914
Coaching Experience: Philadelphia (AL): 1924-50

Earle was the first big-league son to play for his father. He also spent 26 years as a coach for his father. In Connie Mack's autobiography, *My 66 Years in the Big Leagues*, Mack proclaimed that, as a player, Earle "never embarrassed" him. In that same book, one finds a picture of all the Mack sons, as well as one captioned to explain that in his later years Connie refused to allow Earle to continue his third-base coaching job because "he was getting up in years." As a manager, Earle compiled a 45-77 record.

RECORDS

Connie Mack (11 years)

G	AB	R	H	2B	3B	HR	RBI	BB	SO	SB	BA	SA
723	2,695	391	659	79	28	5	265	169	127	127	.245	.300

Earle Mack (3 years)

G	AB	R	H	2B	3B	HR	RBI	BB	SO	SB	BA	SA
5	16	0	2	0	1	0	1	0	*	1	.125	.250

* Not available

Cards

Connie Mack
1887-90 Old Judge   1914 Cracker Jack   1915 Cracker Jack   1940PB—#132   1951TCMAS   1960F—#14
1961F—#123

Earle Mack
None

◆ HARL MAGGERT

Harl Vestin
Born: February 13, 1883
Birthplace: Cromwell, Indiana
Died: January 7, 1963
Bats: Left   **Throws:** Right
Height: 5′8″   **Weight:** 155
Played for: Pittsburgh: 1907; Philadelphia (AL): 1912

Harl was an outfielder who appeared in two more games in 1907 after his September 4th debut. He appeared in 61 games in 1912.

◇ HARL MAGGERT

Harl Warren
Born: May 4, 1914
Birthplace: Los Angeles, California
Died: July 10, 1986
Bats: Right   **Throws:** Right
Height: 6′   **Weight:** 190
Played for: Boston (NL): 1938

Harl was an outfielder and third baseman who first appeared on April 19, 1938.

RECORDS												

Harl Maggert (2 years)

G	AB	R	H	2B	3B	HR	RBI	BB	SO	SB	BA	SA
77	248	40	62	8	6	1	13	38	*	11	.250	.343

* Not available

Harl Maggert

G	AB	R	H	2B	3B	HR	RBI	BB	SO	SB	BA	SA
66	89	12	25	3	0	3	19	10	20	0	.281	.416

Cards
None

◆ CHARLIE MALAY

Charles Francis
Born: June 13, 1879
Birthplace: Brooklyn, New York
Died: September 18, 1949
Bats: Switch   **Throws:** Right
Height: 5'11"   **Weight:** 175
Played for: Brooklyn: 1905

In his only major league season, Charlie cracked the regular lineup, playing 75 games at second base, 25 in the outfield, and 1 at first base for the Brooklyn Superbas.

◇ JOE MALAY

Joseph Charles
Born: October 25, 1905
Birthplace: Brooklyn, New York
Died: March 19, 1989
Bats: Left   **Throws:** Left
Height: 6'   **Weight:** 175
Played for: New York (NL): 1933, 1935

Eight of Joe's nine big league appearances came as a first baseman for the 1933 pennant-winning New York Giants. He did not appear in any of the World Series games.

RECORDS

Charlie Malay

G	AB	R	H	2B	3B	HR	RBI	BB	SO	SB	BA	SA
102	349	33	88	7	2	1	31	22	*	13	.252	.292

* Not available

Joe Malay (2 years)

G	AB	R	H	2B	3B	HR	RBI	BB	SO	SB	BA	SA
9	25	0	4	0	0	0	2	0	0	0	.160	.160

Cards

None

◆ **BARNEY MARTIN**

Barnes Robertson
Born: March 3, 1923
Birthplace: Columbia, South Carolina
Bats: Right   **Throws:** Right
Height: 5'11"   **Weight:** 170
Played for: Cincinnati: 1953

Barney's only major league outing was on April 22, 1953.

◇ **JERRY MARTIN**

Jerry Lindsey
Born: May 11, 1949
Birthplace: Columbia, South Carolina
Bats: Right   **Throws:** Right
Height: 6'1"   **Weight:** 195
Played for: Philadelphia (NL): 1974-78; Chicago (NL): 1979-80; San Francisco: 1981; Kansas City: 1982-83; New York (NL): 1984

Jerry made his career as a platoon outfielder, pinch hitter, and late-inning defensive replacement. He played on three division winners while at Philadelphia.

RECORDS													

Barney Martin

W	L	Pct.	Sv.	G	GS	CG	IP	H	BB	SO	ShO	ERA
0	0	NA	0	1	0	0	2	3	1	1	0	9.00

Jerry Martin (11 years)

G	AB	R	H	2B	3B	HR	RBI	BB	SO	SB	BA	SA
1,018	2,652	337	666	130	17	85	345	207	574	38	.251	.409

Cards

Barney Martin
None

Jerry Martin

1976SS—#475	1977T—#596	1978T—#222	1979T—#382	1980T—#493	1981D—#555
1981F—#295	1981T—#103	1981T—#798	1982D—#298	1982F—#394	1982T—#722
1982TT—#65	1983D—#138	1983F—#117	1983T—#626	1984T—#74	1984FU—#74
1984TT—#74	1985T—#517				

◆ WALLY MATTICK

Walter Joseph
Nickname: Chick
Born: March 12, 1887
Birthplace: St. Louis, Missouri
Died: November 5, 1968
Bats: Right   **Throws:** Right
Height: 5'10"   **Weight:** 180
Played for: Chicago (AL): 1912-13; St. Louis (NL): 1918

Chick played 78 games in the outfield in 1912 and was considered one of the White Sox regulars in 1913, when he logged 63 outfield games. (Some sources record his nickname as "Chink.")

◇ BOBBY MATTICK

Robert James
Born: December 5, 1915
Birthplace: Sioux City, Iowa
Bats: Right   **Throws:** Right
Height: 5'11"   **Weight:** 178
Played for: Chicago (NL): 1938-40; Cincinnati: 1941-42
Coaching Experience: Toronto: 1980-81 (Manager)

Bobby played one game at short for the 1938 pennant-winning Cubs. He became a regular in 1940, playing 126 games at shortstop. However, it appears that his light hitting may have kept him out of the regular lineup. At present, he is a vice-president in the Toronto Blue Jays organization.

RECORDS

Wally Mattick (3 years)

G	AB	R	H	2B	3B	HR	RBI	BB	SO	SB	BA	SA
169	506	60	115	15	10	1	47	47	19	18	.227	.302

Bobby Mattick (5 years)

G	AB	R	H	2B	3B	HR	RBI	BB	SO	SB	BA	SA
206	690	54	161	31	1	0	64	33	60	7	.233	.281

Cards

None

◆ DAVE MAY

David La France
Nickname: Daisy
Born: December 23, 1943
Birthplace: New Castle, Delaware
Bats: Left   **Throws:** Right
Height: 5'10"   **Weight:** 186
Played for: Baltimore: 1967-70; Milwaukee (AL): 1970-74; Atlanta: 1975-76; Texas: 1977; Milwaukee (AL): 1978; Pittsburgh: 1978

Dave registered an unsuccessful pinch-hit appearance during the 1969 ALCS and again during Baltimore's futile Series with the "Miracle Mets." After the Mets traded Dave to Milwaukee, the Brewers inserted him into their regular lineup. Dave enjoyed a career year in 1973, hitting .303 in 624 at-bats, with 25 homers and 93 RBIs. However, Dave's main claim to baseball fame came November 2, 1974 when the Brewers traded him to Atlanta for none other than baseball legend Hammerin' Hank Aaron. He spent his career as an outfielder and sometimes designated hitter.

◇ DERRICK MAY

Derrick Brant
Born: July 14, 1968
Birthplace: Rochester, New York
Bats: Left   **Throws:** Right
Height: 6'4"   **Weight:** 210
Played for: Chicago (NL): 1990-91

The Cubs' first-round draft in the June 1986 draft, Derrick moved up steadily through their system and received his first exposure to major league pitching in 1990.

RECORDS

Dave May (12 years)

G	AB	R	H	2B	3B	HR	RBI	BB	SO	SB	BA	SA
1,253	3,670	462	920	130	20	96	422	344	501	60	.251	.375

Derrick May

	G	AB	R	H	2B	3B	HR	RBI	BB	SO	SB	BA	SA
1990	17	61	8	15	3	0	1	11	2	7	1	.246	.344
1991	15	22	4	5	2	0	1	3	2	1	0	.227	.455

Cards

Dave May
1968T—#56R	1969T—#113	1970T—#081	1971T—#493	1972T—#549	1973T—#152
1974T—#012	1975T—#650	1976T—#281	1978T—#362		

Derrick May
1990F—#645	1990UD—#736	1991DRR—#36	1991F—#427	1991S—#379	1991T—#288
1991UD—#334					

◆ PINKY MAY

Merrill Glend
Born: January 18, 1911
Birthplace: Laconia, Indiana
Bats: Right   **Throws:** Right
Height: 5'11"   **Weight:** 165
Played for: Philadelphia (NL): 1939-43; Military Service in 1944-45
Honors: National League All-Star in 1940.

Merrill cracked the starting nine as a rookie. Playing third for a last-place team, Pinky hit .293 in 1940. Military service during World War II cut short a promising career.

◇ MILT MAY

Milton Scott
Born: August 1, 1950
Birthplace: Gary, Indiana
Bats: Left   **Throws:** Right
Height: 6'   **Weight:** 190
Played for: Pittsburgh: 1970-73; Houston: 1974-75; Detroit: 1976-79; Chicago (AL): 1979; San Francisco: 1980-83; Pittsburgh: 1983-84
Coaching Experience: Pittsburgh: 1987-88

Milt appeared twice as a pinch hitter in the 1971 World Series, getting a hit and an RBI. He duplicated those stats in the 1972 National League Championship Series. When Milt went over to Houston, he became their starting catcher and hit .289 in 127 games. A broken ankle limited his playing time in 1976, but he bounced back to become the Tigers' starting catcher the next year. Milt hit .310 in 97 games for the 1981 Giants.

RECORDS

Pinky May (5 years)

G	AB	R	H	2B	3B	HR	RBI	BB	SO	SB	BA	SA
665	2,215	210	610	102	11	4	215	261	121	13	.275	.337

Milt May (15 years)

G	AB	R	H	2B	3B	HR	RBI	BB	SO	SB	BA	SA
1,192	3,693	313	971	147	11	77	443	305	361	4	.263	.371

Cards

Pinkie May

1939PB—#45	1940PB—#98	1941PB—#9	1941DP—#46

Milt May

1971T—#343R	1972T—#247	1973T—#529	1974T—#293	1975T—#279	1976T—#532
1976TT—#532	1976SS—#53	1977T—#98	1978T—#176	1979T—#316	1980T—#708
1981D—#193	1981F—#442	1981T—#463	1982D—#503	1982F—#395	1982T—#242
1982T—#576SP	1983D—#312	1983F—#268	1983T—#84	1984D—#386	1984F—#254
1984T—#788	1985D—#410	1985T—#509			

◆ HAL MCRAE

Harold Abraham
Born: July 10, 1945
Birthplace: Avon Park, Florida
Bats: Right   **Throws:** Right
Height: 5'11"   **Weight:** 180
Played for: Cincinnati: 1968, 1970-72; Kansas City: 1973-87

Hal McRae came up through the Cincinnati organization and made his debut as a second baseman during the 1968 season. He converted to the outfield and came back up in 1970. Hal contributed to the Reds' 1972 NL championship season with pinch hitting and occasional starts, and hit 4 for 9 in the World Series. In 1973, two events coincided to reshape baseball and Hal's career. The American League adopted the Designated Hitter rule, and the Reds traded Hal to Kansas City. From that point until his retirement, Hal helped define the role of the DH. He recorded six .300+ seasons and two others within three percentage points of .300. McRae followed each game intently. He developed and advocated the belief that the DH needed to keep himself mentally in the game, not merely taking his chances at the plate.

◇ BRIAN MCRAE

Brian Wesley
Born: May 29, 1967
Birthplace: Bradenton, Florida
Bats: Switch   **Throws:** Right
Height: 6'   **Weight:** 175
Played for: Kansas City: 1990-91

Kansas City brought Brian up for 46 games in 1990. The young outfielder responded with a .286 average, .405 slugging percentage, and .322 on-base percentage.

RECORDS												

Hal McRae (19 years)

G	AB	R	H	2B	3B	HR	RBI	BB	SO	SB	BA	SA
2,084	7,218	940	2,091	484	66	191	1,097	648	779	109	.290	.454

Brian McRae

G	AB	R	H	2B	3B	HR	RBI	BB	SO	SB	BA	SA
1990												
46	168	21	48	8	3	2	23	4	29	9	.286	.405
1991												
152	629	86	164	28	9	8	64	24	99	20	.261	.372

Cards

Hal McRae

1968T—#384	1970T—#683	1971T—#177	1972T—#291	1972T—#292	1973T—#28
1974T—#563	1975T—#268	1976T—#72	1977T—#340	1978T—#465	1979T—#585
1980T—#185	1981D—#463	1981F—#41	1981T—#295	1982D—#196	1982F—#416
1982T—#625	1983D—#238	1983F—#119	1983T—#25	1983T—#703SP	1984D—#11
1984D—#297	1984F—#350	1984T—#340	1984T—#96SP	1985D—#588	1985F—#207
1985T—#773	1986D—#521	1986F—#14	1986T—#415	1986T—#606	1987D—#471
1987F—#375	1987T—#573				

Brian McRae

1991D—#575	1991F—#563	1991S—#331	1991T—#222	1991UD—#543

◆ FRANK MEINKE

Frank Louis
Born: October 18, 1863
Birthplace: Chicago, Illinois
Died: November 8, 1931
Bats: Unavailable   **Throws:** Unavailable
Height: 5'10"   **Weight:** 172
Played for: Detroit (NL): 1884, 1885

Frank displayed plenty of versatility, playing second, third, shortstop, and the outfield, and even pitching for the Detroit Wolverines, a club that folded after the 1888 season.

◇ BOB MEINKE

Robert Bernard
Born: June 25, 1887
Birthplace: Chicago, Illinois
Died: December 29, 1952
Bats: Right   **Throws:** Right
Height: 5'10"   **Weight:** 135
Played for: Cincinnati: 1910

Bob's debut came on August 22, 1910. He was a shortstop.

RECORDS

Frank Meinke (2 years)

G	AB	R	H	2B	3B	HR	RBI	BB	SO	SB	BA	SA
93	344	28	56	5	7	6	24	6	90	0	.163	.270

Bob Meinke

G	AB	R	H	2B	3B	HR	RBI	BB	SO	SB	BA	SA
2	1	0	0	0	0	0	0	1	0	0	.000	.000

Cards

None

◆ WILLIE MILLS

William Grant
Nickname: Wee Willie
Born: August 15, 1877
Birthplace: Schenevus, New York
Died: July 5, 1914
Bats: Right   **Throws:** Right
Height: 5'7"   **Weight:** 150
Played for: New York (NL): 1901

Wee Willie and Art became the first father-son combination to both pitch in the major leagues. Willie's first game was on July 13, 1901.

◇ ART MILLS

Arthur Grant
Born: March 2, 1903
Born: Utica, New York
Died: July 23, 1975
Bats: Right   **Throws:** Right
Height: 5'10"   **Weight:** 155
Played for: Boston (NL): 1927-28
Coaching Experience: Detroit: 1944-48

Art's first game for Boston was on April 16, 1927. During a season when the hapless Braves went 60-94 and finished 34 games off the pace, Art appeared in 15 games.

RECORDS												

Willie Mills

W	L	Pct.	Sv.	G	GS	CG	IP	H	BB	SO	ShO	ERA
0	2	.000	0	2	2	2	16	21	4	3	0	8.44

Art Mills (2 years)

W	L	Pct.	Sv.	G	GS	CG	IP	H	BB	SO	ShO	ERA
0	1	.000	0	19	1	0	46	58	26	7	0	5.36

Cards
None

◆ RENE MONTEAGUDO

Born: March 12, 1916
Birthplace: Havana, Cuba
Died: September 14, 1973
Bats: Left   **Throws:** Left
Height: 5'7"   **Weight:** 165
Played for: Washington (AL): 1938, 1940; Philadelphia (NL): 1945

Rene pitched and played the outfield for the Senators.

◇ AURELIO MONTEAGUDO

Aurelio Faustinu
Born: November 19, 1943
Birthplace: Caibarien, Cuba
Bats: Right   **Throws:** Right
Height: 6'2"   **Weight:** 213

Played for: Kansas City: 1963-66; Houston: 1966; Chicago (AL): 1967; Kansas City: 1970; California: 1973

Aurelio left Cuba just four days before the Bay of Pigs invasion. He arrived in the U.S. with $5 in his pocket and the clothes on his back, but bearing a contract from the Kansas City organization. They sent him to the Albuquerque Dukes, then a Class D team, but he made it to the majors just two years later. In 1974, he went to the Mexican League, where he pitched until 1980, compiling a 101-71 record. He later managed in the Mexican League and worked as a pitching coach in the Venezuelan League from 1976 to the present. (See *Baseball America*, May 25, 1990.) Take a peek at their records, then try to imagine family arguments about whose career was better.

RECORDS

Rene Monteagudo (3 years)

W	L	Pct.	Sv.	G	GS	CG	IP	H	BB	SO	ShO	ERA
3	7	.300	2	46	11	5	169	221	95	93	0	6.39

Aurelio Monteagudo (7 years)

W	L	Pct.	Sv.	G	GS	CG	IP	H	BB	SO	ShO	ERA
3	7	.300	4	72	7	0	132	122	62	58	0	5.08

Cards

Rene Monteagudo
None

Aurelio Monteagudo
1964T—#466   1965T—#286   1966T—#532   1967T—#453   1971T—#129   1972T—#458
1974T—#139   1974TT—#139

◆ GENE MOORE, SR.

Eugene
Nickname: Blue Goose
Born: November 9, 1885
Birthplace: Lancaster, Texas
Died: August 31, 1938
Bats: Left   **Throws:** Left
Height: 6′2″   **Weight:** 185
Played for: Pittsburgh: 1909-10; Cincinnati: 1912

The Blue Goose first flew into action sometime during the 1909 season, but got his wings clipped in his only appearance that season. In two innings of work, he struck out two, but walked three and gave up four hits, resulting in an astronomical ERA of 18.00. He put together a 2-1 mark in 1910 and evened up his career stats with a loss for the Reds in 1912.

◇ GENE MOORE, JR.

Eugene
Nickname: Rowdy

Born: August 26, 1909
Birthplace: Lancaster, Texas
Died: March 12, 1978
Bats: Left   **Throws:** Left
Height: 5′11″   **Weight:** 175
Played for: Cincinnati: 1931; St. Louis (NL): 1933-35; Boston (NL): 1936-38; Brooklyn (NL): 1939-40; Boston (NL): 1940-41; Washington (AL): 1942-43; St. Louis (AL): 1944-45

Gene got into just three games in the outfield for the famous 1934 Cardinals and did not appear in post-season play. He became a regular when he went over to Boston (1936) and compiled a .290 average, playing 151 games for the Braves. A knee injury limited Gene's action to 54 games during 1938, but he was back in the regular lineup the next season for Brooklyn. After he was traded back to Boston, he hit .292 in 94 games. In the only all-St. Louis World Series (1944), Gene played outfield all six games, but batted a disappointing .182.

RECORDS

Gene Moore, Sr. (3 years)

W	L	Pct.	Sv.	G	GS	CG	IP	H	BB	SO	ShO	ERA
2	2	.500	1	10	3	0	34	40	21	17	0	4.76

Gene Moore, Jr. (14 years)

G	AB	R	H	2B	3B	HR	RBI	BB	SO	SB	BA	SA
1,042	3,543	497	958	179	53	58	436	317	401	31	.270	.400

Cards

Gene Moore, Sr.
None

Gene Moore, Jr.
1939PB—#160   1940PB—#143   1941PB—#25   1941DP—#37   1941DP—#122

◆ GUY MORTON, SR.

Nickname: The Alabama Blossom
Born: June 1, 1893
Birthplace: Vernon, Alabama
Died: October 18, 1934
Bats: Right **Throws:** Right
Height: 6'1" **Weight:** 175
Played for: Cleveland (AL): 1912-24

Despite a respectable 3.02 ERA, Guy's rookie season resulted in a 1-13 record. He never had another losing season until his final year in baseball, when he went 0-1. A leg injury hampered The Alabama Blossom in 1916, but he managed a 12-6 record. Military service shortened his 1918 campaign, but he was still 14-8. He posted an 8-6 record during the Indians' 1920 American League championship, but he did not appear in the World Series.

◇ GUY MORTON, JR.

Nickname: Moose
Born: November 4, 1930
Birthplace: Tuscaloosa, Alabama
Bats: Right **Throws:** Right
Height: 6'2" **Weight:** 200
Played for: Boston (AL): 1954

Moose's only appearance came on September 17, 1954. He struck out.

RECORDS												

Guy Morton, Sr. (11 years)

W	L	Pct.	Sv.	G	GS	CG	IP	H	BB	SO	ShO	ERA
98	88	.527	6	317	185	82	1,629	1,520	583	830	20	3.13

Guy Morton, Jr.

G	AB	R	H	2B	3B	HR	RBI	BB	SO	SB	BA	SA
1	1	0	0	0	0	0	0	0	1	0	.000	.000

Cards
None

◆ MANNY MOTA

Manuel Rafael
Born: February 18, 1938
Birthplace: Santo Domingo, Dominican Republic
Bats: Right   **Throws:** Right
Height: 5'10"   **Weight:** 160
Played for: San Francisco: 1962; Pittsburgh: 1963-68; Montreal: 1969; Los Angeles: 1969-80, 1982
Coaching Experience: Los Angeles: 1980-89

Manny broke in with the 1962 Giants and contributed to their pennant with games in the outfield and at second and third. He didn't appear in any of the 1962 World Series games, but if the Giants had known the future, they might have employed him as a pinch hitter in that tight Series. Over the course of 20 major league seasons, Manny banged out 150 pinch hits, the current major league record. Manny's .297 pinch-hit average places him eighth on the all-time list. He retired to the coaching box in 1980, but stepped up to the plate one last time in 1982 at the age of 44. Two Motas — Andy and Jose—recorded games in the majors during 1991, and two others were in the minors; three other sons are still too young to sign. Thus stories with titles like *Baseball America's* "Manny Mota's Many Motas."

◇ ANDY MOTA

Andreas
Born: March 4, 1966
Birthplace: Santo Domingo, Dominican Republic
Bats: Right   **Throws:** Right
Height: 5'10"   **Weight:** 180
Played for: Houston: 1991

Andy won two minor league batting titles but struggled with major league pitching. The 1992 season will be crucial for the 26 year old to prove he belongs. He plays second base.

◇ JOSE MOTA

Born: March 16, 1965
Birthplace: Santo Domingo, Dominican Republic
Bats: Right   **Throws:** Right
Height: 5'9"   **Weight:** 155
Played for: San Diego: 1991

The Padres tried Manny's oldest son at second base in 1991, and he should be competing for the job in 1992. Jose has kicked around the minors for several years, recording time with the Pirates, Dodgers, and Indians organizations. If he doesn't make the team as a starter, he has a chance to win a spot on the bench.

RECORDS

Manny Mota

G	AB	R	H	2B	3B	HR	RBI	BB	SO	SB	BA	SA
1,536	3,779	496	1,149	125	52	31	438	289	320	50	.304	.389

Andy Mota

G	AB	R	H	2B	3B	HR	RBI	BB	SO	SB	BA	SA
1991												
27	90	4	17	2	0	1	6	1	17	2	.189	.250

Jose Mota

G	AB	R	H	2B	3B	HR	RBI	BB	SO	SB	BA	SA
1991												
17	36	4	8	0	0	0	2	2	7	0	.222	.230

Cards

Manny Mota

1963T—#141	1964T—#246	1965T—#463	1966T—#112	1967T—#66	1968T—#325
1969T—#236	1970T—#157	1971T—#112	1972T—#596	1973T—#412	1974T—#368
1975T—#414	1976T—#548	1977T—#386	1978T—#228	1979T—#644	1980T—#3
1980T—#104	1981D—#299	1981F—#141			

Andy Mota
None (as of 1991)

Jose Mota
None (as of 1991)

◆ WALTER MUELLER

Walter John
Born: December 6, 1894
Birthplace: Central, Missouri
Died: August 16, 1971
Bats: Right   **Throws:** Right
Height: 5'8"   **Weight:** 160
Played for: Pittsburgh: 1922-24, 1926

Walter hit .306 in 26 games as a Pittsburgh outfielder in 1923. Walter's brother Clarence (Heinie) played the outfield and first base between 1920-35, compiling a .282 career batting average and .389 slugging average.

◇ DON MUELLER

Donald Frederick
Nickname: Mandrake the Magician
Born: April 14, 1927
Birthplace: St Louis, Missouri

Bats: Left   **Throws:** Right
Height: 6'   **Weight:** 185
Played for: New York (NL): 1948-57; Chicago (AL): 1958-59
Honors: National League All-Star in 1954 and 1955.

During the 1951 National League play-off between the Brooklyn Dodgers and the New York Giants, Mueller injured his ankle sliding into third in the third game, but he rejoiced from his stretcher in the locker room when Bobby Thomson hit his famous home run. He was a heavy contributor to the Giants' success in 1954, when he hit .342 during the regular season and .389 in the Series. He led the league in hits that year, with 212. Don was one of baseball's toughest men to strike out; his at-bats per strikeout ratio is 29.9, 11th on the all-time career list. He recorded a .280 career average as a pinch hitter, good enough to place him 17th on the all-time list.

RECORDS

Walter Mueller (4 years)

G	AB	R	H	2B	3B	HR	RBI	BB	SO	SB	BA	SA
121	345	46	95	10	7	2	49	13	19	4	.275	.362

Don Mueller (12 years)

G	AB	R	H	2B	3B	HR	RBI	BB	SO	SB	BA	SA
1,245	4,364	499	1,292	139	37	65	520	167	146	11	.296	.390

Cards

Walter Mueller
None

Don Mueller

1950B—#221	1951B—#268	1952B—#18	1952T—#52	1953B—#74	1954B—#73
1954T—#42	1956T—#241	1957T—#148	1958T—#253	1959T—#368	

◆ BILL NARLESKI

William Edward
Nickname: Cap
Born: June 9, 1899
Birthplace: Perth Amboy, New Jersey
Died: July 22, 1964
Bats: Right   **Throws:** Right
Height: 5'9"   **Weight:** 160
Played for: Boston (AL): 1929-30

Bill was a utility infielder, playing second, shortstop, and third in 96 games as a 30-year-old rookie. Bill's two seasons with the Red Sox came at the tail end of nearly a decade of futility for this once-proud franchise. From 1922 until 1930, Boston finished dead last eight times and seventh once. In 1929, they finished 59-96, 48 games out of first; the succeeding season saw them fall to 52-102, a full half century (50 games) off the pace.

◇ RAY NARLESKI

Raymond Edmund
Born: November 25, 1928
Birthplace: Parma Heights, Ohio
Bats: Right   **Throws:** Right
Height: 6'1"   **Weight:** 175
Played for: Cleveland (AL): 1954-58; Detroit: 1959
Honors: American League All-Star in 1958

Ray saw action in two World Series games during his rookie year. Ray came into the game at a time when the idea of the "relief ace" was coming into its own, and the Cleveland bullpen (with Ray and Don Mossi) was one reason. In 1955, he led the American League in saves (19) and appearances (60). An elbow injury slowed him down in 1956, but he bounced back with an 11-5 mark and 16 saves in 1957. The Indians gave Ray 24 starts in 1958. In 1959, he went to Detroit and rejoined former teammate Mossi, as well as baseball sons Dave Sisler and George Susce.

RECORDS

Bill Narleski (2 years)

G	AB	R	H	2B	3B	HR	RBI	BB	SO	SB	BA	SA
135	358	41	95	25	1	0	32	28	27	4	.265	.341

Ray Narleski (6 years)

W	L	Pct.	Sv.	G	GS	CG	IP	H	BB	SO	ShO	ERA
43	33	.566	58	266	52	17	702	606	335	454	1	3.60

Cards

Bill Narleski
None

Ray Narleski

1955T—#160	1955B—#96	1956T—#133	1957T—#144	1958T—#439	1959T—#442
1960T—#161					

◆ JULIO NAVARRO

Ventura
Nickname: Whiplash
Born: January 9, 1936
Birthplace: Vieques, Puerto Rico
Bats: Right   **Throws:** Right
Height: 6'   **Weight:** 175
Played for: Los Angeles (AL): 1962-64; Detroit: 1964-66; Atlanta: 1970

The Topps company issued Julio's rookie card two years prior to his actual major league debut. He appeared on a 1960 "Rookie Star" card, but didn't actually pitch in the big leagues until

September 3, 1962, when he pitched for the Los Angeles Angels.

◇ JAIME NAVARRO

Born: March 27, 1967
Birthplace: Baymon, Puerto Rico
Bats: Right   **Throws:** Right
Height: 6'4"   **Weight:** 210
Played for: Milwaukee (AL): 1989-91

Jaime joined the Brewers' staff after less than two seasons of minor league ball. He throws a 90-mile-an-hour fastball and a slider.

RECORDS

Julio Navarro (6 years)

	W	L	Pct.	Sv.	G	GS	CG	IP	H	BB	SO	ShO	ERA
	7	9	.438	17	130	1	0	212	191	70	151	0	3.65

Jaime Navarro

	W	L	Pct.	Sv.	G	GS	CG	IP	H	BB	SO	ShO	ERA
1989	7	8	.467	0	19	17	1	110	119	32	56	0	3.12
1990	8	7	.533	1	32	22	3	149	176	41	75	0	4.46
1991	15	12	.556	0	34	34	10	234	237	73	114	2	3.92

Cards

Julio Navarro
1960T—#140   1963T—#169   1964T—#489   1965T—#563   1966T—#527

Jaime Navarro
1990F—#331   1990S—#569   1990UD—#646   1991D—#216   1991F—#592   1991S—#102
1991T—#548   1991UD—#476

◆ CHET NICHOLS, SR.

Chester Raymond
Born: July 2, 1897
Birthplace: Woonsocket, Rhode Island
Died: July 11, 1982
Bats: Right   **Throws:** Right
Height: 5'11"   **Weight:** 160
Played for: Pittsburgh: 1926-27; New York (NL): 1928; Philadelphia (NL): 1930-32

Chet posted an 0-3 record during Pittsburgh's 1927 pennant-winning season. He was a hold-out during the 1930 season, but he still saw action in 16 games.

◇ CHET NICHOLS, JR.

Chester Raymond
Born: February 22, 1931

Birthplace: Providence, Rhode Island
Bats: Switch   **Throws:** Left
Height: 6'1"   **Weight:** 180
Played for: Boston (NL): 1951; Military Service in 1952-53; Milwaukee (NL): 1954-56; Boston (AL): 1960-63; Cincinnati: 1964

As a 20-year-old rookie, Chet pitched his way to an 11-8 record for a Braves team that went 76-78. He also posted a 2.88 ERA, good enough to lead the National League, ahead of such pitching giants as Sal Maglie, Warren Spahn, and Robin Roberts. Despite this, he disappeared from the major leagues until 1954, and although he stayed around until 1964, he never again recaptured the form he demonstrated during his rookie year. A broken bone in his hand hampered him in 1961, but he still managed a 3-2 record with three saves in 26 games.

RECORDS

Chet Nichols, Sr. (6 years)

W	L	Pct.	Sv.	G	GS	CG	IP	H	BB	SO	ShO	ERA
1	8	.111	1	44	5	1	123	167	56	33	0	7.19

Chet Nichols, Jr. (9 years)

W	L	Pct.	Sv.	G	GS	CG	IP	H	BB	SO	ShO	ERA
34	36	.486	10	189	71	23	604	600	280	266	4	3.64

Cards

Chet Nichols, Sr.
None

Chet Nichols, Jr.

1952T—#288	1952B—#120	1955B—#72	1956T—#278	1961T—#301	1962T—#403
1963T—#307					

◆ RON NORTHEY

Ronald James
Nickname: The Round Man
Born: April 26, 1920
Birthplace: Mahoney City, Pennsylvania
Died: April 16, 1971
Bats: Left   **Throws:** Right
Height: 5'10"   **Weight:** 195
Played for: Philadelphia (NL): 1942-44; Military Service in 1945; Philadelphia (NL): 1946-47; St. Louis (NL): 1947-49; Cincinnati: 1950; Chicago (NL): 1950, 1952; Chicago (AL): 1955-57; Philadelphia (NL): 1957
Coaching Experience: Pittsburgh: 1961-63

Ron posted a .291 mark during 94 games as an outfielder for the 1947 Cardinals. However,

Ron's pinch-hitting abilities were mainly what kept him in the majors so long. His .276 career pinch-hitting average is 24th on the all-time list. He hammered eight career grand slams. Today, The Round Man would probably have been a full-time DH.

◇ SCOTT NORTHEY

Scott Richard
Born: October 15, 1946
Birthplace: Philadelphia, Pennsylvania
Bats: Right   **Throws:** Right
Height: 6'   **Weight:** 175
Played for: Kansas City: 1969

Scott was an outfielder.

RECORDS												

Ron Northey (12 years)

G	AB	R	H	2B	3B	HR	RBI	BB	SO	SB	BA	SA
1,084	3,172	385	874	172	28	108	513	361	297	7	.276	.450

Scott Northey

G	AB	R	H	2B	3B	HR	RBI	BB	SO	SB	BA	SA
20	61	11	16	2	2	1	7	7	19	6	.262	.410

Cards

Ron Northey
1949B—#79   1950B—#81   1951B—#70   1952T—#204   1957T—#31

Scott Northey
1970T—#241R   1971T—#633R

◆ FRANK OKRIE

Frank Anthony
Nickname: Lefty
Born: October 28, 1896
Birthplace: Detroit, Michigan
Died: October 16, 1959
Bats: Left   **Throws:** Left
Height: 5'11"   **Weight:** 175
Played for: Detroit: 1920

Lefty made his pro debut on April 20, 1920.

◇ LEN OKRIE

Leonard Joseph
Born: July 16, 1923
Birthplace: Detroit, Michigan
Bats: Right   **Throws:** Right
Height: 6'1"   **Weight:** 185
Played for: Washington (AL): 1948, 1950-51; Boston (AL): 1952
Coaching Experience: Boston (AL): 1961-62, 1965-66; Detroit: 1970.

Len was a catcher.

RECORDS

Frank Okrie

W	L	Pct.	Sv.	G	GS	CG	IP	H	BB	SO	ShO	ERA
1	2	.333	0	21	1	1	41	44	18	9	0	5.27

Len Okrie (4 years)

G	AB	R	H	2B	3B	HR	RBI	BB	SO	SB	BA	SA
42	78	3	17	1	1	0	3	9	16	0	.218	.256

Cards
None

◆ JIM O'ROURKE

James Henry
Nickname: Orator Jim
Born: August 24, 1852
Birthplace: Bridgeport, Connecticut
Died: January 8, 1919
Bats: Right   **Throws:** Right
Height: 5'8"   **Weight:** 185
Played for: Boston (NL): 1876-78; Providence (NL): 1879; Boston (NL): 1880; Buffalo (NL): 1881-84; New York (NL): 1885-89; New York (Players Association): 1890; New York (NL): 1891-92; Washington (NL): 1893; New York (NL): 1904
Coaching Experience: Buffalo (NL): 1881-84 (Player/Manager); Washington (NL): 1893 (Player/Manager)
Hall of Fame: Elected in 1945, by the Committee on Old-Timers

A graduate of Yale Law School, Orator Jim earned his nickname with his speech-making ability. Orator Jim was a true baseball pioneer, recording the first hit ever in the National League. O'Rourke batted over .300 11 times and his RBI total places him fifth in the 1876-92 era. His batting average is eighth for that period. In 1904, at the age of 52 years and 29 days, Jim caught a complete game. O'Rourke managed Buffalo (NL) from 1881 to 1884 and Washington (NL) in 1893. His record as a manager is 246-258. O'Rourke also worked as an umpire and was a minor league president. Jim's brother John also played.

◇ QUEENIE O'ROURKE

James Stephen
Born: December 26, 1883
Birthplace: Bridgeport, Connecticut
Died: December 22, 1955
Bats: Right   **Throws:** Right
Height: 5'7"   **Weight:** 160
Played for: New York (AL): 1908

Queenie played 14 games in the outfield, 11 at shortstop, 4 at second, and 3 at third.

RECORDS												

Jim O'Rourke (19 years)

G	AB	R	H	2B	3B	HR	RBI	BB	SO	SB	BA	SA
1,762	7,368	1,439	2,300	385	139	51	1,010	481	349	211*	.312	.423

* From 1886-1904; stolen bases weren't recorded 1872-85.

Queenie O'Rourke

G	AB	R	H	2B	3B	HR	RBI	BB	SO	SB	BA	SA
34	108	5	25	1	0	0	3	4	*	4	.231	.241

* Not available

Cards

Jim O'Rourke
Orator Jim appears on an Old Judge card and various Hall of Fame cards.

Queenie O'Rourke
None

◆ PATSY O'ROURKE

Joseph Leo, Sr.
Born: April 13, 1881
Birthplace: Philadelphia, Pennsylvania
Died: April 18, 1956
Bats: Right   **Throws:** Right
Height: 5'7"   **Weight:** 160
Played for: St. Louis (NL): 1908

St. Louis utilized eight players at shortstop during the 1908 season. Patsy's 53 games there made him the regular.

◇ JOE O'ROURKE

Joseph Leo, Jr.
Born: October 28, 1904
Birthplace: Philadelphia, Pennsylvania
Bats: Left   **Throws:** Right
Height: 5'7"   **Weight:** 145
Played for: Philadelphia (NL): 1929

The Phillies used Joe as a pinch hitter for the first time early in the 1929 season (April 19th). He got up two more times, both times as a pinch hitter, but never played so much as a third of an inning in the field and left baseball with one of the sorriest records in the books.

RECORDS

Patsy O'Rourke

G	AB	R	H	2B	3B	HR	RBI	BB	SO	SB	BA	SA
53	164	8	32	4	2	0	16	14	*	2	.195	.244

* Not available

Joe O'Rourke

G	AB	R	H	2B	3B	HR	RBI	BB	SO	SB	BA	SA
3	3	0	0	0	0	0	0	0	1	0	.000	.000

Cards

None

◆ TINY OSBORNE

Earnest Preston
Born: April 9, 1893
Birthplace: Porterdale, Georgia
Died: January 5, 1969
Bats: Left   **Throws:** Right
Height: 6'4"   **Weight:** 215
Played for: Chicago (NL): 1922-24; Brooklyn: 1924-25

As a 29-year-old rookie, Tiny showed promise with a 9-5 record. However, he slipped to 8-15 the following year. Tiny rallied for a 6-5 record after he was traded to Brooklyn, but he suffered another 8-15 mark his final season in the majors.

◇ BOBO OSBORNE

Lawrence Sidney
Born: October 12, 1935
Birthplace: Chattahoochie, Georgia
Bats: Left   **Throws:** Right
Height: 6'1"   **Weight:** 205
Played for: Detroit: 1957-59, 1961-62; Washington (AL): 1963

Bobo played first and third. The Osbornes might not have produced very distinguished baseball records, but you've got to love their nicknames, especially when you stop for a moment to contrast them with their given names, which sound really serious. Then ponder the significance of a 215-pound man called "Tiny" walking into a room.

RECORDS

Tiny Osborne (4 years)

W	L	Pct.	Sv.	G	GS	CG	IP	H	BB	SO	ShO	ERA
31	40	.437	6	142	74	31	646	693	315	263	2	4.72

Bobo Osborne (6 years)

G	AB	R	H	2B	3B	HR	RBI	BB	SO	SB	BA	SA
359	763	93	157	30	2	17	86	104	171	2	.206	.317

Cards

Tiny Osborne
None

Bobo Osborne

| 1959T—#524 | 1960T—#201 | 1961T—#208 | 1962T—#583 | 1963T—#514 |

◆ STEVE PARTENHEIMER

Harold Philip
Born: August 30, 1891
Birthplace: Greenfield, Massachusetts
Died: June 16, 1971
Bats: Right   **Throws:** Right
Height: 5'8"   **Weight:** 145
Played for: Detroit: 1913

Steve appeared on June 18, 1913. He played third base.

◇ STAN PARTENHEIMER

Stanwood Wendell
Nickname: Party
Born: October 21, 1922
Birthplace: Chicoppee Falls, Massachusetts
Died: January 28, 1989
Bats: Right   **Throws:** Left

Height: 5'11"   **Weight:** 175
Played for: Boston (AL): 1944; St. Louis (NL): 1945

Sometimes, a baseball player's record contains just enough information to provoke speculation. Stan's nickname, for example, was probably a play on his family name. But then again, was it the sort of nickname that also reflects a person's character? If so, one can't help but wonder if Stan's career might have been better served if he hadn't tried quite so hard to live up to his nickname. To be sure, baseball history is filled with party-hearty players, but you still can't give up 18 walks in 14 innings of work and expect to stay in the majors long. Then again, maybe Stan just realized his limitations all along and decided to make the best of it before everybody else discovered what he already knew ....

RECORDS												
Steve Partenheimer												
G	AB	R	H	2B	3B	HR	RBI	BB	SO	SB	BA	SA
1	2	0	0	0	0	0	0	0	0	0	.000	.000
Stan Partenheimer (2 years)												
W	L	Pct.	Sv.	G	GS	CG	IP	H	BB	SO	ShO	ERA
0	0	NA	0	9	3	0	14	15	18	6	0	7.07

Cards
None

◆ HERM PILLETTE

Herman Polycarp
Nickname: Old Folks
Born: December 26, 1895
Birthplace: St. Paul, Oregon
Died: April 30, 1960
Bats: Right   **Throws:** Right
Height: 6'2"   **Weight:** 190
Played for: Cincinnati: 1917; Detroit: 1922-24

Baseball historian Bill Deane projected Herm as the hypothetical 1922 American League Rookie of the Year. That year (1922), Herm compiled a 19-12 record with four shutouts and a 2.84 ERA. However, the following year, Herm led the league in losses with a 14-19 record. A sore arm ended Herm's career. Just how do you suppose he got that nickname, anyway?

◇ DUANE PILLETTE

Duane Xavier
Nickname: Dee
Born: July 24, 1922
Birthplace: Detroit, Michigan
Bats: Right   **Throws:** Right
Height: 6'3"   **Weight:** 195
Played for: New York (AL): 1949-50; St. Louis (AL): 1950-53; Baltimore: 1954-55; Philadelphia (NL): 1956

Duane never managed to put together a winning season. When he led the Ameican League with 14 losses in 1951, he achieved the dubious distinction of making the Pillettes the only father-son combination both to lead their league in losses.

RECORDS

Herm Pillette (4 years)

W	L	Pct.	Sv.	G	GS	CG	IP	H	BB	SO	ShO	ERA
34	32	.515	3	107	76	33	564	600	192	148	4	3.45

Duane Pillette (8 years)

W	L	Pct.	Sv.	G	GS	CG	IP	H	BB	SO	ShO	ERA
38	66	.365	2	188	119	34	904	985	391	305	4	4.40

Cards

Herm Pillette
None

Duane Pillette
1951B—#316   1952T—#82   1953T—#269   1953BBW—#59   1954T—#107   1954B—#133
1955T—#168   1955B—#244

◆ MEL QUEEN, SR.

Melvin Joseph
Born: March 14, 1918
Birthplace: Maxwell, Pennsylvania
Died: April 4, 1982
Bats: Right   **Throws:** Right
Height: 6'   **Weight:** 204
Played for: New York (AL): 1942, 1944; Military Service in 1945; New York (AL): 1946-47; Pittsburgh: 1947-52

When Mel was traded from New York to Pittsburgh, he went from a team that finished first to one that finished last.

◇ MEL QUEEN, JR.

Melvin Douglas
Born: March 26, 1942
Birthplace: Johnson City, New York
Bats: Left   **Throws:** Right
Height: 6'1"   **Weight:** 190
Played for: Cincinnati: 1966-69; California: 1970-72
Coaching Experience: Cleveland (AL): 1982; Toronto: 1990

During Mel's rookie season, he played 32 games in the outfield and appeared in seven as a pitcher. Concentrating on his pitching, he posted a 14-8 record as a starter in 1967. He suffered a shoulder injury in 1968.

RECORDS

Mel Queen, Sr. (8 years)

W	L	Pct.	Sv.	G	GS	CG	IP	H	BB	SO	ShO	ERA
27	40	.403	1	146	77	15	556	567	329	328	3	5.10

Mel Queen, Jr. (7 years)

W	L	Pct.	Sv.	G	GS	CG	IP	H	BB	SO	ShO	ERA
20	17	.541	14	140	33	6	390	336	143	306	2	3.14

As an Outfielder

G	AB	R	H	2B	3B	HR	RBI	BB	SO	SB	BA	SA
269	274	20	49	7	0	2	25	21	50	2	.179	.226

Cards

Mel Queen, Sr.
1951B—#309   1952B—#171

Mel Queen, Jr.
1964T—#33R   1966T—#556   1967T—#374   1968T—#283   1969T—#81   1971T—#736
1974T—#447M   1975T—#443M

◆ CAL RIPKEN, SR.

Calvin Edwin
Born: December 17, 1935
Birthplace: Aberdeen, Maryland
Bats: Unavailable   **Throws:** Unavailable
Height: 5'11"   **Weight:** 170
Coaching Experience: Baltimore: 1976-91 (Manager in 1987)

A minor league catcher, Cal never appeared in a major league game. He joined the Baltimore coaching staff in 1976 and managed in 1987. Cal was the first to manage two big league offspring.

◇ CAL RIPKEN, JR.

Calvin Edwin
Born: August 24, 1960
Birthplace: Havre de Grace, Maryland
Bats: Right   **Throws:** Right
Height: 6'4"   **Weight:** 215
Played for: Baltimore: 1981-91
Honors: AL Rookie-of-the-Year in 1982. Most Valuable Player in 1983. American League All-Star in 1983-89, 1991.

Cal followed an outstanding rookie season with an even more impressive sophomore campaign. He was named the American League MVP and led Baltimore to a World Series Championship. During this year, he led the AL in hits (211), doubles (47), and runs (121). He also hit .318 with 27 homers and 102 RBIs. In succeeding years, Cal established himself as a superstar and an iron man. During the 1990 season, he set the second-longest playing streak in baseball history when he played in his 1,308th consecutive game. During this time, he played in 12,888 out of a possible 12,930 innings (99.7 percent). Cal also established new major league records for play chances by a shortstop without an error.

◇ BILLY RIPKEN

William Oliver
Born: December 16, 1964
Birthplace: Havre de Grace, Maryland
Bats: Right   **Throws:** Right
Height: 6'1"   **Weight:** 180
Played for: Baltimore: 1987-91

Billy teams with Cal as the Oriole's double play combination. In 1989, collectors paid hundreds of dollars for one of his cards that had an obscenity printed on a bat he was holding. Billy possesses an above-average glove, but has proved inconsistent as a hitter. After leading the team in hitting in 1990 with a .291 average, he slipped to .216 in 1991.

RECORDS

Cal Ripken, Jr.

G	AB	R	H	2B	3B	HR	RBI	BB	SO	SB	BA	SA
1981-87												
992	3,834	626	1,084	211	23	160	570	394	494	14	.283	.475
1988												
161	575	87	152	25	1	23	81	102	69	2	.264	.431
1989												
162	646	80	166	30	0	21	93	57	72	3	.257	.401
1990												
161	600	78	150	28	4	21	84	82	66	3	.250	.415
1991												
162	650	99	210	46	5	34	114	53	46	6	.323	.566

Billy Ripken

G	AB	R	H	2B	3B	HR	RBI	BB	SO	SB	BA	SA
1987												
58	234	27	72	9	0	2	20	21	23	4	.308	.372
1988												
150	512	52	106	18	1	2	34	33	63	8	.207	.258
1989												
115	318	31	76	11	2	2	26	22	53	1	.239	.305
1990												
129	406	48	118	28	1	3	38	28	43	5	.291	.387
1991												
104	287	24	62	11	1	0	14	15	31	0	.216	.261

Cards

Cal Ripken, Sr.

1988D—#625	1988T—#444	1989B—#260

Cal Ripken, Jr.

1982D—#405	1982F—#176	1982T—#21	1982TT—#98	1983D—#279	1983F—#70
1983T—#163	1984D—#106	1984F—#17	1984T—#409	1984T—#426	1984T—#400
1985D—#14	1985D—#169	1985F—#187	1985F—#626	1985F—#641	1985T—#30
1985T—#704	1986D—#210	1986F—#284	1986F—#633	1986SPF—#8	1986SPF—#54
1986SPF—#57	1986SPF—#69	1986SPF—#73	1986SPF—#128	1986T—#715	1987D—#89
1987F—#478	1987SPF—#9	1987SPF—#113	1987T—#609	1987T—#784	1988D—#26
1988D—#171	1988D—#625	1988F—#570	1988F—#635	1988F—#640	1988S—#651
1988SPF—#152	1988T—#650	1989B—#9	1989B—#260	1989D—#51	1989F—#617
1989S—#15	1989SPF—#66	1989T—#250	1989UD—#467	1989UD—#682	1990D—#96
1990F—#187	1990S—#2	1990T—#8	1990T—#388	1990T—#570	1990UD—#266
1991D—#223	1991F—#490	1991S—#95	1991T—#150	1991UD—#347	

Billy Ripken

1988D—#336	1988D—#625	1988F—#569	1988F—#640	1988S—#200	1988SPF—#216
1988T—#216	1989B—#9	1989B—#260	1989D—#259	1989F—#616	1989S—#18
1989T—#571	1989UD—#283	1990D—#164	1990F—#186	1990S—#174	1990T—#468
1990UD—#184	1991D—#167	1991F—#489	1991S—#487	1991T—#677	1991UD—#550

◆ WALT RIPLEY

Walter Franklin
Born: November 26, 1916
Birthplace: Worcester, Massachusetts
Died: October 7, 1990
Bats: Right   **Throws:** Right
Height: 6'   **Weight:** 168
Played for: Boston (AL): 1935

Walt was only 18 when he made his major league debut (August 17, 1935) for a Red Sox staff whose average age was 29. For whatever reason, though, Walt never reappeared in the majors after this season.

◇ ALLEN RIPLEY

Allen Stevens
Born: October 18, 1952
Birthplace: Norwood, Massachusetts
Bats: Right   **Throws:** Right
Height: 6'3"   **Weight:** 200
Played for: Boston (AL): 1978-79; San Francisco: 1980-81; Chicago (NL): 1982

Allen began his major league career with the Red Sox in April 1978. Used primarily as a starter, he struggled to a 2-5 record. Long-suffering BoSox fans sorrowfully remember that year because the Sox went from 10½ games on top in late July to collapse and finish the season a game behind the Yankees. The Sox moved Allen to a middle relief role the next season. The Giants made him a starter again.

RECORDS

Walt Ripley

W	L	Pct.	Sv.	G	GS	CG	IP	H	BB	SO	ShO	ERA
0	0	NA	0	2	0	0	4	7	3	0	0	9.00

Allen Ripley (5 years)

W	L	Pct.	Sv.	G	GS	CG	IP	H	BB	SO	ShO	ERA
23	27	.460	1	101	67	4	465	521	148	229	0	4.51

Cards

Walt Ripley
None

Allen Ripley

1979T—#702R	1980T—#413	1981F—#454	1981T—#144	1982D—#125	1982F—#399
1982T—#529	1982TT—#99	1983D—#57	1983F—#506	1983T—#73	

◆ RALPH SAVIDGE

Ralph Austin
Nickname: The Human Whipcord
Born: February 3, 1879
Birthplace: Jerseytown, Pennsylvania
Died: July 22, 1959
Bats: Right   **Throws:** Right
Height: 6'2   **Weight:** 210
Played for: Cincinnati: 1908-09

The Human Whipcord made his professional debut on September 22, 1908. Four of his five big league appearances and his only decision came during the 1908 season.

◇ DON SAVIDGE

Donald Snyder
Born: August 28, 1908
Birthplace: Berwick, Pennsylvania
Died: March 22, 1983
Bats: Right   **Throws:** Right
Height: 6'1"   **Weight:** 180
Played for: Washington (AL): 1929

Don's debut was August 6, 1929.

RECORDS

Ralph Savidge (2 years)

W	L	Pct.	Sv.	G	GS	CG	IP	H	BB	SO	ShO	ERA
0	1	.000	0	5	1	1	25	28	11	9	0	5.76

Don Savidge

W	L	Pct.	Sv.	G	GS	CG	IP	H	BB	SO	ShO	ERA
0	0	NA	0	3	0	0	6	12	2	2	0	9.00

Cards

None

◆ DICK SCHOFIELD

John Richard
Nickname: Ducky
Born: January 7, 1935
Birthplace: Springfield, Illinois
Bats: Switch   **Throws:** Right
Height: 5'9"   **Weight:** 163
Played for: St. Louis (NL): 1953-58; Pittsburgh: 1958-65; San Francisco: 1965-66; New York (AL): 1966; Los Angeles (NL): 1966-67; St. Louis (NL): 1968; Boston (AL): 1969-70; St. Louis (NL): 1971; Milwaukee (AL): 1971

Ducky appeared in the majors as an 18-year-old. A versatile reserve, he played second, shortstop, and third, and sometimes the outfield. During Pittsburgh's 1960 championship season, he filled in ably for the Pirates' Dick Groat (23 games at short) and Bill Mazeroski (10 games at second) and contributed 34 hits in 102 at-bats (.333). He appeared at shortstop three games during the Series and duplicated his regular season batting average by going 1 for 3. 1963 marked Dick's first year as a regular; he hit .246 in 138 games. A marvel of consistency, he hit exactly .246 the next season as well. St. Louis utilized his versatility in 69 games in their 1968 pennant-winning season.

◇ DICK SCHOFIELD

Richard Craig
Born: November 21, 1962
Birthplace: Springfield, Illinois
Bats: Right   **Throws:** Right
Height: 5'10"   **Weight:** 170
Played for: California: 1983-91

Dick claimed a starting role his first full season with California and became the first rookie in history to lead American League shortstops in fielding. He accomplished this despite missing a month with a sprained right ankle. Dick excelled in his first postseason exposure, hitting .300 in the 1986 ALCS. Although not known for his hitting, he has four career grand slams.

RECORDS

Dick Schofield (19 Years)

G	AB	R	H	2B	3B	HR	RBI	BB	SO	SB	BA	SA
1,321	3,083	394	699	113	20	21	211	390	526	12	.227	.297

Dick Schofield

	G	AB	R	H	2B	3B	HR	RBI	BB	SO	SB	BA	SA
1983-87	581	1,829	212	418	65	15	37	169	159	275	58	.229	.341
1988	155	527	61	126	11	6	6	34	40	57	20	.239	.320
1989	91	302	42	69	11	2	4	26	28	47	9	.228	.320
1990	99	310	41	79	8	1	1	18	52	61	3	.255	.300
1991	134	427	44	96	9	3	0	31	50	69	8	.225	.260

Cards

Dick Schofield

1954T—#191	1955T—#143	1958T—#106	1959T—#68	1960T—#104	1961T—#453
1962T—#484	1963T—#34	1964T—#284	1965T—#218	1966T—#156SP	1966T—#474
1967T—#381	1968T—#588	1969T—#18	1970T—#251	1971T—#396	1978MA—#199
1985T—#138SP					

Dick Schofield

1984D—#35	1984FU—#105	1984TT—#107	1985D—#329	1985F—#311	1985T—#629
1985T—#138SP	1986D—#133	1986F—#167	1986T—#311	1987D—#283	1987F—#92
1987T—#502	1988D—#233	1988F—#504	1988S—#274	1988T—#43	1989B—#46
1989D—#108	1989F—#488	1989S—#16	1989T—#477	1989UD—#201	1990D—#288
1990F—#144	1990S—#44	1990T—#189	1990UD—#669	1991D—#262	1991F—#325
1991S—#776	1991T—#736	1991UD—#169			

◆ JOE SCHULTZ, SR.

Joseph Charles
Nickname: Germany
Born: July 24, 1893
Birthplace: Pittsburgh, Pennsylvania
Died: April 13, 1941
Bats: Right   **Throws:** Right
Height: 5'11"   **Weight:** 172
Played for: Boston (NL): 1912-13; Brooklyn (NL): 1915; Cincinnati: 1915; Pittsburgh: 1916; St. Louis (NL): 1919-24; Philadelphia (NL): 1924-25; Cincinnati: 1925

Joe was one of 48 players to wear a Boston Braves uniform during the 1913 season. He played his first season as a regular outfielder for the 1920 Cardinals. He hit .309 in 92 games during the 1921 campaign, and .314 in 112 games the subsequent year. In short, Germany was no star, but he was a steady journeyman/platoon type of outfielder.

◇ JOE SCHULTZ, JR.

Joseph Charles
Nickname: Dode
Born: August 29, 1918
Birthplace: Chicago, Illinois
Bats: Left   **Throws:** Right
Height: 5'11"   **Weight:** 180
Played for: Pittsburgh: 1939-41; St. Louis (AL): 1943-48
Coaching Experience: St. Louis (AL): 1949; St. Louis (NL): 1963-68; Seattle: 1969 (Manager); Kansas City: 1970; Detroit: 1971-76 (Manager in 1973)

Joe spent his career as a backup catcher and pinch hitter. As a pinch hitter, he managed 43 for 160, for a .269 mark (his father was 46 for 170 hitting off the bench). The Schultzes can claim the obscure distinction of being the only father-son pair to become league-leading pinch hitters.

RECORDS

Joe Schultz, Sr. (11 years)

G	AB	R	H	2B	3B	HR	RBI	BB	SO	SB	BA	SA
703	1,959	235	558	83	19	15	249	116	102	35	.285	.370

Joe Schultz, Jr. (9 years)

G	AB	R	H	2B	3B	HR	RBI	BB	SO	SB	BA	SA
240	328	18	85	13	1	1	46	37	21	0	.259	.314

Cards

Joe Schultz, Sr.
None

Joe Schultz, Jr.
1969T—#254   1973T—#323

◆ DIEGO SEGUI

Diego Pablo
Nickname: Gonzales
Born: August 17, 1937
Birthplace: Holguin, Cuba
Bats: Right   **Throws:** Right
Height: 6'   **Weight:** 190
Played for: Kansas City: 1962-65; Washington (AL): 1966; Kansas City: 1967; Oakland: 1968; Seattle: 1969; Oakland: 1970-72; St. Louis (NL): 1972-73; Boston (AL): 1974-75; Seattle: 1977

Diego won 17 and lost 11 in his first two seasons, then completely reversed his fortunes as he posted an 8-17 record in 1964; he led the American League in losses. He proved to be the ace of the Seattle Pilots with a 12-6 record. Diego led the majors with a 2.56 ERA in 1970. He got into the World Series as a member of the 1972 Boston Red Sox.

◇ DAVID SEGUI

David Vincent
Born: July 19, 1966
Birthplace: Kansas City, Kansas
Bats: Switch   **Throws:** Left
Height: 6'1"   **Weight:** 170
Played for: Baltimore: 1990-91

This switch-hitting first baseman works hard on all aspects of his game. Managers in the AAA International League voted David both the best hitting prospect and the best defensive first baseman in the league. *Baseball America* (October 10, 1990) named David the number two prospect in the league in 1990 as well. He's a good contact hitter, utilizing the whole field. The Orioles brought him up several times in 1990, and he played fairly regularly in 1991.

RECORDS

Diego Segui (15 Years)

W	L	Pct.	Sv.	G	GS	CG	IP	H	BB	SO	ShO	ERA
92	111	.453	71	639	171	28	1808	1656	786	1298	7	3.81

David Segui

G	AB	R	H	2B	3B	HR	RBI	BB	SO	SB	BA	SA
1990												
40	123	14	30	7	0	2	15	11	15	0	.244	.350
1991												
86	212	15	59	7	0	2	22	12	19	1	.278	.340

Cards

Diego Segui

1963T—#157	1964T—#508	1965T—#197	1966T—#309	1968T—#517	1969T—#511
1970T—#2	1971T—#67	1971T—#215	1972T—#735	1973T—#383	1974T—#151
1974TT—#151	1975T—#232	1977T—#653			

David Segui

1991D—#730	1991F—#492	1991S—#362	1991T—#724	1991UD—#342

◆ EARL SHEELY

Earl Homer
Nickname: Whitey
Born: February 12, 1893
Birthplace: Bushnell, Illinois
Died: September 16, 1952
Bats: Right   **Throws:** Right
Height: 6'3"   **Weight:** 190
Played for: Chicago (AL): 1921-27; Pittsburgh: 1929; Boston (NL): 1931

Playing first base in all 154 games of the 1921 season, Earl hit .304 with 95 RBIs. Whitey spent most of his career with mediocre teams. Nevertheless, this durable player hit over .300 four times and annually played nearly all games on the schedule. His finest season was 1924, when he hit .320 with 103 RBIs. His .426 on-base percentage that season placed him fifth in the American League. Earl's 43 doubles in 1925 were second on the circuit and his 111 RBIs were fifth. In 1926 (May 20th and 21st), Whitey slammed six doubles in two games.

◇ BUD SHEELY

Hollis Kimball
Born: November 26, 1920
Birthplace: Spokane, Washington
Died: October 17, 1985
Bats: Left   **Throws:** Right
Height: 6'1"   **Weight:** 200
Played for: Chicago (AL): 1951-53

Bud was 30 when he became the White Sox backup catcher. In 1952, his age matched his number of games behind the plate. By the time he completed the 1953 season, Bud's age exceeded his number of games (32-31).

RECORDS												
Earl Sheely (9 years)												
G	AB	R	H	2B	3B	HR	RBI	BB	SO	SB	BA	SA
1,234	4,471	572	1,340	244	27	48	747	563	205	33	.300	.399
Bud Sheely (3 years)												
G	AB	R	H	2B	3B	HR	RBI	BB	SO	SB	BA	SA
101	210	7	44	5	0	0	12	27	22	0	.210	.233

Cards
None

◆ DICK SIEBERT

Richard Walther
Born: February 19, 1912
Birthplace: Fall River, Massachusetts
Died: December 9, 1978
Bats: Left   **Throws:** Left
Height: 6'   **Weight:** 170
Played for: Brooklyn (NL): 1932, 1936; St. Louis (NL): 1937-38; Philadelphia (AL): 1938-45; Held out in 1946

Knee and arm problems plagued Dick's career. When healthy, he was a decent hitter and first baseman, hitting .334 in 123 games for the eighth-place Philadephia Athletics in 1941.

◇ PAUL SIEBERT

Paul Edward
Born: June 5, 1953
Birthplace: Minneapolis, Minnesota
Bats: Left   **Throws:** Left
Height: 6'2"   **Weight:** 205
Played for: Houston: 1974-76; New York (NL): 1977-78

Paul was used primarily as a middle inning reliever.

RECORDS

Dick Siebert (11 years)

G	AB	R	H	2B	3B	HR	RBI	BB	SO	SB	BA	SA
1,035	3,917	439	1,104	204	40	32	482	276	185	30	.282	.379

Paul Siebert

W	L	Pct.	Sv.	G	GS	CG	IP	H	BB	SO	ShO	ERA
3	8	.273	3	87	7	1	129	130	73	59	1	3.77

Cards

Dick Siebert
1940PB—#192   1941DP—#128

Paul Siebert
1975T—#614R

◆ GEORGE SISLER

George Harold
Nickname: Gorgeous George
Born: March 24, 1893
Birthplace: Manchester, Ohio
Died: March 26, 1973
Bats: Left   **Throws:** Left
Height: 5'11"   **Weight:** 170
Played for: St. Louis (AL): 1915-22; Injured in 1923; St. Louis (AL): 1924-27; Washington (AL): 1928; Boston (NL): 1928-30
Coach: St. Louis (AL): 1924-26 (Player/Manager); Boston (NL): 1930
Hall of Fame: Elected in 1939, by the Baseball Writers of America
Honors: Most Valuable Player in 1921. (*At this time, players were only eligible to win once.*)
Records: Most hits in a season, with 257 (1920)

Many consider Sisler one of the greatest first basemen of all time, certainly one of the best prior to Gehrig. He hit over .400 twice in his career and compiled 1,535 career assists. The 257 hits this Michigan alum recorded in 1920 still stands as a single season major league record. The Sizzler's .340 lifetime average puts him 15th on that list, and he was one of baseball's toughest strikeouts; his ratio of 25.3 at-bats per strikeout is 19th overall. In 1918, his 45 steals led the league. A severe sinus infection resulting in double vision caused Gorgeous George to miss the entire 1923 season. Sisler came into the league as a pitcher, and one of his greatest baseball thrills came during his rookie season when he hurled a 2-1 victory against Walter Johnson, his boyhood idol. He switched from pitcher to first base after the 1915 season. George managed the St. Louis Browns from 1924 to 1926 and recorded 218 wins and 241 losses.

◇ DICK SISLER

Richard Allen
Born: November 2, 1920
Birthplace: St. Louis, Missouri
Bats: Left   **Throws:** Right
Height: 6'2"   **Weight:** 205
Played for: St. Louis (NL): 1946-47; Philadelphia (NL): 1948-51; Cincinnati: 1952; St. Louis (NL): 1952-53
Coach: Cincinnati: 1961-64 (Manager 1964-65); St. Louis (NL): 1966-70; San Diego: 1975-76; New York (NL): 1979-80
Honors: National League All-Star in 1950

Dick and George constitute the only father-son combination other than the Macks to have both managed. Dick played primarily at first, although he sometimes patrolled the outfield. His greatest moment in baseball came in 1950, when his 10th-inning, three-run homer against Brooklyn clinched Philadelphia's first pennant since 1915. This was a career year for Dick, who batted .296 and drove in 83 runs. Dick's managerial record, compiled from 1964-65 with the Reds, was 215-121.

◇ DAVE SISLER

David Michael
Born: October 16, 1931
Birthplace: St. Louis, Missouri
Bats: Right   **Throws:** Right
Height: 6'4"   **Weight:** 200
Played for: Boston (AL): 1956-59; Detroit: 1959-60; Washington (AL): 1961; Cincinnati: 1962

Dave played basketball at Princeton. He appeared in 39 games and started 14 during his rookie season. Dave spent most of his career this way, as a spot starter and long reliever.

RECORDS

George Sisler

W	L	Pct.	Sv.	G	GS	CG	IP	H	BB	SO	ShO	ERA
5	6	.455	2	24	12	9	111	91	52	63	1	2.35
G	AB	R	H	2B	3B	HR	RBI	BB	SO	SB	BA	SA
2,055	8,267	1,284	2,812	425	164	102	1,175	472	327	375	.340	.468

Dick Sisler

G	AB	R	H	2B	3B	HR	RBI	BB	SO	SB	BA	SA
799	2606	302	720	118	28	55	360	226	253	6	.276	.406

Dave Sisler

W	L	Pct.	Sv.	G	GS	CG	IP	H	BB	SO	ShO	ERA
38	44	.463	29	247	59	12	655	622	368	355	1	4.33

Cards

George Sisler
1940PB—#179   1960F—#13   1961F—#78   1961F—#89SP   1972K—#5   1979T—#411SP

Dick Sisler
1949L—#143   1949B—#205   1950B—#119   1951TBB—#8   1951B—#52   1951BR—#C8
1952T—#113   1952B—#127   1953BBW—#10   1964T—#162SP   1965T—#158   1976SS—#622

Dave Sisler
1957T—#56   1958T—#59   1959T—#346SP   1959T—#384   1960T—#186   1960L—#64
1961T—#239   1961P—#44   1962T—#171   1963T—#284

◆ BOB SKINNER

Robert Ralph
Born: October 3, 1931
Birthplace: La Jolla, California
Bats: Left   **Throws:** Right
Height: 6'4"   **Weight:** 190
Played for: Pittsburgh: 1954, 1956-63; Cincinnati: 1963-64; St. Louis (NL): 1964-66
Coaching Experience: Philadelphia (NL): 1968-69 (Manager); 1970-73; Pittsburgh: 1974-76; San Diego: 1977 (Manager for one game); California (AL) 1978; Pittsburgh: 1979-85; Atlanta: 1986-88
Honors: National League All-Star in 1958 and 1960

A journeyman outfielder good enough to be named to two All-Star squads, Bob hit .321 in 141 games during the 1958 season, fifth best in the NL. His .390 on-base mark that season was also fifth best. During the Pirates' 1960 Championship campaign, Bob's 86 RBIs were the team's second best total (Clemente had 94), and his 33 doubles ranked third in the NL. He played only two of the seven Series games, hitting .200 (1 for 5) with two runs and an RBI. Bob joined the 1964 Cardinals in time to pinch hit and play 31 games in the outfield as they squeezed past his former Cincinnati teammates to win the pennant by one game. He appeared in four Series games, but his only at-bats against the Yankees came as a pinch hitter; he registered an impressive 2 for 3 with a walk and an RBI for the victorious Redbirds. Skinner's mark as a manager was 92-123 in 1968 and 1969, and in 1977 he compiled a perfect 1-0 record as interim manager of the Padres.

◇ JOEL SKINNER

Joel Patrick
Born: February 21, 1961
Birthplace: La Jolla, California
Bats: Right   **Throws:** Right
Height: 6'4"   **Weight:** 205
Played for: Chicago (AL): 1983-86; New York (AL): 1986-88; Cleveland (AL): 1989-91

Joel made his career as a reliable backup catcher known for his rifle arm.

RECORDS

Bob Skinner (12 Years)

G	AB	R	H	2B	3B	HR	RBI	BB	SO	SB	BA	SA
1,381	4,318	642	1,198	197	58	103	531	485	646	67	.277	.421

Joel Skinner

G	AB	R	H	2B	3B	HR	RBI	BB	SO	SB	BA	SA
1983-87												
249	589	47	127	19	2	9	60	36	162	2	.216	.301
1988												
88	251	23	57	15	0	4	23	14	72	0	.227	.335
1989												
79	178	10	41	10	0	1	13	9	42	1	.230	.303
1990												
49	139	16	35	4	1	2	16	7	44	3	.252	.338
1991												
99	284	23	69	14	0	1	24	14	67	0	.243	.303

Cards

Bob Skinner

1955T—#88	1955TDH—#56	1956T—#297	1957T—#209	1958T—#94	1959T—#320
1959T—#543SP	1960T—#113	1961T—#204	1961P—#131	1962T—#115	1962P—#174
1963T—#18SP	1963T—#215	1963P—#141	1964T—#377	1965T—#591	1966T—#471
1969T—#369	1973T—#12C	1974T—#489C	1985T—#139SP		

Joel Skinner

1984D—#27	1985D—#574	1985F—#646	1985T—#488	1985T—#139SP	1986D—#330
1986T—#239	1987D—#545	1987F—#115	1987T—#626	1988D—#474	1988S—#532
1988T—#109	1989D—#427	1989F—#270	1989S—#447	1989T—#536	1989UD—#328
1990D—#73	1990F—#501	1990T—#54	1990UD—#369	1991D—#120	1991F—#377
1991S—#809	1991T—#783	1991UD—#121			

◆ ROY SMALLEY, JR.

Roy Frederick
Born: June 9, 1926
Birthplace: Springfield, Missouri
Bats: Right   **Throws:** Right
Height: 6'3"   **Weight:** 190
Played for: Chicago (NL): 1948-53; Milwaukee (NL): 1954; Philadelphia (NL): 1955-58

Roy established himself as the Cubs' regular shortstop during his first season in the majors. He held onto the position for six years until the Cubs' management traded him to make way for a youngster named Ernie Banks. In 1950, Roy hit for the cycle.

◇ ROY SMALLEY, III

Roy Frederick
Born: October 25, 1952
Birthplace: Los Angeles, California
Bats: Switch   **Throws:** Right
Height: 6'1"   **Weight:** 190

Played for: Texas: 1975-76; Minnesota: 1976-82; New York (AL): 1982-84; Chicago (AL): 1984; Minnesota: 1985-87

Like his father, Roy was primarily a shortstop, although he could play all infield positions. In the last part of his career he was a valued utility infielder/designated hitter. He contributed to the Twins' 1987 World Series victory with two pinch hits in four at-bats. Roy's career stats are good enough that Peter Palmer's Total Player Rating lists him 141st lifetime, ahead of Roy Campanella, Zach Wheat, Joe Tinker, Roger Bresnehan, and several other Hall of Famers. At the end of a 13-year career, Roy finally got to play on a winner, as the Twins won the West (85-77), defeated the Tigers (4-1) for the pennant, and edged St. Louis (4-3) in the Series. Not many players ever get to play in the World Series, and fewer still get to end their careers as a World Champ, but Roy did as he retired as an active player after the 1987 season.

RECORDS

Roy Smalley, Jr. (11 years)

G	AB	R	H	2B	3B	HR	RBI	BB	SO	SB	BA	SA
872	2,644	277	601	103	33	61	305	257	541	4	.227	.360

Roy Smalley, III (13 years)

G	AB	R	H	2B	3B	HR	RBI	BB	SO	SB	BA	SA
1,653	5,657	745	1,454	244	25	163	694	771	908	27	.257	.395

Cards

Roy Smalley, Jr.
1948L—#77	1950B—#115	1951TBB—#17	1951B—#44	1952T—#173	1952B—#64
1953BBW—#56	1954T—#231	1954B—#109	1955B—#252	1957T—#397	1976T—#70SP
1985T—#140SP					

Roy Smalley, III
1976T—#70SP	1976T—#657	1976SS—#267	1977T—#66	1978T—#471	1979T—#219
1980T—#570	1981D—#487	1981F—#551	1981T—#115	1982D—#22	1982D—#573
1982F—#560	1982T—#767	1982TT—#107	1983D—#209	1983F—#397	1983T—#460
1984D—#225	1984F—#142	1984T—#305	1985D—#622	1985F—#527	1985T—#26
1985T—#140SP	1985FU—#105	1985TT—#108	1986D—#486	1986F—#404	1986T—#613
1987D—#443	1987F—#552	1987T—#744	1988D—#566	1988F—#22	1988S—#606
1988T—#239					

◆ ED SPRAGUE

Edward Nelson
Born: September 16, 1945
Birthplace: Boston, Massachusetts
Bats: Right   **Throws:** Right
Height: 6'4"   **Weight:** 195
Played for: Oakland: 1968-69; Cincinatti: 1971-73;
St. Louis (NL): 1973; Milwaukee (AL): 1974-76

Ed appeared in 33 games for the 1972 NL champion Reds, mostly in middle relief. He did not register any appearances in the championship series or in the October classic. A knee injury hampered him during the 1974 season, but he still managed a 7-2 record in 20 games; it proved to be his only winning season.

◇ ED SPRAGUE

Born: July 25, 1967
Birthplace: Castro Valley, California
Bats: Right   **Throws:** Right
Height: 6'2"   **Weight:** 215
Played for: Toronto: 1991

The Blue Jays made Ed the first selection in the June 1988 draft and then converted him to a catcher. However, when he came up in 1991, he played at third.

RECORDS

Ed Sprague

W	L	Pct.	Sv.	G	GS	CG	IP	H	BB	SO	ShO	ERA
17	23	.425	9	198	23	3	408	406	206	188	0	3.84

Ed Sprague

G	AB	R	H	2B	3B	HR	RBI	BB	SO	SB	BA	SA
1991												
61	160	17	44	7	0	4	20	19	43	0	.275	.394

Cards

Ed Sprague
1969T—#638   1972T—#121   1975T—#76

Ed Sprague
1988T—#113USOC

◆ EBBA ST. CLAIRE

Edward Joseph
Born: August 5, 1921
Birthplace: Whitehall, New York
Died: August 22, 1982
Bats: Switch   **Throws:** Right
Height: 6'1"   **Weight:** 219
Played for: Boston (NL): 1951-52; Milwaukee (NL): 1953; New York (NL): 1954

A catcher, Ebba and son Randy constitute one of three father-son batteries. Ebba didn't appear in the majors until he was 29. That year a broken finger limited his playing time to 62 games behind the plate; he hit a respectable .282 in 220 at-bats. He was the New York Giants third-string catcher in 1954, appearing in 16 games during the regular season but none during the Series.

◇ RANDY ST. CLAIRE

Randy Anthony
Born: August 23, 1960
Birthplace: Glens Falls, New York
Bats: Right   **Throws:** Right
Height: 6'3"   **Weight:** 180
Played for: Montreal: 1984-88; Cincinnati (NL): 1988; Minnesota: 1989; Atlanta: 1991

Randy has bounced around for several years but never securely established himself in the majors.

RECORDS

Ebba St. Claire (4 years)

G	AB	R	H	2B	3B	HR	RBI	BB	SO	SB	BA	SA
164	450	39	112	23	2	7	40	35	52	0	.249	.356

Randy St. Claire

	W	L	Pct.	Sv.	G	GS	CG	IP	H	BB	SO	ShO	ERA
1984-88	10	6	.625	8	101	0	0	163	157	54	93	0	3.81
1988	11	6	.647	8	117	0	0	184	181	64	107	0	3.82
1989	1	0	1.000	1	14	0	0	22	19	44	63	0	5.32
1991	0	0	NA	0	19	0	0	29	31	9	30	0	4.08

Cards

Ebba St. Claire
1952B—#172   1952T—#393   1953B—#34   1953T—#91   1954B—#128

Randy St. Claire
1985D—#575   1986D—#463   1986F—#261   1986T—#89   1987FU—#113   1987T—#467
1988D—#426   1988F—#197   1988S—#397   1988T—#279   1989T—#666   1989UD—#29
1990T—#503

◆ DAVE STENHOUSE

David Rotchford
Born: September 12, 1933
Birthplace: Westerly, Rhode Island
Bats: Right   **Throws:** Right
Height: 6'   **Weight:** 195
Played for: Washington (AL): 1962-64

Dave was the ace of the Washington Senators' staff in 1962, compiling an 11-12 record for a won-lost percentage (.478) more than 100 points above that of the team's (60-11, .373). He started that year's second All-Star Game. Elbow and arm injuries brought a early end to Dave's career.

◇ MIKE STENHOUSE

Michael Steven
Born: February 29, 1958

Birthplace: Pueblo, Colorado
Bats: Left   **Throws:** Right
Height: 6'1"   **Weight:** 195
Played for: Montreal: 1982-84; Minnesota: 1985; Boston (AL): 1986

Mike played outfield and first base. In 1984, the Donruss company introduced their "Rated Rookies" to baseball card collectors. Mike was one of them, and from the back of his card we learn: "Was drafted by Expos out of Harvard U and is 1st Ivy Leaguer to play for Montreal." Veteran baseball card readers would immediately pick this up as a signal to look more closely. Sure enough, this is a baseball card copywriter's way of telling us, "Jeez, this guy is certainly smart enough to know how to hit, but I don't know if he has the reflexes to hit big league pitching." He didn't.

RECORDS													
Dave Stenhouse (3 years)													
W	L	Pct.	Sv.	G	GS	CG	IP	H	BB	SO	ShO	ERA	
16	28	.364	1	76	56	12	372	339	174	214	3	4.14	
Mike Stenhouse (5 years)													
G	AB	R	H	2B	3B	HR	RBI	BB	SO	SB	BA	SA	
207	416	40	79	15	0	9	40	71	66	1	.190	.291	

Cards					
Dave Stenhouse					
1962T—#592	1963F—#30	1963T—#263	1964T—#498	1965T—#304	1985T—#141SP
Mike Stenhouse					
1984D—#29	1985D—#376	1985F—#411	1985T—#658	1985T—#141SP	1985FU—#110
1985TT—#112	1986F—#406	1986T—#17			

◆ JOE STEPHENSON

Joseph Chester
Born: June 30, 1921
Birthplace: Detroit, Michigan
Bats: Right   **Throws:** Right
Height: 6'2"   **Weight:** 185
Played for: New York (NL): 1943; Chicago (NL): 1944; Military Service in 1945; Chicago (AL): 1947

A catcher, Joe and his son Jerry form one of only three father-son batteries to have both played in the major leagues.

◇ JERRY STEPHENSON

Jerry Joseph
Born: October 6, 1943
Birthplace: Detroit, Michigan
Bats: Left   **Throws:** Right
Height: 6'2"   **Weight:** 185
Played for: Boston (AL): 1963, 1965-68; Seattle: 1969; Los Angeles (NL): 1970

Jerry's career was plagued by arm problems. In the 1967 World Series against St. Louis, Jerry appeared in one game, pitched two innings, gave up three hits and a walk, and was saddled with a 9.00 ERA.

RECORDS												

Joe Stephenson (3 years)

G	AB	R	H	2B	3B	HR	RBI	BB	SO	SB	BA	SA
29	67	8	12	1	0	0	4	2	15	1	.179	.194

Jerry Stephenson (7 years)

W	L	Pct.	Sv.	G	GS	CG	IP	H	BB	SO	ShO	ERA
8	19	.296	1	67	33	3	239	265	145	184	0	5.69

Cards

Joe Stephenson
None

Jerry Stephenson

1965T—#74	1966T—#396	1968T—#519	1969T—#172	1971T—#488

◆ RON STILLWELL

Ronald Roy
Born: December 3, 1939
Birthplace: Los Angeles, California
Bats: Right   **Throws:** Right
Height: 5'11"   **Weight:** 165
Played for: Washington (AL): 1961-62

Ron was a middle infielder.

◇ KURT STILLWELL

Kurt Andrew
Nickname: Opie
Born: June 4, 1965
Birthplace: Glendale, California
Bats: Switch   **Throws:** Right
Height: 5'11"   **Weight:** 165
Played for: Cincinnati: 1986-87; Kansas City: 1988-91

Kurt played his first major league ball with the Reds; they traded him to Kansas City for pitcher Danny Jackson.

RECORDS

Ron Stillwell (2 years)

G	AB	R	H	2B	3B	HR	RBI	BB	SO	SB	BA	SA
14	38	8	8	1	0	0	3	3	6	0	.211	.237

Kurt Stillwell

	G	AB	R	H	2B	3B	HR	RBI	BB	SO	SB	BA	SA
1986-87	235	674	85	166	26	8	4	59	62	97	10	.246	.326
1988	128	459	63	115	28	5	10	53	47	76	6	.251	.399
1989	130	463	52	121	20	7	7	54	42	64	9	.261	.380
1990	144	506	60	126	35	4	3	51	39	60	0	.249	.352
1991	122	385	44	102	17	1	6	51	33	56	3	.265	.361

Cards

Ron Stillwell
None

Kurt Stillwell

1986FU—#108	1986TT—#104	1987D—#123	1987F—#215	1987T—#623	1988D—#265
1988F—#248	1988S—#221	1988T—#339	1988FU—#35	1988SS—#4	1988TT—#115
1989B—#120	1989D—#322	1989F—#293	1989S—#162	1989T—#596	1989UD—#616
1990D—#120	1990F—#118	1990S—#96	1990T—#222	1990UD—#361	1991DDK—#5
1991D—#520	1991F—#571	1991S—#295	1991T—#478	1991UD—#587	

◆ MEL STOTTLEMYRE, SR.

Melvin Leon
Born: November 13, 1941
Birthplace: Hazelton, Missouri
Bats: Right   **Throws:** Right
Height: 6'1"   **Weight:** 185
Played for: New York (AL): 1964-74
Coaching Experience: New York (NL): 1984-88
Honors: American League All-Star in 1966, 1968, 1969, and 1970

Mel won 20 or more games three times. As a rookie, he appeared in three World Series games, recording a 1-1 record in 20 innings. Mel's first 20-win season came in 1965.

◇ MEL STOTTLEMYRE, JR.

Melvin Leon
Born: December 28, 1963
Birthplace: Prosser, Washington

Bats: Right   **Throws:** Right
Height: 6'   **Weight:** 190
Played for: Kansas City: 1990

Mel endured two rotator cuff and five knee operations before he made his dad the first father to have two sons pitch in the major leagues.

◇ TODD STOTTLEMYRE

Born: May 20, 1965
Birthplace: Yakima, Washington
Bats: Left   **Throws:** Right
Height: 6'3"   **Weight:** 190
Played for: Toronto: 1988-91

Todd pitched his way onto the Blue Jays staff in 1988, but was sent to Syracuse. He joined the Jays' starting rotation in late June 1989. The hard-throwing righthander showed plenty of poise during the stretch drive, winning five straight in August and September.

RECORDS

Mel Stottlemyre, Sr. (11 years)

W	L	Pct.	Sv.	G	GS	CG	IP	H	BB	SO	ShO	ERA
164	139	.541	1	360	356	152	2,661	2,435	809	1,257	40	2.97

Mel Stottlemyre, Jr.

	W	L	Pct.	Sv.	G	GS	CG	IP	H	BB	SO	ShO	ERA
1990	0	1	.000	0	13	2	0	31.1	35	12	14	0	4.88

Todd Stottlemyre

	W	L	Pct.	Sv.	G	GS	CG	IP	H	BB	SO	ShO	ERA
1988	4	8	.333	0	28	16	0	98	109	45	6.7	0	5.69
1989	7	7	.500	0	27	18	0	128	137	44	63	0	3.88
1990	13	17	.433	0	33	33	4	203	214	69	115	0	4.34
1991	15	8	.652	0	34	34	1	219	194	75	116	0	3.78

Cards

Mel Stottlemyre, Sr.

1965T—#550	1966T—#224SP	1966T—#350	1967T—#225	1968T—#120	1969T—#9SP
1969T—#470	1969TS—#25	1969TDE—#13	1970T—#70SP	1970T—#100	1970TS—#27
1970K—#5	1971T—#615	1971TS—#10	1971K—#40	1972T—#325	1972T—#492SP
1972K—#50	1972T—#44	1973T—#520	1975T—#183		

Mel Stottlemyre, Jr.

1989B—#110	1990T—#263	1991D—#257	1991S—#361	1991T—#58

Todd Stottlemyre

1988D—#658	1988DU—#37	1988FU—#68	1988SS—#90	1988TT—#116	1989B—#242
1989D—#620	1989F—#245	1989S—#453	1989T—#722	1989UD—#362	1990D—#669
1990F—#94	1990S—#554	1990T—#591	1990UD—#692	1991D—#155	1991F—#186
1991S—#39	1991T—#348	1991UD—#257			

◆ BILLY SULLIVAN, SR.

William Joseph
Born: February 1, 1875
Birthplace: Oakland, Wisconsin
Died: January 28, 1965
Bats: Right   **Throws:** Right
Height: 5'9"   **Weight:** 155
Played for: Boston (NL): 1899-1900; Chicago
(AL): 1901-12, 1914; Detroit: 1916
Coaching Experience: Chicago (AL): 1909
(Player/Manager)

Billy was the White Sox starting catcher during their pennant-winning 1901 season, the American League's inaugural year. An illness sidelined him for much of the 1903 season, but he was back in the starting lineup next year. He was behind the plate for all six games of the famous 1906 all-Chicago World Series, pitting the mighty Cubs (116-36), one of baseball's greatest teams, against the "Hitless Wonders" (team batting average—.230). Perhaps because he was concentrating on catching Big Ed Walsh's spitball, or perhaps because he was merely living up to the team's reputation, Sullivan failed to get a hit in 21 at-bats during the Series. Incredible as it seems, the Hitless Wonders prevailed with a Series team batting average of .198 — the Cubs could manage only .196!

◇ BILLY SULLIVAN, JR.

William Joseph
Born: October 23, 1910
Birthplace: Chicago, Illinois
Bats: Left   **Throws:** Right
Height: 6'   **Weight:** 170
Played for: Chicago (AL): 1931-33; Cincinnati: 1935; Cleveland (AL): 1936-37; St. Louis (AL): 1938-39; Detroit: 1940-41; Brooklyn (NL): 1942; Military Service in 1944-46; Pittsburgh: 1947

Billy shortened his 1932 and 1933 seasons by his decision to return to school and complete his education. Primarily a catcher, Billy was also capable of filling in at first, third, and the outfield. He hit .351, with a .508 slugging average, in 93 games for Cleveland in 1936.

RECORDS

Billy Sullivan, Sr. (16 years)

G	AB	R	H	2B	3B	HR	RBI	BB	SO	SB	BA	SA
1,147	3,647	363	777	119	33	21	378	170	*	98	.213	.281
												* Not available

Billy Sullivan, Jr.

G	AB	R	H	2B	3B	HR	RBI	BB	SO	SB	BA	SA
962	2,840	347	820	152	32	29	388	240	119	30	.289	.395

Cards

Billy Sullivan, Sr.
T207—#179   1961F—#141

Billy Sullivan, Jr.
None

◆ HAYWOOD SULLIVAN

Haywood Cooper
Born: December 15, 1930
Birthplace: Donalsonville, Georgia
Bats: Right   **Throws:** Right
Height: 6'4"   **Weight:** 215
Played for: Boston (AL): 1955, 1957; Injured in 1958; Boston (AL): 1959-60; Kansas City: 1961-63
Coaching Experience: Kansas City: 1965 (Manager)

Haywood was a University of Florida quarterback and was primarily a catcher during his major league days. When his playing career ended, he became General Manager and later part-owner of the Boston Red Sox.

◇ MARC SULLIVAN

Marc Cooper
Born: July 25, 1958
Birthplace: Quincy, Massachusetts
Bats: Right   **Throws:** Right
Height: 6'4"   **Weight:** 200
Played for: Boston (AL): 1982, 1984-87

Marc was a light-hitting catcher.

RECORDS												

Haywood Sullivan (7 years)

G	AB	R	H	2B	3B	HR	RBI	BB	SO	SB	BA	SA
312	851	94	192	30	5	13	87	109	140	2	.226	.318

Marc Sullivan (5 years)

G	AB	R	H	2B	3B	HR	RBI	BB	SO	SB	BA	SA
137	360	37	67	11	0	5	28	18	92	0	.186	.258

Cards

Haywood Sullivan

1957T—#336	1958T—#197	1959T—#416	1960T—#474	1961T—#212	1961P—#56
1962T—#184	1962P—#99	1963T—#359	1963P—#92		

Marc Sullivan

1986D—#614	1986T—#529	1987D—#643	1987T—#66	1988S—#271	1988T—#354

◆ **GEORGE SUSCE**

George Cyril Methodius
Nickname: Good Kid
Born: August 13, 1908
Birthplace: Pittsburgh, Pennsylvania
Died: February 25, 1986
Bats: Right   **Throws:** Right
Height: 5'11"   **Weight:** 200
Played for: Philadelphia (NL): 1929; Detroit: 1932; Pittsburgh: 1939; St. Louis (AL): 1940; Cleveland (AL): 1941-44
Coaching Experience: Cleveland (AL): 1941-47, 1948-49; Boston (AL): 1950-54; Kansas City: 1955-56; Milwaukee (NL): 1958-59; Washington (AL): 1961-67, 1969-71; Texas: 1972.

George was a catcher during his playing days, making him and his son the third father-son battery. He reportedly got his nickname because he called everybody "Good Kid."

◇ **GEORGE SUSCE**

George Daniel
Born: September 13, 1931
Birthplace: Pittsburgh, Pennsylvania
Bats: Right   **Throws:** Right
Height: 6'1"   **Weight:** 180
Played for: Boston (AL): 1955-58; Detroit: 1958-59

After a promising rookie season (9-7, 3.06 ERA), an illness hampered George's effectiveness during the 1956 season. Primarily a relief pitcher, George registered a 7-3 mark in 1957.

RECORDS													
George Susce (8 years)													
G	**AB**	**R**	**H**	**2B**	**3B**	**HR**	**RBI**	**BB**	**SO**	**SB**	**BA**	**SA**	
146	268	23	61	11	1	2	22	25	21	1	.228	.299	
George Susce (5 years)													
W	**L**	**Pct.**	**Sv.**	**G**	**GS**	**CG**	**IP**	**H**	**BB**	**SO**	**ShO**	**ERA**	
22	17	.564	3	117	36	8	410	407	170	177	1	4.41	

Cards
George Susce
None
George Susce
1955B—#320   1956T—#93   1957T—#229   1958T—#189   1959T—#511

◆ CHUCK TANNER

Charles William
Born: July 24, 1929
Birthplace: New Castle, Pennsylvania
Bats: Left   **Throws:** Left
Height: 6'   **Weight:** 185
Played for: Milwaukee (NL): 1955-57; Chicago (NL): 1957-58; Cleveland (AL): 1959-60; Los Angeles (AL): 1961-62
Coaching Experience: Chicago (AL): 1970-75 (Manager); Oakland: 1976 (Manager); Pittsburgh: 1977-85 (Manager); Atlanta: 1986-88 (Manager)

On April 12, 1955, Chuck became one of only 10 men in baseball history to hit a home run on *the very first pitch thrown to him.* He appeared in 97 games during his rookie season, 62 of them in the outfield. When he was traded to the Cubs during the 1957 campaign, he cracked their starting lineup and hit a respectable .286. However, the following season, he was once again relegated to a backup role. During the remainder of his career, he never accumulated more than 25 at-bats in a season. He launched his managerial career with the 1970 White Sox, and piloted the "We are Family" Pirates to their 1979 World Series victory.

◇ BRUCE TANNER

Bruce Matthew
Born: December 9, 1961
Birthplace: New Castle, Pennsylvania
Bats: Left   **Throws:** Right
Height: 6'3"   **Weight:** 220
Played for: Chicago (AL): 1985

When he was first signed, Bruce was considered one of the White Sox best prospects. However, a poor showing when he was brought up in 1985, combined with arm problems, kept him bouncing around the minors with the A's and Giants' organizations. The Padres gave him a shot in 1990, signing him to a AAA contract.

RECORDS

Chuck Tanner (8 Years)

G	AB	R	H	2B	3B	HR	RBI	BB	SO	SB	BA	SA
396	885	98	231	39	5	21	105	82	93	2	.261	.388

Bruce Tanner

W	L	Pct.	Sv.	G	GS	CG	IP	H	BB	SO	ShO	ERA
1	2	.333	0	10	4	0	27	34	13	9	0	5.33

Cards

Chuck Tanner

1955T—#161	1956T—#69	1957T—#392	1958T—#91	1959T—#234	1960T—#279
1971T—#661	1972T—#98	1973T—#356	1974T—#221	1978T—#494	1980T—#551
1981D—#257	1981F—#367	1981T—#683	1982D—#150	1983D—#124	1983T—#696
1984T—#291	1985T—#268	1986T—#351	1986TT—#107	1987T—#593	1988T—#134

Bruce Tanner

1985FU—#116	1986F—#218

◆ JOSE TARTABULL

Jose Guzman (Milages)
Born: November 27, 1938
Birthplace: Cienfuegos, Cuba
Bats: Left   **Throws:** Left
Height: 5'11"   **Weight:** 165
Played for: Kansas City: 1962-66; Boston (AL): 1966-68; Oakland: 1969-70

After appearing in 85 games in the outfield during his rookie year, Jose became a regular in his second year. He stole 16 bases that season (1963) and was nabbed only once, for a major league-leading 94.1 stolen base percentage. Jose platooned most of his career. He contributed to Boston's 1967 American League championship by appearing in 83 games in the outfield and 115 total games. He appeared in all seven World Series games, scratching out two hits in 13 at-bats as the Red Sox succumbed to the Cardinals, three games to four.

◇ DANNY TARTABULL

Danilo (Mora)
Born: October 30, 1962
Birthplace: San Juan, Puerto Rico
Bats: Right   **Throws:** Right
Height: 6'1"   **Weight:** 180
Played for: Seattle: 1984-86; Kansas City: 1987-91

The Mariners brought Danny up as an infielder, primarily a shortstop, but began playing him in the outfield during the 1986 season, which was his first full year in the American League. The Mariners traded him to Kansas City, and he quickly asserted himself as one of the league's top power hitters. In 1987, he became the second Royal ever to hit .300 with 30 homers and 100 RBIs. He followed that with another outstanding RBI season (102), and his three grand slams set a Royals record.

RECORDS

Jose Tartabull (9 Years)

G	AB	R	H	2B	3B	HR	RBI	BB	SO	SB	BA	SA
749	1,857	247	484	56	24	2	107	115	136	81	.261	.320

Danny Tartabull

	G	AB	R	H	2B	3B	HR	RBI	BB	SO	SB	BA	SA
1984-86	324	1,174	182	344	60	10	62	211	150	310	14	.293	.520
1988	146	507	80	139	38	3	26	102	76	119	8	.274	.520
1989	133	441	54	118	22	0	18	62	69	123	4	.268	.440
1990	88	313	41	84	19	0	15	60	36	93	1	.268	.473
1991	132	484	78	153	35	3	31	100	65	121	6	.316	.593

Cards

Jose Tartabull
1962T—#451	1963T—#449	1964T—#276	1966T—#143	1967T—#56	1968T—#555
1969T—#287	1970T—#481				

Danny Tartabull
1985D—#27	1985F—#647	1986F—#38	1986DU—#45	1986F—#476	1986TT—#108
1986T—#178	1987D—#147	1987F—#598	1987SPF—#23	1987T—#476	1987FU—#117
1987TT—#120	1988D—#5	1988D—#177	1988F—#271	1988S—#106	1988SPF—#19
1988T—#724	1989B—#128	1989D—#61	1989F—#295	1989S—#105	1989SPF—#46
1989T—#275	1989UD—#329	1990D—#322	1990F—#120	1990S—#244	1990T—#540
1990UD—#656	1991D—#463	1991F—#572	1991S—#515	1991T—#90	1991UD—#523

◆ RICARDO TORRES

Ricardo J.
Born: 1894
Birthplace: Cuba
Died: Date of death unknown
Bats: Right   **Throws:** Right
Height: 5'11"   **Weight:** 160
Played for: Washington (AL): 1920-22

Ricardo made his major league debut on May 18, 1920. He was a catcher and first baseman.

◇ GIL TORRES

Don Gilberto (Nunez)
Born: August 23, 1915
Birthplace: Regla, Cuba

Died: January 11, 1983
Bats: Right   **Throws:** Right
Height: 6'   **Weight:** 155
Played for: Washington (AL): 1940, 1944-46

Gil pitched in two games in 1940 and three games in 1946. During 1944, the Washington Senators used Gil 123 games at third, 10 at second, and 4 at first. They moved him to shortstop next season (145 games), as Washington climbed to second place (87-67, only 1½ games behind the Tigers). In 1946, Gil became one of the Senators' interchangeable infielders (31 games at short, 18 at third, and 7 at second), along with Cecil Travis (short: 75, third: 56), Billy Hitchcock (short: 53, third: 46), S. Robertson (third: 28, second: 14, short: 12), and George Myatt (third: 7, second: 2).

RECORDS												

Ricardo Torres (3 years)

G	AB	R	H	2B	3B	HR	RBI	BB	SO	SB	BA	SA
22	37	9	11	1	0	0	3	2	6	0	.297	.324

Gil Torres (4 years)

G	AB	R	H	2B	3B	HR	RBI	BB	SO	SB	BA	SA
346	1,271	99	320	40	11	0	119	53	65	20	.252	.301

Cards
None

◆ MIKE TRESH

Michael
Born: February 23, 1914
Birthplace: Hazelton, Pennsylvania
Died: October 4, 1966
Bats: Right   **Throws:** Right
Height: 5'11"   **Weight:** 170
Played for: Chicago (AL): 1938-48; Cleveland (AL): 1949

Mike caught all the White Sox games in 1945, including 125 complete games. Mike was a decent defensive catcher, and his career batting mark of .249 was respectable for a catcher, but this man had no power. He didn't hit his first home run until the 1940 campaign. Despite the fact that he always appeared in at least 72 games a season and always registered at least 230 at-bats, Mike didn't connect for another round-tripper until the 1948 season, establishing a major league record for home run futility.

◇ TOM TRESH

Thomas Michael
Born: September 20, 1937

Birthplace: Detroit, Michigan
Bats: Switch   **Throws:** Right
Height: 6'1"   **Weight:** 185
Played for: New York (AL): 1961-69; Detroit: 1969
Honors: American League Rookie-of-the-Year in 1962. American League All-Star in 1962 and 1963.

During Tom's outstanding rookie year, he hit .286 with 20 home runs, playing 111 games at shortstop and 43 in the outfield. Tom's home run power certainly came from somewhere in the gene pool other than his father, since in this one season he walloped 10 times more four-baggers than his father managed in 12 years and more than 1,000 games. Tom played all seven games of the 1962 World Series in the outfield, hitting 9 for 28, a .328 mark that led all Yankee hitters. He also contributed four RBIs to the Bronx victory over the Giants. His 91 runs in 1963 tied him for third in the league. While he hit a home run in the Series, the Dodger pitching quartet of Koufax, Drysdale, Podres, and Perranoski limited him to 3 for 15 overall. In the 1964 Series, his two-out, ninth-inning home run off Bob Gibson tied Game Five.

RECORDS

Mike Tresh (12 Years)

G	AB	R	H	2B	3B	HR	RBI	BB	SO	SB	BA	SA
1,027	3,169	326	788	75	14	2	297	402	263	19	.249	.283

Tom Tresh (9 Years)

G	AB	R	H	2B	3B	HR	RBI	BB	SO	SB	BA	SA
1,192	4,251	595	1,041	179	34	153	530	550	698	45	.245	.411

Cards

Mike Tresh
1941DP—#69   1949B—#166

Tom Tresh
| 1962T—#31 | 1963T—#173SP | 1963T—#470 | 1963P—#23 | 1964T—#395 | 1965T—#440 |
| 1966T—#205 | 1967T—#289 | 1968T—#69 | 1969T—#212 | 1970T—#698 | |

◆ HAL TROSKY, SR.

Harold Arthur (Troyavesky)
Born: November 11, 1912
Birthplace: Norway, Indiana
Died: June 18, 1979
Bats: Left   **Throws:** Right
Height: 6'2"   **Weight:** 207
Played for: Cleveland (AL): 1933-41; On Injured List 1942-43; Chicago (AL): 1944; On Injured List 1945; Chicago (AL): 1946

Hal is one of seven Cleveland Indians to have 30 or more homers in at least two seasons. As a 21-year-old first baseman in 1934, Hal hit .330, 45 doubles, and 35 homers with a .598 slugging mark, and was still possibly only the fourth best at his position in the league, behind Gehrig, Greenberg, and Jimmie Foxx! However, these marks were good enough for baseball historian Bill Deane to project Hal as 1934's Hypothetical Rookie of the Year. It would be difficult to shine amidst such sterling competition, but Hal's name regularly appeared among the league offensive leaders during the rest of the 1930s. His lifetime slugging percentage is good enough to rank him 27th on the career list.

◇ HAL TROSKY, JR.

Harold Arthur
Nickname: Hoot
Born: September 29, 1936
Birthplace: Cleveland, Ohio
Bats: Right   **Throws:** Right
Height: 6'3"   **Weight:** 205
Played for: Chicago (AL): 1958

Hoot's debut came September 25, 1958.

RECORDS												

Hal Trosky, Sr. (11 Years)

G	AB	R	H	2B	3B	HR	RBI	BB	SO	SB	BA	SA
1,347	5,161	835	1,561	331	58	228	1,012	545	440	28	.302	.522

Hal Trosky, Jr.

W	L	Pct.	Sv.	G	GS	CG	IP	H	BB	SO	ShO	ERA
1	0	1.000	0	2	0	0	3	5	2	1	0	6.00

Cards

Hal Trosky, Sr.

1934G—#76	1934DS—#70	1935G—#1L	1935G—#2E	1935G—#6E	1935G—#7E
1940PB—#50	1941PB—#16	1941DP—#80	1941DP—#87		

Hal Trosky, Jr.
None

◆ DIZZY TROUT

Paul Howard
Born: June 29, 1915
Birthplace: Otter Creek, Indiana
Died: February 28, 1972
Bats: Right   **Throws:** Right
Height: 6'2"   **Weight:** 205
Played for: Detroit: 1939-52; Boston (AL): 1952; Baltimore: 1957

Dizzy Trout was one of those pitchers who seemed to improve with a few years' experience. After a 9-10 rookie year, he suffered a sophomore slump of 3-7 during Detroit's 1940 pennant-winning season. He started and lost Game Four against the Reds. He pitched his way to an even .500 season in 1942 (9-9), then slumped to a disappointing 12-18. However, he turned things around in 1943, when he led the American League with 20 victories and five shutouts. Dizzy won 27 in 1944, but finished second to teammate Hal Newhouser, who won 29. He did lead the league that season in complete games (33), shutouts (7), ERA (2.12), and innings (352). In 1945, Dizzy's five-hitter in Game Four evened the Series against the Cubs. In Game Six, he came in after a Tiger rally tied the score in the top of the eighth, but lost the game in the bottom of the 12th. Dizzy's overall career stats place him 29th on Palmer's Total Pitcher Index.

◇ STEVE TROUT

Steven Russell
Nickname: Rainbow
Born: July 30, 1957
Birthplace: Detroit, Michigan
Bats: Left   **Throws:** Left
Height: 6'4"   **Weight:** 205
Played for: Chicago (AL): 1978-82; Chicago (NL): 1983-87; New York (AL): 1987; Seattle: 1988-89

Steve won 13 and lost only seven during Chicago's 1984 Division championship season. In the NLCS, he pitched nine innings in two games and won one.

RECORDS

Dizzy Trout (15 Years)

W	L	Pct.	Sv.	G	GS	CG	IP	H	BB	SO	ShO	ERA
170	161	.514	35	521	322	158	2,726	2,641	1,046	1,256	28	3.23

Steve Trout (12 Years)

W	L	Pct.	Sv.	G	GS	CG	IP	H	BB	SO	ShO	ERA
88	92	.489	4	301	236	32	1,501	1,665	578	656	9	4.18

Cards

Dizzy Trout

1939PB—#153	1940PB—#44	1948L—#10	1949B—#208	1950B—#134	1951TBB—#23
1952T—#39	1953T—#169	1985T—#142SP			

Steve Trout

1980T—#83	1981D—#400	1981F—#345	1981T—#552	1982D—#243	1982F—#358
1982T—#299	1983D—#417	1983F—#251	1983T—#461	1983TT—#117	1984D—#533
1984F—#506	1984T—#151	1985D—#198	1985F—#70	1985T—#668	1985T—#142SP
1986D—#117	1986F—#384	1986T—#384	1987D—#201	1987F—#578	1987T—#750
1987T—#581SP	1988D—#524	1988S—#342	1988T—#584	1989S—#522	1989T—#54

◆ AL UNSER

Albert Bernard
Born: October 12, 1912
Birthplace: Morrisonville, Illinois
Bats: Right   **Throws:** Right
Height: 6'1"   **Weight:** 175
Played for: Detroit: 1942-44; Cincinnati: 1945

Al was a backup catcher. In 1944, he was pressed into service as a second baseman for five games.

◇ DEL UNSER

Delbert Bernard
Born: December 9, 1944
Birthplace: Decatur, Illinois
Bats: Left   **Throws:** Left
Height: 6'1"   **Weight:** 180
Played for: Washington (AL): 1968-71; Cleveland (AL): 1972; Philadelphia (NL): 1973-74; New York (NL): 1975-76; Montreal: 1976-78; Philadelphia (NL): 1979-82
Coaching Experience: Philadelphia (NL): 1985-88

Del cracked Washington's starting lineup in 1968, playing 156 games in the outfield. He placed second in the Rookie of the Year vote. Del spent most of his career as a regular. Later in his career he also played first as well as pinch-hitting. In the 1980 NLCS, he appeared in five games, hitting 2 for 5 with one RBI. He helped Philadelphia with their World Series victory, appearing in three games, with a 3 for 6 plate record and two RBIs.

RECORDS

Al Unser (4 Years)

G	AB	R	H	2B	3B	HR	RBI	BB	SO	SB	BA	SA
120	338	41	85	15	4	4	30	32	43	0	.251	.355

Del Unser (15 Years)

G	AB	R	H	2B	3B	HR	RBI	BB	SO	SB	BA	SA
1,799	5,215	617	1,344	179	42	87	481	481	675	64	.258	.358

Cards

Al Unser
None

Del Unser

1969T—#338	1970T—#336	1971T—#33	1972T—#687	1973T—#247	1974T—#69
1975T—#138	1976T—#268	1977T—#471	1978T—#348	1979T—#628	1980T—#6
1980T—#27	1981D—#164	1981F—#26	1981T—#566	1982D—#273	1982F—#261
1982T—#713					

◆ OZZIE VIRGIL, SR.

Osvaldo Jose (Pichardo)
Born: May 1, 1933
Birthplace: Montecristi, Dominican Republic
Bats: Right   **Throws:** Right
Height: 6'1"   **Weight:** 174
Played for: New York (NL): 1956-57; Detroit: 1958, 1960-61; Kansas City: 1961; Baltimore: 1962; Pittsburgh: 1965; San Francisco: 1966, 1969

Ozzie played second, third, and shortstop, and even filled in behind the plate occasionally. Some sources spell his name Ossie.

◇ OZZIE VIRGIL, JR.

Osvaldo Jose
Born: December 7, 1956
Birthplace: Mayaguez, Puerto Rico
Bats: Right   **Throws:** Right
Height: 6'1"   **Weight:** 205
Played for: Philadelphia (NL): 1980-85; Atlanta: 1986-88; Toronto: 1989

Ozzie caught only one game in both the 1980 and 1981 seasons. After that he was used primarily as a backup until the 1984 season, when he became a regular. When Ozzie retired from the major leagues, he teamed up with his dad to become the first father-son combination in the Senior Professional Baseball League. Dad coached and Junior caught, played first, and DHed for the St. Petersburg Pelicans.

RECORDS

Ozzie Virgil, Sr. (9 Years)

G	AB	R	H	2B	3B	HR	RBI	BB	SO	SB	BA	SA
324	753	75	174	19	7	14	73	34	91	6	.231	.331

Ozzie Virgil, Jr. (11 Years)

G	AB	R	H	2B	3B	HR	RBI	BB	SO	SB	BA	SA
739	2,258	258	549	84	6	98	307	248	453	4	.243	.416

Cards

Ozzie Virgil, Sr.

1957T—#365	1958T—#107	1959T—#203	1961T—#67	1962T—#327	1965T—#571
1967T—#132	1985T—#143SP				

Ozzie Virgil, Jr.

1982T—#231	1983D—#606	1983F—#175	1983T—#383	1984D—#326	1984F—#49
1984T—#484	1985D—#82	1985F—#267	1985T—#611	1985T—#143SP	1986D—#137
1986F—#456	1986T—#95	1986FU—#122	1986TT—#119	1987D—#67	1987F—#532
1987T—#571	1988D—#143	1988F—#552	1988S—#129	1988SPF—#217	1988T—#755
1989D—#145	1989F—#605	1989S—#111	1989SPF—#94	1989T—#179	1989UD—#104

◆ HOWARD WAKEFIELD

Howard John
Born: February 2, 1884
Birthplace: Bucyrus, Ohio
Died: April 16, 1941
Bats: Right   **Throws:** Right
Height: 6'1"   **Weight:** 205
Played for: Cleveland (AL): 1905; Washington (AL): 1906; Cleveland (AL): 1907

Howard qualified as the Senators' regular catcher in 1906, his second season in the majors, with only 60 games. The Senators employed a slew of backstops that season. In addition to Howard, three other players donned the "tools of ignorance" (players' slang for catcher's gear at one time) for at least 27 games. He hit .280 and stole six bases that season. Something must have happened to young Howard, since the following season he caught only 11 games for the Indians, hit a meager .135, and never again appeared in a major league game.

◇ DICK WAKEFIELD

Richard Cummings
Born: May 6, 1921
Birthplace: Chicago, Illinois
Died: August 26, 1985
Bats: Left   **Throws:** Right
Height: 6'4"   **Weight:** 210
Played for: Detroit: 1941, 1943-44; Military Service in 1945; Detroit: 1946-49; New York (AL): 1950; Chicago (AL): 1950; New York (NL): 1952

In 1943, Dick's first full major league season, he led the American League in at-bats (633), hits (200), and doubles (38). He appeared in 78 games in the outfield in 1944, and was hitting .355 when his career was interrupted by military service. Nevertheless, he finished fifth in that season's Most Valuable Player voting. Except for four games, he was a hold-out in 1950 and didn't get back into a major league uniform until 1952, when he went 0 for 2.

RECORDS

Howard Wakefield (3 years)

G	AB	R	H	2B	3B	HR	RBI	BB	SO	SB	BA	SA
113	274	24	68	11	2	1	25	10	*	6	.248	.314

* Not available

Dick Wakefield (9 years)

G	AB	R	H	2B	3B	HR	RBI	BB	SO	SB	BA	SA
638	2,132	334	625	102	29	56	315	360	270	10	.293	.447

Cards

Howard Wakefield
None

Dick Wakefield
1949B—#91

◆ DIXIE WALKER

Ewart Gladstone
Born: June 1, 1887
Birthplace: Brownsville, Pennsylvania
Died: November 14, 1965
Bats: Left   **Throws:** Right
Height: 6'1"   **Weight:** 192
Played for: Washington (AL): 1909-12

Given a chance, Ewart came up with a 3-1 record for a team that went 42-110. The next year, while the Senators struggled to a seventh place finish (66-85), Walker was 11-11. The following season, the Senators had a .416 winning percentage; he sunk to .364 with an 8-14 season. He could only muster a 3-4 record in 1912, his last season.

◇ DIXIE WALKER

Fred
Nickname: The People's Cherce
Born: September 24, 1910
Birthplace: Villa Rica, Georgia
Died: May 17, 1982
Bats: Left   **Throws:** Right
Height: 6'1"   **Weight:** 175
Played for: New York (AL): 1931, 1933-36; Detroit: 1938-39; Brooklyn (NL): 1939-47; Pittsburgh: 1948-49

When Dixie finally got a chance to play regularly, he responded by hitting .308, patrolling the outfield for Detroit in 114 games in 1938. He quickly established himself as one of the most popular players in Brooklyn history, helping bring Brooklyn its first pennant in 21 years in 1941. In 1944, he led the league in hitting, with a .357 average. Dixie's outspoken opposition to Jackie Robinson's playing with the Dodgers resulted in him completing his career in Pittsburgh.

◇ HARRY WALKER

Harry William
Nickname: The Hat
Born: October 22, 1916
Birthplace: Pascagoula, Mississippi
Bats: Left   **Throws:** Right
Height: 6'2"   **Weight:** 175
Played for: St. Louis (NL): 1940-43; Military Service in 1944-45; St. Louis (NL): 1946-47; Philadelphia (NL): 1947-48; Chicago (NL): 1949; Cincinnati: 1949; St. Louis (NL): 1950-51, 1955
Coaching Experience: St. Louis (NL): 1955 (Player/Manager); St. Louis: 1959-62; Pittsburgh: 1965-67 (Manager); Houston: 1968-72 (Manager)

Harry won the 1947 National League batting crown (.363) and led the National League in triples (16). He became a playing manager during the 1955 season, and coached in St. Louis (NL) from 1959 to 1962. Harry the Hat resumed his career as a manager in 1965, piloting the Pirates to a 90-72 third place finish. He continued managing (Pittsburgh and Houston) until 1972, and finished with a 630-604 career mark.

RECORDS

Dixie Walker (4 years)

W	L	Pct.	Sv.	G	GS	CG	IP	H	BB	SO	ShO	ERA
25	31	.446	0	74	62	40	481	485	142	203	5	3.52

Dixie Walker (18 years)

G	AB	R	H	2B	3B	HR	RBI	BB	SO	SB	BA	SA
1,905	6,740	1,037	2,064	376	96	105	1,023	817	325	59	.306	.437

Harry Walker (11 years)

G	AB	R	H	2B	3B	HR	RBI	BB	SO	SB	BA	SA
807	2,651	385	786	126	37	10	214	245	175	42	.296	.383

Cards

Dixie Walker
None

Dixie Walker
1934G—#39   1941DP—#21   1953T—#190

Harry Walker
1949B—#130   1950B—#180   1953T—#190   1960T—#468SP   1965T—#438   1966T—#318
1967T—#448   1969T—#633   1970T—#32   1971T—#312   1972T—#249

◆ ED WALSH

Edward Augustine
Nickname: Big Ed
Born: May 14, 1881
Birthplace: Plains, Pennsylvania
Died: May 26, 1959
Bats: Right   **Throws:** Right
Height: 6'1"   **Weight:** 193
Played for: Chicago (AL): 1904-16; Boston (NL): 1917
Hall of Fame: Elected in 1946.

Ed worked in the Wilkes-Barre (Pennsylvania) area coal mines, pitching semi-pro ball when he was noticed. Charles Comiskey purchased his contract for $750. He came up to the White Sox from Newark and pitched a 4-0 shutout against Washington in his first major league outing. Some sources credit Big Ed with introducing the spitball to the major leagues, but other sources say he learned it from Elmer Stricklett, who learned it from George Hildebrand. He certainly popularized the pitch, and became the game's greatest spitball pitcher, throwing the pitch at a time when it was legal. Walsh threw four variations of the "cuspidorous curve," and reputedly could control them all.

However, it would be an injustice to think of Walsh as solely owing his success to this pitch. His career ERA is 1.82, making him the all-time leader. He led the league in innings pitched four times, including 464 innings in 1908, the year he won 40 games. He pitched seven games during that season's final nine games, including a double-header win over Boston. Ed also hit one of his team's three homers that year. He injured his arm in 1913 and never regained his form. Nevertheless, he must be considered one of the game's all-time greats. Opponents hit a meager .215 against him, placing him eleventh on the all-time roster. Furthermore, his opponents' on-base percentage is .270; he is the all-time leader in that category. He ranks 11th on Peter Palmer's career Total Pitching Index.

◇ ED WALSH

Edward Arthur
Born: February 11, 1905
Birthplace: Meriden, Connecticut
Died: October 31, 1937
Bats: Right   **Throws:** Right
Height: 6'1"   **Weight:** 180
Played for: Chicago (AL): 1928-30, 1932

Ed pitched for his father at Notre Dame. Later, he teamed up with the son of his father's former battery mate, Billy Sullivan, Jr., on their fathers' former team, the White Sox. Ed died in his parents' home following a long illness; he suffered from an acute heart ailment induced by chronic rheumatism. While Ed, Jr. doesn't appear on any baseball card lists, he does, in fact, appear on a card. He can be found on an uncorrected error in the 1960 Fleer Baseball Greats issue.

RECORDS												
Ed Walsh (14 years)												
W	**L**	**Pct.**	**Sv.**	**G**	**GS**	**CG**	**IP**	**H**	**BB**	**SO**	**ShO**	**ERA**
195	126	.607	40	430	315	250	2,964	2,346	617	1,736	57	1.82
Ed Walsh (4 years)												
W	**L**	**Pct.**	**Sv.**	**G**	**GS**	**CG**	**IP**	**H**	**BB**	**SO**	**ShO**	**ERA**
11	24	.314	0	79	38	11	331	399	149	107	0	5.57

Cards

Big Ed Walsh
T206—#368	T201—#39	1911 Turkey Red—#125	T202 Triple Folder—#22A
1914 Cracker Jack	1915 Cracker Jack	1960F—#49 (Actually Ed, Jr.)	1961F—#83

Little Ed Walsh
Uncorrected Error, 1960F, issued as his father

◆ JOJO WHITE

Joyner Clifford
Born: June 1, 1909
Birthplace: Red Oak, Georgia
Died: October 8, 1986
Bats: Left   **Throws:** Right
Height: 5'11"   **Weight:** 165
Played for: Detroit: 1932-38; Cincinnati: 1943-44
Coaching Experience: Cleveland (AL): 1960 (Manager)

JoJo played 100 games in the outfield, hit .313, and scored 97 runs during Detroit's 1934 pennant-winning campaign. He played all seven games in the Series against the Cardinals, getting only three hits in 23 at-bats, but scoring six runs in a losing cause. In 1935, he improved his World Series mark, with five hits in 19 at-bats and collected a World Series ring as the Tigers clawed past the Cubs in a match-up made in sportwriters' metaphor heaven. JoJo earned his nickname from the way he pronounced the name of his native state.

◇ MIKE WHITE

Joyner Michael
Born: November 18, 1938
Birthplace: Detroit, Michigan
Bats: Right   **Throws:** Right
Height: 5'8"   **Weight:** 160
Played for: Houston: 1963-65

After getting a "cup of coffee" in 1963, Mike broke into Houston's starting lineup as a rookie with 72 appearances in the outfield, 10 at second, and 3 at third. He hit .271 in 280 at-bats. However, the following year he was 0 for 9 in eight games, and his major league career was over.

RECORDS

JoJo White (9 Years)

G	AB	R	H	2B	3B	HR	RBI	BB	SO	SB	BA	SA
878	2,652	456	678	83	42	8	229	386	276	92	.256	.328

Mike White (3 years)

G	AB	R	H	2B	3B	HR	RBI	BB	SO	SB	BA	SA
100	296	30	78	11	3	0	27	21	49	1	.264	.321

Cards

JoJo White
1934DS—#45   1939PB—#79   1940PB—#84   1960T—#460SP   1963T—#460C

Mike White
1964T—#492   1965T—#31

◆ MAURY WILLS

Maurice Morning
Born: October 2, 1932
Birthplace: Washington, District of Columbia
Bats: Switch   **Throws:** Right
Height: 5'11"   **Weight:** 170
Played for: Los Angeles (NL): 1959-66; Pittsburgh: 1967-68; Montreal: 1969; Los Angeles (NL): 1969-72
Coaching Experience: Seattle: 1980-81 (Manager)
Honors: Most Valuable Player in 1962

Perhaps more than any player of his era, Maury Wills redefined how the game was played, effectively re-introducing the stolen base in the National League and paving the way for the likes of Lou Brock. Maury stole 104 bases in his 1962 Most Valuable Player season. He led the National League in stolen bases 1960-65. In the 1965 Series, he led in at-bats (30), hits (11), and doubles (3). He finished third in that season's Most Valuable Player vote. He played third base for Pittsburgh, but switched back to short when he returned to Los Angeles.

◇ BUMP WILLS

Elliot Taylor
Born: July 27, 1952
Birthplace: Washington, District of Columbia
Bats: Switch   **Throws:** Right
Height: 5'8"   **Weight:** 175
Played for: Texas: 1977-81; Chicago (NL): 1982

Bump hit .287 as a rookie second baseman. Though he was never the player his dad was, Bump was a pretty fair infielder and a decent base thief himself. In 1978, his total of 52 stolen bases was third in the American League, and he placed fifth in 1979, with 35.

RECORDS

Maury Wills (14 Years)

G	AB	R	H	2B	3B	HR	RBI	BB	SO	SB	BA	SA
1,942	7,588	1,067	2,134	177	71	20	458	552	684	586	.281	.331

Bump Wills (6 Years)

G	AB	R	H	2B	3B	HR	RBI	BB	SO	SB	BA	SA
831	3,030	472	807	128	24	36	302	310	441	196	.266	.360

Cards

Maury Wills

1961P—#164	1962P—#104	1963F—#43	1963P—#115	1967T—#570	1968T—#175
1969T—#45	1969TS—#49	1969TDE—#24	1970T—#595	1971T—#385	1972T—#437
1972T—#438SP	1975T—#200SP	1977T—#435SP	1978MA—#70	1981F—#595	1981TT—#672
1987T—#315					

Bump Wills

1977T—#494R	1978T—#23	1979T—#369	1980T—#473	1981D—#25	1981F—#628
1981T—#173	1982D—#289	1982F—#334	1982T—#272	1982TT—#129	1983D—#351
1983F—#511	1983T—#643				

◆ BOBBY WINE

Robert Paul, Sr.
Born: September 17, 1938
Birthplace: New York, New York
Bats: Right   **Throws:** Right
Height: 6'1"   **Weight:** 185
Played for: Philadelphia (NL): 1960, 1962-68; Montreal: 1969-72
Coaching Experience: Atlanta: 1985 (Manager)

Bobby played shortstop and third base. A back injury resulted in limited action in 1966, but he returned to the lineup in 1967. He suffered a broken wrist in 1971 and was limited to 119 games.

◇ ROBBIE WINE

Robert Paul, Jr.
Born: July 13, 1962
Birthplace: Norristown, Pennsylvania
Bats: Right   **Throws:** Right
Height: 6'2"   **Weight:** 200
Played for: Houston: 1986-87

Robbie is a light-hitting catcher who never lived up to his potential.

RECORDS

Bobby Wine (12 Years)

G	AB	R	H	2B	3B	HR	RBI	BB	SO	SB	BA	SA
1,164	3,172	249	682	104	16	30	268	214	538	7	.215	.286

Robbie Wine

G	AB	R	H	2B	3B	HR	RBI	BB	SO	SB	BA	SA
23	41	3	6	2	0	0	0	2	14	0	.146	.195

Cards

Bobby Wine

1963T—#71	1964T—#347	1965T—#36	1966T—#284	1967T—#466	1968T—#396
1969T—#648	1970T—#332	1971T—#171	1972T—#657	1973T—#486SP	1974T—#119SP
1986T—#57SP					

Robbie Wine

1988D—#508	1988F—#459	1988S—#496	1988T—#119

◆ SMOKEY JOE WOOD

Howard Ellsworth
Born: February 25, 1889
Birthplace: Kansas City, Missouri
Died: July 27, 1985
Bats: Right   **Throws:** Right
Height: 5'11"   **Weight:** 180
Played for: Boston (AL): 1908-15, 1917; Cleveland (AL): 1919-22

Smokey Joe won 34 games in 1912, including 16 straight. When chronic thumb pain forced him to abandon his pitching career, he came back as an outfielder for Cleveland. Joe's career began when he signed a contract in 1906 for $20 to play with the Kansas City Bloomer Girls, a barnstorming team composed of both men and women. As a pitcher, Wood struck out 231 batters and pitched a no-hitter during the 1911 season. In the 1912 season, he logged sixteen consecutive wins and ten shutouts, and he also recorded three of his club's four World Series victories. When he made his comeback as an outfielder, he hit .298 from 1917 to 1922. Wood coached at Yale University from 1923 to 1942 and was awarded an honorary doctorate by that institution in 1984. Despite his shortened pitching career, he is ranked 67th on the Palmer Total Pitching Index.

◇ JOE WOOD

Joseph Frank
Born: May 20, 1916
Birthplace: Shoshola, Pennsylvania
Bats: Right   **Throws:** Right
Height: 6'   **Weight:** 190
Played for: Boston (AL): 1944

Joe made his debut on May 1, 1944.

RECORDS												

Smokey Joe Wood (14 Years)

W	L	Pct.	Sv.	G	GS	CG	IP	H	BB	SO	ShO	ERA
116	57	.671	11	225	158	121	1,436	1,138	421	989	28	2.03

G	AB	R	H	2B	3B	HR	RBI	BB	SO	SB	BA	SA
696	1,952	266	553	118	30	24	325	208	*	23	.283	.411

* Not available

Joe Wood

W	L	Pct.	Sv.	G	GS	CG	IP	H	BB	SO	ShO	ERA
0	1	.000	0	3	1	0	10	13	3	5	0	6.30

Cards

Smokey Joe Wood
1915 Cracker Jack

Joe Wood
None

◆ DEL YOUNG

Delmer John
Born: October 24, 1885
Birthplace: Macon City, Missouri
Died: December 17, 1959
Bats: Left   **Throws:** Right
Height: 5'11"   **Weight:** 195
Played for: Cincinnati: 1909; Buffalo (Federal League): 1914-15

Del played two games in the outfield for the Reds in 1909. In 1914, he jumped to the Buffalo Buffeds in the short-lived Federal League and never played another major league game after the Federal League folded in 1915.

◇ DEL YOUNG

Delmer Edward
Born: May 11, 1912
Birthplace: Cleveland, Ohio
Died: December 8, 1979
Bats: Switch   **Throws:** Right
Height: 5'11"   **Weight:** 168
Played for: Philadelphia (NL): 1937-40

Although Del cracked Philadephia's starting lineup as a rookie second baseman, this light-hitting middle infielder never established himself as a serious major leaguer.

RECORDS

Del Young (3 years)

G	AB	R	H	2B	3B	HR	RBI	BB	SO	SB	BA	SA
94	196	17	52	5	5	4	23	5	13	1	.265	.403

Del Young (4 years)

G	AB	R	H	2B	3B	HR	RBI	BB	SO	SB	BA	SA
309	950	87	213	31	7	3	76	48	115	7	.224	.281

Cards

Del Young
None

Del Young
1939PB—#33

PART III

Cardboard Fathers, Cardboard Sons

Vern Law plays the harmonica. Ken Griffey, Sr. draws cartoons. Hal Lanier collects baseball cards. Dizzy Trout did a daily radio show in Detroit. Fritz Brickell was the smallest man on the 1959 Yankees.

To the uninitiated, these snippets of information would seem disparate and random. But a more worldly, discerning observer might peer at you and then assert, "Been reading the backs of them baseball cards again, haven't you?" Yes, these tidbits represent merely a tiny fraction of what can be gleaned from the backs of baseball cards. Welcome to the pasteboard universe.

Volumes have already been written about baseball card collecting. Some treat the subject with scholarly sanctity, equating baseball card collecting with some primordial urge to return to the past. Others anticipate the golden future, professing to guide you through shrewd investment and trading to the promised land of Big Bucks. The books most worth reading, though, are those that are simply fun. Because after all, folks, these are pieces of cardboard we are talking about. They're meant to be fun, and that's how we're going to treat them. No heavy duty investment tips or hot cards, so if that's what you're after, look elsewhere. On the other hand, if you are serious about your fun, read on.

To begin, let's face some facts. The proliferation of baseball card issues and the popularity of card collecting as a hobby has resulted in a situation rendering it virtually impossible for all but the most ardent or well-heeled collector to purchase every set every year. I know, I know, some people still try and I admire their effort. But just cataloguing such a collection would require a master's degree in library science, significant knowledge of data collection and entry, and computer programming skills, not to mention specialized training in archival storage and retrieval. After all, we're talking about thousands of cards a year. And, speaking of storage, do you realize how much space four or five or more sets a year accumulated over a decade would require?

Fact number two. It's costly and going up all the time.

That being said, consider the advantages of building a father-son baseball card collection.

First, you won't have to build a special wing of the house or rent extra storage space to house your collection. One or two shoeboxes will probably take care of the whole collection. Second, it's generally affordable, although there are a few cards like the "One million dollar one-of-a-kind Freddie Lindstrom" card being hyped recently. Third, you get to assemble a really interesting collection that has some old stuff, some new stuff, and quite a number of interesting cards. Finally, and most important, it's fun.

Compare the resemblances between Ray and Bob Boone. If you didn't know that 20-some years separated the issue, you could be looking at a pair of brothers. On the other hand, you've got to look close to see a similarity between Ron Northey and his son Scott. You can use your father-son collection to build a "type" set, acquiring one of as many varieties of cards as you can discover. Or, you could specialize in certain issues, acquiring at least one card for every year of issue.

To date, fifty-one combinations of fathers who had baseball cards issued and sons who had cards issued exist. Ten fathers had cards issued but not their sons, and twenty-three sons only with cards complete our list. (See below.)

Study the list carefully. What do you notice? Well, aside from the occasional superstar like Yogi Berra, you'll be surprised at how many of these cards are commons. Even guys who were pretty well respected in their own day — Ray Boone, Tito Francona, or Jim Hegan, to name but a few—seem to hold little collector interest and can be picked out of a lot of dealers' bargain bins.

Granted, there are some hard-to-locate items. But, a surprising number of these cards are available within most collecting budgets. This is especially true if you are willing to accept some of the older, harder-to-find material in less than Mint or Near Mint condition. Here are a few other tips that will help you build your collection without smashing your collecting budget.

Few exhibitors bring their full stock of commons to card shows. However, most of them will be delighted to provide you the opportunity to look through their commons stock; you can frequently arrange private deals.

Second, if you are willing, perhaps temporarily, to accept some substitutes for the more expensive items, you'll discover a treasure trove of readily available material. Take the Hall of Famers, for example. You could pick them all up in one swoop with the purchase of a Hall of Fame set. If that doesn't appeal to you, consider the range of other sets that include old-timers and Hall of Famers. For example, Fleer's 1960 and 1961 "Baseball Greats" are a terrific source. More recently, the Pacific "Legends of Baseball" sets yield players such as Earl Averill, Yogi Berra, Gus Bell, Tito Francona, Harry Walker, and Tom Tresh. There is a host of other sets like these on the market. I've included a list of some of the sets I'm familiar with, but I'm sure you can locate others.

Third, given the proliferation of reprint sets, you can pick up many interesting and attractive cards at a fraction of their original cost. The 1951 Bowman reprint set, for example, includes thirteen fathers and three sons. There are even reprints of the rare and famous T206 set, or the Goudey sets of the 1930s.

Finally, another acceptable substitute for some of the older or higher-priced cards lies in the fact that a lot of the desired individuals can be located on manager or coach cards. Compare the cost of a Yogi Berra coach or manager card against the cost of a Berra player card.

You could start with players currently active and then look for their fathers. You might consider limiting yourself to material produced after World War II. And, with the growing interest in minor league cards, this offers yet another collecting opportunity.

Unless you are relatively sure you're not going to get a certain card at a better price, be patient. Keep watching the ads for sales, especially of older material. If you're lucky enough to know a dealer who is knowledgeable and whom you trust, don't hesitate to ask for his help in putting your collection together. The chances are good that they will be more than willing to help.

Remember, know what you're looking for, be patient, but learn to know a bargain when you truly come across one. Your rewards will be a unique and exciting collection, a greater understanding of baseball history and baseball card history, and a lasting appreciation of baseball's families. Good hunting!

FATHERS AND SONS CARDS AVAILABLE

Fathers and Sons

Bobby and Mike Adams
Sandy, Sr., Roberto, and Sandy, Jr. Alomar
Felipe and Moises Alou
Earl and Earl Averill
Jim, Sr. and Jim, Jr. Bagby
Charlie and Charlie Beamon
Gus and Buddy Bell
Yogi and Dale Berra
Bobby and Barry Bonds
Ray and Bob Boone
Fred and Fritz Brickell
Mike and Mike Brumley
Dolf and Doug Camilli
Cam and Mark Carreon
Joe and Joe Coleman
Dick and Steve Ellsworth
Tito and Terry Francona
Peaches and Jack Graham
Fred and Gary Green
Ken, Sr. and Ken, Jr. Griffey
Jim and Mike Hegan
Ken and Tom Heintzelman
Randy and Todd Hundley
Julian and Stan Javier
Bob and Terry Kennedy
Marty and Matt Keogh
Bill and Jeff Kunkel
Max and Hal Lanier
Vern and Vance Law
Thornton and Don Lee
Dave and Derrick May
Pinkie and Milt May
Hal and Brian McRae
Julio and Jaime Navarro
Ron and Scott Northey
Mel and Mel Queen
Cal, Sr., Cal, Jr., and Billy Ripken
Dick and Dick Schofield
Dick and Paul Siebert
George, Dick, and Dave Sisler
Bob and Joel Skinner
Roy and Roy Smalley
Ed and Ed Sprague
Ebba and Randy St. Claire
Dave and Mike Stenhouse
Mel, Mel, Jr., and Todd Stottlemyre
Haywood and Marc Sullivan

Fathers and Sons (cont.)
Bruce and Chuck Tanner
Jose and Danny Tartabull
Mike and Tom Tresh
Dizzy and Steve Trout
Ozzie, Sr. and Ozzie, Jr. Virgil
Jo-Jo and Mike White
Maury and Bump Wills
Bobby and Robbie Wine

Fathers Only
Eddie Collins, Sr.
Glenn Liebhardt, Sr.
Fred Lindstrom
Jack Lively
Connie Mack
Orator Jim O'Rourke
Billy Sullivan
Hal Trosky, Sr.
Big Ed Walsh
Smokey Joe Wood

Sons Only
Charlie Berry
Jim Campanis
Ed Connolly, Jr.
Bill Crouch
Len Gabrielson
Ross Grimsley, Jr.
Jerry Hairston
Lew Krausse, Jr.
Bill Landrum
Jerry Martin
Aurelio Monteagudo
Gene Moore, Jr.
Don Mueller
Ray Narleski
Chet Nichols, Jr.
Bobo Osborne
Allen Ripley
Joe Schultz, Jr.
Jerry Stephenson
Kurt Stillwell
George Susce
Del Unser
Dick Wakefield

Replacement Cards
The following sets contain cards of some of the difficult-to-obtain or expensive players you might want in your set. All cards listed can be purchased for as little as 5 cents. The most expensive are likely to be those in the 1960 and 1961 Fleer sets, and they can generally be found for no more than a couple dollars. You might also try sets such as Hostess, Kellogg's, Post, etc., which have not been catalogued here.

1960 Fleer
#13 George Sisler
#14 Connie Mack
#20 Eddie Collins
#49 Ed Walsh
#71 Earl Averill

1961 Fleer
#5 Earl Averill
#16 Eddie Collins
#78 Ed Walsh
#89 George Sisler/Traynor
#92 Jim Bagby
#97 Dolph Camilli
#123 Connie Mack
#141 Billy Sullivan
#145 Hal Trosky
#151 Dixie Walker

1975 Fleer Pioneers
#20 Eddie Collins

1980-83 Cramer Legends
#4 Earl Averill
#26 Eddie Collins
#67 Yogi Berra
#100 Fred Lindstrom
#108 George Sisler

1985 Circle K
#33 Yogi Berra

1988 Pacific Legends
#22 Mel Stottlemyre
#25 Tom Tresh
#53 Yogi Berra
#58 Felipe Alou
#65 Gus Bell

1989 Pacific Legends
#133 Tito Francona
#158 Thornton Lee
#162 Joe Schultz
#190 Harry Walker
#203 Earl Averill
#207 Randy Hundley

1989 Swell Baseball Greats
#34 Harry Walker
#52 Tom Tresh
#76 Tito Francona

Father-Son Card Guide, 1887-1941
While material on cards from 1948 through the present is readily available, it is harder to locate information on earlier issues. In order to help prospective collectors, here is a guide concentrating on cards issued prior to 1948.

1887-1890 Old Judge
#392 Orator Jim O'Rourke

1909-1911 T206
- #72 Eddie Collins
- #144 Peaches Graham
- #346 Billy Sullivan
- #368 Ed Walsh

1911 Gold Border
- #4 Eddie Collins
- #5 Eddie Collins
- #38 Peaches Graham
- #181 Ed Walsh

1911 T201 Mecca Double Folder
- #1 Eddie Collins
- #24 Peaches Graham
- #39 Ed Walsh

1911 Turkey Reds
- #87 Eddie Collins
- #95 Peaches Graham
- #121 Billy Sullivan
- #125 Ed Walsh

1912 T202 Hassan Triple Folders
- #6 Eddie Collins
- #22A Ed Walsh
- #23 Joe Wood
- #25ABC Eddie Collins
- #63 Joe Wood

1912 T207 (Brown Background)
- #34 Eddie Collins
- #106 Jack Lively
- #179 Billy Sullivan
- #203 Joe Wood

1914 Cracker Jack™
- #7 Eddie Collins
- #12 Connie Mack
- #22 Joe Wood
- #36 Ed Walsh

1915 Cracker Jack™
- #7 Eddie Collins
- #12 Connie Mack
- #22 Joe Wood
- #36 Ed Walsh

1933 Goudey
- #38 Fred Brickell
- #42 Eddie Collins
- #133 Fred Lindstrom
- #194 Earl Averill

1934 Goudey
- #76 Hal Trosky
- #91 Dolph Camilli

1935 Goudey 4-in-1
- #1L Earl Averill/Hal Trosky
- #2E Earl Averill/Hal Trosky
- #4C Charlie Berry
- #6C Fred Brickell
- #7C Charlie Berry
- #12C Charlie Berry
- #13C Fred Brickell
- #15C Fred Brickell
- #16E Earl Averill/Hal Trosky
- #17E Earl Averill/Hal Trosky

1936 Goudey
- #5 Dolph Camilli

1939 Playball
- #40 Jim Bagby, Jr.
- #45 Pinky May
- #85 Johnny Cooney
- #86 Dolph Camilli
- #143 Earl Averill
- #153 Dizzy Trout
- #160 Gene Moore

1940 Playball
- #32 Jim Bagby, Jr.
- #44 Dizzy Trout
- #46 Earl Averill
- #50 Hal Trosky
- #60 John Cooney
- #68 Dolph Camilli
- #98 Pinky May
- #132 Connie Mack
- #143 Gene Moore
- #179 George Sisler
- #190 Charlie Berry
- #192 Dick Siebert

1941 Double Play
- #20 Dolph Camilli
- #21 Dixie Walker
- #41 Johnny Cooney
- #45 Pinky May
- #69 Mike Tresh
- #79 Hal Trosky
- #87 Hal Trosky
- #122 Gene Moore
- #127 Dick Siebert

1941 Playball
- #9 Pinky May
- #16 Hal Trosky
- #25 Gene Moore
- #50 Johnny Cooney
- #51 Dolph Camilli

A LAST WORD

Amazing, isn't it, how so much baseball history lives through its fathers and sons—from Orator Jim to Cal, Barry, and Ken. No doubt many of you know anecdotes and facts that should be added to this volume. That, of course, is part of the fun and part of the allure of this great game. Each and every fan has a story to pass along. And each generation gets to pass along something of its common experience through these shared stories.

Wouldn't you love to peer into a crystal ball and see which of today's players will become baseball fathers? Of course, none of us can predict the future. We can, however, make educated guesses and informed observations. So the next time you go to the ballpark, or if perhaps you are one of the lucky ones who makes it to spring training, take a good look around. Take heed of those four year olds hefting bats and hurling balls, and watch to see which fathers take the time to encourage them. Chances are some of them will be putting on real uniforms before you know it. And while they may be lucky enough to play catch with their dads at a big league park, I'll bet none of us lucky enough to have played catch with our own dads has ever forgotten it.

SEE YOU AT THE BALLPARK.

WHEN DAY IS DONE: IN THE DUGOUT

Baseball fathers have managed from one game to many years; they have known unbridled success and abject failure. Eighteen fathers (seven sons to date) have led a major league team.

Orator Jim O'Rourke herded the Buffalo Bisons from 1881-84. As was then the custom, O'Rourke was a playing manager and Orator Jim inserted himself in the lineup at catcher, first, third, short, and the outfield. He even pitched a few times. The Bisons were overmatched and never placed higher than third during O'Rourke's years at the helm.

Two other Hall of Fame fathers took a turn as player-managers — Eddie Collins and George Sisler. Sisler took charge of the Browns from 1924-26, and Collins gave it a shot for the White Sox in 1925 and 1926. Neither distinguished himself as a manager, but interestingly enough, on the last day of the 1925 season, Sisler and Ty Cobb both pitched in relief—the only time two playing managers pitched against each other.

Ten men in baseball history have had onegame managerial careers. Baseball father JoJo White took his turn in 1960. White played nine seasons in the big leagues and coached for a decade. In 1960, he took over the Indians for one game. The Indians won, giving White a perfect record as a manager. Connie Mack represents the other end of the longevity spectrum. Mack recorded 53 seasons as a manager—7,755 games, 9 pennants, and 5 World Series championships.

Chuck Tanner is the only other baseball father to win a World Series. Tanner began his managerial career in 1970 as the third of three managers of a White Sox team that finished dead last in the AL West. His Pittsburgh Pirates won the World Series in 1979, but in Chuck's last five seasons, he finished fifth in his division once and sixth five times with miserable Pittsburgh and Atlanta teams, finishing his career in 1988 with an Atlanta Braves team that got off to a 12-27 start before Chuck's dismissal.

Yogi Berra never won a World Series, but when his 1973 Mets won the National League he became only the second manager to win pennants in both leagues. Hal Lanier won a division title his first time around the block with the 1986 Houston ball club. The Astros slid into third the next year and bounced into fifth in 1988, Lanier's last year with the club. Joe Schultz claims the distinction of being the one and only manager the Seattle Pilots ever employed. The Pilots came into being in the 1969 expansion and finished sixth in the division with a 64-98 record. The franchise folded and reorganized itself in Milwaukee, sans Joe, after only one year in existence. The managerial records of baseball's fathers and sons follows:

Manager	Year/Teams	Won	Loss	Pct.
Yogi Berra	1964, 1984, 1985/New York (AL); 1972-75/New York (NL)	484	444	.522
Earle Brucker, Sr.	1952/Cincinnati (NL)	3	2	.600
Johnny Cooney	1949/Boston (NL)	20	25	.444
Red Corriden	1950/Chicago (AL)	52	72	.419
John Ganzel	1908/Cincinnati (NL) (Playing); 1915/Brooklyn (Federal League)	90	99	.476
Bob Kennedy	1963-65/Chicago (NL); 1968/Oakland (AL)	264	278	.487
Hal Lanier	1986-88/Houston	254	232	.523
Connie Mack	1894-96/Pittsburgh; 1901-50/Philadelphia (AL)	3,731	3,948	.486
Earle Mack	1937, 1939/Philadelphia (AL)	45	77	.369
	(Earle managed on those rare occasions when Connie was absent or thrown out of a game.)			
Bobby Mattick	1980-81/Toronto	104	164	.388
Jim O'Rourke	1881-84/Buffalo (NL) (Playing); 1893/Washington (NL)	246	258	.488
Cal Ripken, Sr.	1985, 1987-88/Baltimore	68	101	.402
Joe Schultz	1969/Seattle (AL); 1973/Detroit	78	112	.411
George Sisler	1924-26/St. Louis (AL) (Playing)	218	241	.475
Dick Sisler	1964-65/Cincinnati	121	94	.563
Bob Skinner	1968-69/Pittsburgh; 1977/San Diego	93	123	.431
Billy Sullivan	1909/Chicago (AL) (Playing)	78	74	.513
Haywood Sullivan	1965/Kansas City (AL)	54	82	.397
Chuck Tanner	1970-75/Chicago; 1976/Oakland; 1977-85/Pittsburgh; 1986-88/Atlanta	1,352	1,381	.495
Harry Walker	1955/St. Louis (NL) (Playing); 1965-67/Pittsburgh; 1968-72/Houston	630	604	.511
Ed Walsh	1924/Chicago (AL)	1	2	.333
JoJo White	1960/Cleveland	1	0	1.000

Index